...AND HURL THEM BACK AT HIM, BEFORE HE CAN CONJURE UP NEW DEFENSES!
TAKEN BY SHEER SURPRISE... STRUCK BY THE FORCE AND FURY OF THE SPELLS HE HAD TRIED TO DEFEAT DR. STRANGE WITH... BARON MORDO IS CAST OUT OF THE ANCIENT ONE'S CASTLE, IN COMPLETE DEFEAT!
AT THAT VERY INSTANT, THE EVIL SPELLS HE HAD CAST ARE BROKEN, AND THE HOME OF DR. STRANGE REAPPEARS IN ITS RIGHTFUL PLACE, AS THE MASTER OF BLACK MAGIC ONCE AGAIN REGAINS HIS PHYSICAL FORM!
AND, IN FAR OFF TIBET, THE ANCIENT ONE SCENDS HIS DAIS AGAIN AND SINKS DOWN PON THE SOFT CUSHIONS OF HIS SEAT...
ACH TIME MORDO TTACKS, HE GROWS STRONGER, MORE DANGEROUS!
DO NOT FEAR, MASTER! NO MATTER *HOW* AWESOME HIS POWER, I SHALL DEVOTE MY LIFE TO VANQUISHING HIM!

ditko shrugged

The Uncompromising Life of the Artist-Creator of Spider-Man and the Rise of Marvel Comics

Foreword by Mark S. Ditko

By David Currie

Hermes Press

Daniel Herman, Editor
Proofreading, Erica McNatt, Kandice Hartner, and L.A. Geer

Cover image: digitally restored original art from *Out of This World* #4, 1957, Charlton Comics; original colors by Troy Musguire.
Cover and book design by Daniel Herman; cover and book design ©2020 Hermes Press
First printing, 2020

Published by Hermes Press an imprint of Herman and Geer Communications, Inc.
2100 Wilmington Road
Daniel Herman, Publisher
Troy Musguire, Production Manager
Sabrina Herman, Managing Editor/Vice President
Alissa Fisher, Senior Graphic Designer
Kandice Hartner, Senior Editor
Neshannock Township, Pennsylvania 16105
(724) 652-0511
www.HermesPress.com; info@hermespress.com

Opposite page: Steve Ditko, pencils and inks, original art for the splash page from *Tales of Suspense* #42, 1963, ©1963 Marvel Characters; Page 3: Steve Ditko, pencils and inks, original cover art for *Out of This World* #4, 1957, ©1957 Charlton Comics; Page 6: Steve Ditko, pencils and inks, original interior page art for *Tales of Suspense* #41, 1963, ©1963 Marvel Characters; Page 7: Steve Ditko, pencils and inks, original cover artwork from *Out of This World* #5, 1957, ©1957 Charlton Comics; Page 8: Cover from *Outer Space* #21, 1959, Steve Ditko, pencils and inks, ©1959 Charlton Comics; Page 10: Steve Ditko, pencils and inks, original interior page artwork from *The Amazing Spider-Man* #18, 1964, ©1964 Marvel Characters; and Page 11: Steve Ditko, pencils and inks, original interior page artwork from *Showcase* #73, 1968, ©1968 DC Comics.

From Dan, Louise, Sabrina, Jacob, Ruk'us, Noodle, and Ginger for D'Zur and Mellow

LCCN Applied for: 10 9 8 7 6 5 4 3 2 1 0
ISBN 978-1-61345-177-9

Image scanning and digital corrections by H + G Media

Printed in China

Supense #42-18

CDC
OUT OF THIS WORLD
№4
OUT OF THIS WORLD
APPROVED BY THE COMICS CODE AUTHORITY
10¢
DITKO ST.
DITKO
YELLOW
BLACK
RED
BLUE
VANDERCOOK

"Stan had his own office and I got along with him fine but he was all business and was probably told by Goodman not to get too friendly with the staff" – Allen Bellman (2018)

"By 1995, it was clear just how important Marvel's intellectual property was, whether it was presented in comics or on TV or in the movies or in videogames. It wasn't playtime anymore" – Danny Fingeroth (2019)

"Throughout the centuries there were men who took first steps down new roads, armed with nothing but their own vision"– Ayn Rand (1943)

"It's like when Stan Lee and Steve Ditko created Spider-Man, Stan Lee may get all the credit but Steve Ditko knows he was just as important, even though Stan Lee gets to be in all the Marvel movies and is far richer and is a household name, whereas if you say Ditko, it sounds like a company that makes Dits!"– Sheldon to Leonard as an allegory for not receiving credit, *Big Bang Theory* television episode (December 2014)

"The attacks just spread. There were editors at both Marvel and DC who wouldn't use me now and even pressured other editors into not giving me any assignments" – Steve Ditko (2014)

"I'm sure there will be lots written about him (Ditko) as time goes by and I will be one of the guys who buys the first book" – Stan Lee (2018)

"In times of deceit, telling the truth becomes a revolutionary act" – George Orwell (1949)

"He looked like he had spent a lifetime at the drawing board" – Neil Gaiman (2019)

YOU ARE GAZING AT THE FAR FUTURE! IT IS THE YEAR 3,000---THE YEAR THAT MANKIND IS ABOUT TO PROBE THE END OF THE UNIVERSE! AND NOW, LET US TURN OUR ATTENTION TO THE ACADAMY OF SCIENCE, WHERE AN IMPORTANT MEETING IS TAKING PLACE...
GENTLEMEN, OUR SPACE SHIPS HAVE FINALLY BEEN DEVELOPED TO THE POINT WHERE THEY CAN EXCEED THE SPEED OF LIGHT! AND THAT MEANS, AT LONG LAST, WE CAN REACH THE VERY LIMITS OF SPACE!
OUR NEXT SPACE PROJECT SHALL BE OUR FINAL ONE--- WE MUST FIND A VOLUNTEER WHO WILL FLY OUR FASTEST SHIP... FLY IT TO THE END OF THE UNIVERSE ITSELF, AND RETURN TO TELL US WHAT HE FOUND!
BUT, FINDING THE RIGHT VOLUNTEER IS NOT AN EASY TASK, FOR THE ASSIGNMENT IS THE MOST DANGEROUS EVER OFFERED TO A MAN...
IT MUST BE UNDERSTOOD THAT THE ODDS ARE AGAINST THE PILOT RETURNING SAFELY!
FOR NO MAN CAN SUSPECT WHAT NAMELESS DANGERS MAY BE WAITING AT THE END OF THE UNIVERSE!
BUT FINALLY, AFTER MONTHS OF SEARCHING, TESTING, INTERVIEWING...
I'M THE MAN YOU WANT! I DON'T CARE WHETHER I LIVE OR DIE!
HMMMMM... YOU SEEM TO HAVE ALL THE QUALIFICATIONS!
I'VE GOT NO FAMILY--- NO FRIENDS! NO JOB AND NO FUTURE!
I CAN'T GET AWAY FROM EARTH FAST ENOUGH TO SUIT ME! AND IF I NEVER COME BACK, THAT'LL SUIT ME FINE TOO!
MISTER, YOU JUST GOT YOURSELF A JOB!
2.

contents

OUT OF THIS WORLD
No 5
-DITKO-

OUTER SPACE
CDC
MARCH
APPROVED BY THE COMICS CODE AUTHORITY
10¢
WIN
8000 PRIZES
DETAILS IN
THIS ISSUE
U.S.A.
USA
Steve Ditko

NOW THERE'S NOTHING TO STOP ME FROM BEING SPIDER-MAN AGAIN!! AUNT MAY HAS ENOUGH GUMPTION FOR BOTH OF US! I WON'T HAVE TO WORRY ABOUT HER ANY MORE!!
AS FOR J. JONAH JAMESON, BEFORE I'M THROUGH, HE'LL BE EATING HIS WORDS ABOUT ME!!
RIP!
FATE GAVE ME SOME TERRIFIC SUPER-POWERS, AND I REALIZE NOW THAT IT'S MY DUTY TO USE THEM... WITHOUT DOUBT... WITHOUT HESITATION...!!
...AND THAT MEANS SPIDER-MAN IS GOING INTO ACTION AGAIN! I'LL FIGHT AS I'VE NEVER FOUGHT BEFORE!! NOTHING WILL STOP ME NOW! FOR I KNOW AT LAST THAT A MAN CAN'T CHANGE HIS DESTINY... AND I WAS BORN TO BE... SPIDER-MAN!!!
WE TOLD YOU THIS TALE WOULD BE DIFFERENT, DIDN'T WE?? SO FAR AS WE KNOW, IT'S THE FIRST TIME IN HISTORY THAT AN ADVENTURE HERO HAD NO ACTUAL FIGHT WITH ANY FOE!
BUT... NOW THE RESPITE IS OVER! NEXT ISH WILL FEATURE SPIDER-MAN FIGHTING AS ONLY HE CAN! SO, GET THOSE WEBS UNTANGLED, AND BE WITH US WHEN SPIDEY SHOWS THE WHOLE WIDE WORLD WHAT HE'S REALLY MADE OF!!
THE END ...FOR NOW
22.

WE CAN CHANGE CLOTHES HERE. THEN WE'LL CLEAR OUT AND GET RID OF THE PROFESSOR'S BODY!
WE DIDN'T EXACTLY FAIL YOU ENTIRELY, MAJOR SMEJ. WE DID GET PROFESSOR YATZ BACK FOR YOU!
YOU FOOL! WHAT GOOD IS A DEAD MAN? HE CAN'T TELL US HIS SECRETS! I'LL SEE THAT YOU---WHAT'S THAT LAUGH?
HA! HA! HA!
SORRY, BOYS! YOUR CAR ISN'T READY YET! IT'S STILL BEING WASHED!
HA! HA! HA! HA! HA! HA! HA! HA! HA! HA!
BOFF!
IT---IT'S THAT THING AGAIN! KILL HIM! KILL HIM!
AIEEEE!
UGHHHHH!
14

Foreword
Uncle Steve

Mark S. Ditko

Steve Ditko was my uncle, my dad's older brother, so I've known him my entire life. It seemed like he was always around at family get-togethers and holidays and was just another fun family member to me and my siblings. You have to understand that in small town Johnstown, especially in the 1960's, family was pretty important and central to our activities. As a little kid in the 60's, I didn't think much at all about what my aunts and uncles did for a living, only whether or not they were fun to be around. And my Uncle Steve had some great skills that a "kid" would love. He was playful, could draw anything you asked him, was funny, and very friendly. At the same time, and I never put two and two together, there were always new comics lying around the house. I loved them! ...and didn't even know that my uncle Steve was the artist behind them. But then again, I was a kid, and only four or five years old during my *Konga* comic phase.

As I grew older, my uncle was always still around. And by that time I knew what he had done in the comic industry, but it wasn't the focus of our relationship. When I was in my late teens I started to see him more and more as someone who stood out amongst others in a unique way. Someday I'll offer more details about this time period, but for now, I'll just say that I began to see him as someone to look up to and admire. The level of his conviction, certainty, integrity and rationality was captivating to this young college kid. When I left Johnstown and moved to Phoenix, we continued our relationship through pages upon pages of written correspondence.

Fast forward to early 2019, when I first saw the notice for this upcoming book, and thought to myself, "*Ditko Shrugged* ...Great title. I wonder how the actual book will be." At the same time I wondered who David Currie was, and then left it at that. Then in mid-June, I got a message from David about his book on my uncle.

Skipping over the fine details that occurred over the next month, I'll say this — through our correspondence, I have grown to see that not only is David qualified to write what he wrote, but more importantly his heart is in the right place. When it comes to people discussing my Uncle Steve, it's difficult for me to hear the incorrect and embellished stories being told about his earlier years and the persistent and continued speculation and innuendos about his life. Thankfully, David allowed me to read his book, and welcomed my seemingly endless pages of commentary with open arms.

As I told David in my first batch of comments on his book, "From a 'Ditko' perspective, this really good book could be turned into a really great book that we could support. I hope that you are not overwhelmed and shocked by this review, but at the same time ... we can only support the truth as we know it. My sole ambition is to present him in the clearest possible light and promote his works to the best of my ability."

I'm very happy to say that this *is* a really great book. David, and his correspondence with my uncle and others, uncovered and documented things that would otherwise have been left unknown or subject to complete speculation ...if ever even considered.

Note that my role in the review of this book was mainly about my uncle's personal life as we know it and not necessarily his professional career. But David clearly has a good grasp on that aspect of him.

I really have to acknowledge my dad for helping me to sort out, debunk, and clarify personal stories that have been told about my uncle for decades. As Steve Ditko's brother, his knowledge was invaluable.

Regarding my Uncle Steve ... I miss him.

PS: Keep your ear to the ground and your eyes open for upcoming material regarding Steve Ditko from the DitkoVerse. (Mark@DitkoVerse.com.)

Opposite page: Steve Ditko with nephews Mark (left) and Stephen on the lawn of the house where Ditko grew up in Johnstown, circa 1963, ©2020 Ditkoverse/Mark S. Ditko.

Mark was born and raised in the hills of small-town Johnstown, Pennsylvania and grew up in an artistic family. After high school his dad, a self-employed architect, encouraged him to pursue a career in Civil Engineering, which he did. Eventually moving to Phoenix, AZ and then to Los Angeles, CA, he now runs his own niche civil engineering consulting business supporting engineers all over the world. He has over two dozen published technical books and is seen as a renowned expert in his field. As a true entrepreneur, he has a love of art, comics, writing, philosophy, fast cars and many, many other areas of life.

715
S. Ditko

Introduction
The Last of the First

Back during the early years of the 21st Century, no-one would have paid any attention to the bespectacled, wispy-haired old man with ink-stained hands as he shuffled through the crowds, clutching black art portfolios while making his daily attendance to a small office near New York's ever-bustling Times Square. He'd done this for over 60 years to one Manhattan office or another, reporting to a drawing board with unfailing duty and to no authority other than his own. Creating art and comic strips to express his thoughts and to feed his quenchless artistic drive, still burning bright as he advanced, sturdily, into his eighties. He knew, and cared little, that very few people ever saw the results he currently produced — but that wasn't always the case over his long career as a legendary comic book artist. For Steve Ditko was the last of two generations of original American comic book artist creators who were inspired architects of fantastic mythologies, unique in depth and scope; who created pen-and-ink fables for the modern age, fueling billion-dollar industries. A principal player, along with Jack Kirby, of a band of artistic visionaries who pitched their relentless creativity to the corporate "dream stealers" of a publishing system that was ultimately stacked against them. Along the way to his office, Ditko would have passed daily reminders of the phenomenal success of one of his past creations in particular. As he side-stepped the increasing number of street entertainers dressed in garish red-and-blue, web-patterned costumes, posing awkwardly for tourist dollars and hanging from street lights. As he passed the Foxwood Theatre (between 2010 and 2014) and its advertising proclamations, "Broadway is the only place to see Spider-Man onstage!" As he passed numerous and varied images of his design on sale from street vendors on t-shirts, caps, plaques and posters. When he first arrived in New York back in 1950 to pursue a career as a comic book artist, Ditko would seek his own visual inspiration in the neon-lit movie theatres — now he walked beneath illuminated advertising for movie releases starring his own creation, while passing shops packed with Spider-Man toys, apparel and comic books. Every day, his famous and world-beloved character would be a permanent fixture of the landscape he walked. Perhaps it was hardly noticed or easily dismissed. To the artist it was simply a job done in the distant past, and any time given to ponder the whys and wherefores would be wasted time. There was, after all, new art and new characters to be created that very day. Ditko replied to the author in May 2013 when asked about his daily walk, "One can't live in the past. The now and tomorrow are where one's focus needs to be." Adding, "Times Square has always been an ongoing side-show, a magnet, to be some kind of part of it — usually a victim in some way." On rare occasions there may have been a knock on the old man's office door that bore the metal nameplate "S. Ditko," as he worked within, radio music on to drown out traffic noise. A fan or a journalist looking for an interview; to praise him; to question him; to meet him. These intrusions would always have been handled exactly the same way: politely but curtly. No interviews. No autographs. No photos. For anyone. Ever. Steve Ditko would then return to his art board and continue the act of production. He never married nor had children in any sense other than his art creations. He was content with that and with the creative opportunities his own company allowed him. The artist wrote to me in 2013, "It's an age-old problem that everyone should or must belong to their tribe or some group, (or) collective. Human nature, being what it is, the different will always be seen as threatening to many." Concluding, "They don't like any Lone Wolf type."

Opposite page: Door of Steve Ditko's studio, 1650 Broadway, room 715, New York City, circa 2010.

Another elderly man by the name of Stan Lee would return to his native New York most years each October for an annual public appearance, a tradition that was upheld up until his 93rd year in 2016 when his seemingly inexhaustible energy finally began to falter. As tens of thousands of devotees, industry professionals and inventively-garbed, attention-seeking cosplayers descended on the riverside Javits Centre — just a few blocks from Ditko's office — for the New York Comicon, writer/editor and toasted celebrity Lee would fly into the city from the sun-soaked shores of the West Coast of America, his chosen home since the early 1980s. Increasingly becoming a media event with wider appeal, the contemporary version of the NYCC was an iteration of one of many conventions, calling the Big Apple their home base. The first "Comicon" held on July 27,

1964 had been set up by a youthful group of fans and was attended by both Stan Lee and Steve Ditko. It was the first and last comic convention Ditko would ever attend during his lifetime.

Stan Lee was the unquestioned star of the recreated NYCC, run by professional "convention-company" Reed Exhibitions, in a line-up of contenders that included A-list actors and directors, and was recognized the world over as the most famous comic book writer/creator who ever lived. Celebrated as the main (and often sole) creator of Spider-Man, The Avengers, The X-Men, The Hulk and countless other Marvel comic characters, he led a million-dollar lifestyle, constantly courted attention and eventually became as famous as the comic characters he'd once scripted, decades earlier. Everybody knew who Stan Lee was, even if they'd never read a single comic book in their lives. He was the sprightly old man that made all those jokey cameo appearances in 30-plus Marvel movies. The charmer always smiling in numerous television interviews as he excitedly told tales of spandex-suited heroes. He'd appeared in every media possible, stage, screen, print, online, in search of new "true believers," becoming a cultural reference point cited in such mass-audience entertainments as *The Simpsons*, *The Big Bang Theory* and many others. Unyieldingly jovial, gently-humoured, quick-witted and forever sharp, Lee had spent nearly 80 years writing and editing then promoting comics and the Marvel brand, since he first joined the company (then known as Timely) at the tender age of 17 in 1939, through his uncle Robby Solomon. This was all as the company went through of succession of owners, from its original owner (also a relative of Lee's, albeit a distant one) Martin Goodman to eventually settle into the hands of the corporation borne by the personality Lee most wanted to emulate as a younger man, Walt Disney. Lee enjoyed a long life in the celebrity spotlight and was revered by many as their childhood guru and feted by the rest as the most prolific comic book character creator of them all. His intuitive ability to be able connect with audiences, to make

Above: Steve Ditko, pencils and inks, original artwork featuring Mr. A from ***Eon Fanzine***, 1969, ©1969 Steve Ditko.

them feel included and always in on the jokes his snappy dialogue was peppered with, was his true mastery. He coined catch-phrases by the dozen ("Excelsior!," "Nuff Said!," and "Face Front, True Believers!"") and swiftly developed his "face of Marvel" persona with unerring skill and through the auspices of the company itself. A shamelessly-corny, ever-smiling spokesperson for a world of dreams. Ditko wrote to the author in July 2016, "Stan promoting Marvel titles worked more promoting himself. He took advantage of an opportunity and it keeps paying off." Lee adored the attention and played his role exceedingly well over many decades — a friendly-neighbourhood grandfather figure to the world who brought you comic books, tales of heroic deeds and a character for every occasion. Behind the mask, however, his celebrity and vast wealth would bring him unfortunate complications, family dramas and business scandals to mire his final years. Ditko wrote to the author that, "Wanting, needing some public recognition status, being a public celebrity, a false ego-building, pandering to others, fans, crowds with interviews etc., is self-defeating." Ditko also wrote to me in 2013 on the subject of fame, adding, "The public viewing must be continually maintained or feel abandoned, alone, helpless." Still singing the cause back when he entered his 90s, an appearance by Stan Lee at the NYCC was a guaranteed crowd-puller — all eager to pay $100 or more for a photo, or an autograph. For $300 plus, you could buy a one-on-one with Stan as part of a small group of people, get two items signed and that coveted photo with "The Man." His final appearance at the New York Comic Con in October 2016 saw Stan Lee billed as the "Creator of Spider-Man."

And back then, all the while in solitude, Steve Ditko drew on…

Steve Ditko's body was discovered in his New York apartment on June 29, 2018. A social worker assigned to him after a hospital stay hadn't heard anything from him for couple of days and decided to check up on his welfare. It was estimated that he had died alone of a heart attack two days earlier on June 27. Over a week later, when his passing was officially announced on July 7, 2018, his name was the top trend on Twitter for most of that day. As the world blinked and saw the name attributed to the creation of Spider-Man, Doctor Strange and many other famous characters, a flood of tributes poured in and the words "legendary," "genius" and "reclusive" were often used to describe the late, 90-year-old comic book artist. For perhaps the first time, some people were asking, however briefly, and in the tradition of John Galt, a fictional character the artist would have identified with, "Who is Steve Ditko?"

Stan Lee's death at 95 from heart and respiratory failure, prefaced by pneumonia, on November 12, 2018 — just some five months after Ditko's — was afforded the attention befitting a world-status media personality. He wasn't just the top trend on Twitter that day, he was the top five trends. The outpouring of love and gratitude expressed by millions encapsulated the feeling that an entire era in the particularly American art-form of comic books had also passed when the celebrated writer took his final breath. In various headlines he was referred to as the "Boss of Marvel" "Marvel's Real-life Superhero" and "The Man who Created the Marvel Universe." As numerous celebrities stumbled over themselves in their speed to eulogize Stan on social media, one post in particular stood out as one which perhaps both Steve Ditko and Jack Kirby, little mentioned in most articles, would have found great irony in. Hugh Jackman, the Australian actor who played the Marvel character Wolverine in no less than nine movies and who met Lee on more than one occasion, wrote, "I'm proud to have been a small part of his legacy and to have helped bring one of his characters to life." Wolverine was first introduced in 1974, some two years after Lee had stopped writing comic books altogether and the actual creators, a potential four in number, have their own mixed memories of who actually did what, as later examined in this book. Ditko wrote to me in May 2015, "Comic books never had a strict division of labour. At the time, who created what was of no importance," to illustrate how casually collaborative the process often was. In such a process and with the passing of time, the lines between creative credit can be easily blurred, especially by memory but also sometimes potentially by intent. As writer/editor Roy Thomas, Lee's former assistant and protégé during the latter part of Marvel Comics' 1960s halcyon years, wrote to me in 2013, referencing the origins of Wolverine, "Creation is a word of infinite stretchability."

Using Ditko's own previously unpublished words, along with interviews with many other creators, the story of Steve Ditko and of American comic books of the 20th Century — along with of the rise of the media giant Marvel — is told in this book. It's a story of supremely-gifted artists who created enduring modern mythology on what was effectively zero-hour contracts; a story of heroes and villains, both fictional and real, and a story of one particular man's dedication to his art and his principals. Set against the backdrop of the times they took place in, the achievements of that one man and his resolute approach to life provide all the necessary ingredients for an intrinsically American tale of a genius outsider artist. Because the word most often used to describe Steve Ditko by people that knew him and even by those that knew only of his legend was "uncompromising." He wrote to me in May 2013, "One can set the terms for one's own life or let others influence and dominate, pragmatically going along for some new gratification or short-term benefit. Choices always have to be made with positive or negative consequences. It's always a freewill choice."

TAKE IT AWAY! ITS BRIGHTNESS IS APALLING TO ME!
But NO MATTER WHERE THE EVIL MORDO TURNS, THE RAYS OF THE ENCHANTED LIGHT REACH OUT AND BATHE HIM IN THEIR BRILLIANT GLOW!
IT IS JUST AS THE ANCIENT ONE HAS EVER SAID! THE POWER OF GOOD SHALL ALWAYS BANISH EVIL! NOW I SHALL GATHER ALL THE SINISTER SPELLS OF MORDO..
...AND HURL THEM BACK AT HIM, BEFORE HE CAN CONJURE UP NEW DEFENSES!
TAKEN BY SHEER SURPRISE... STRUCK BY THE FORCE AND FURY OF THE SPELLS HE HAD TRIED TO DEFEAT DR. STRANGE WITH... BARON MORDO IS CAST OUT OF THE ANCIENT ONE'S CASTLE, IN COMPLETE DEFEAT!
AT THAT VERY INSTANT, THE EVIL SPELLS HE HAD CAST ARE BROKEN, AND THE HOME OF DR. STRANGE REAPPEARS IN ITS RIGHTFUL PLACE, AS THE MASTER OF BLACK MAGIC ONCE AGAIN REGAINS HIS PHYSICAL FORM!
AND, IN FAR OFF TIBET, THE ANCIENT ONE ASCENDS HIS DAIS AGAIN AND SINKS DOWN UPON THE SOFT CUSHIONS OF HIS SEAT...
EACH TIME MORDO ATTACKS, HE GROWS STRONGER, MORE DANGEROUS!
DO NOT FEAR, MASTER! NO MATTER HOW AWESOME HIS POWER, I SHALL DEVOTE MY LIFE TO VANQUISHING HIM!
8.
BUT, AS DR. STRANGE RETURNS TO HIS SILENT ABODE IN GREENWICH VILLAGE, LITTLE DOES HE DREAM THAT HIS NEXT THREAT WILL NOT COME FROM BARON MORDO... BUT FROM A FAR DIFFERENT, A FAR STRANGER MENACE... AS WE SHALL SEE NEXT ISSUE!!
The End

Prologue
Sturdy Against the "Dream Stealers"

In late November 1965, when Steve Ditko hand-delivered his very last Spider-Man comic art pages to the small offices of underdog-but-rising comic book publisher Marvel Comics on New York's Madison Avenue, he walked away from what would prove to be his most enduring artistic legacy. At least, as far as the world was concerned, while the artist himself would cite his creation Mr. A as "the one character from the past that I would like to see in the present and the future," as he once wrote to his nephew Mark S. Ditko.

But in Spider-Man, Ditko had crafted a timeless, heroic-yet-identifiable character who would eventually be known and loved around the globe, forming the centre of a billion-dollar industry as a result. He had given the art pages, along with his final Doctor Strange story, to Marvel's Production Editor Sol Brodsky, as he had done for the past six months since any communication between Ditko and the comic strip's credited writer and editor Stan Lee had long since broken down and ceased. Ditko had created Spider-Man, along with scripter/editor Lee, three years earlier in 1962 but within a process of creation that encouraged the artist to be responsible for many uncredited aspects that would today unambiguously be considered elements of creationist writing: Plot narrative, emotional drive, story pacing, introduction of characters, super-villains, situations. Eventually named "The Marvel Method" by its inventor Stan Lee, the process enabled Lee to write dialogue, edit and co-ordinate an ever-increasing number of comic book titles, while dispensing of the need for a full script for each one but effectively keeping the artists constantly busy. This was an innovation designed solely to benefit Lee's workload, and this free-wheeling style was not the norm in the business during this period.

Over at DC Comics, the industry leader at the time, for example, the writer would provide the artist with a comprehensive full script that told a complete story with fully formed characters, dialogue and often suggesting page layout breakdowns. But, at the very birth of Marvel Comics' rise to popularity with initially just a slim roster of titles to handle, Lee, by this time a seasoned comic book editor, was already dispensing of such formalities and instead offering only verbal instructions or suggestions to select artists whose story-telling skills he trusted, especially Jack Kirby and Steve Ditko. As Ditko himself confirmed to the author in March 2015, "There were never any written Spider-Man scripts." From the early to middle 1960s, it was Ditko's sinewy and highly stylistic art which defined Spider-Man in both look and tone: the genius costume design; the tortured elegance of the character's elbows-and-knees poses; the web-swinging with vertiginous views of Manhattan; the inventive parade of sinister villains he fought and the dramas of the teenage mistakes he made as his alter-ego Peter Parker — all wrapped up in a real-world based morality play. And Ditko's artwork revealed that world to be dark and un-glamorous with his strangely compelling depictions of busy-handed people that appeared frantic or paranoid or outright ugly as they lived and survived in the shadowy canyons of New York City, almost a third main character in the yarn. To the comparatively few readers of the singular monthly comic book, which had only reached 38 issues and two annuals at this stage, Ditko *was* Spider-Man and his abrupt departure seemed baffling to the extreme. No explanation was given to them, as none was offered by Ditko to his editor or readers, but the decision to leave an increasingly bestselling title just as it was gaining momentum, seemed bizarre.

For the majority of comic book artists in the mid-1960s, the working conditions were exactly the same as they had been in the New York controlled publishing industry since the field enjoyed its heyday in the seminal 1940s period — strictly free-lance "work-for-hire." This meant the publishers, which fluctuated from a multitude during boom periods to a handful during leaner, offered writers and artists work on a month-to-month basis with no guarantee of further work and no ongoing benefits, such as health insurance and pensions, even if your work was sufficient enough to ensure those months of employment turned into years. In modern parlance, the majority of freelance comic book creators from this time all worked zero-hour contracts. To flourish or even survive in this environment, the writers and artists had to be good, fast, reliable and relentlessly creative. Although the creators had little rights within this contract of non-employment, the publishers enjoyed many,

Opposite page: Ditko, pencils and inks, original artwork from ***Strange Tales*** #117, February, 1964, ©1964 Marvel Characters.

primarily the exclusive copyright on any and all images, characters, created by the artists for publication in their titles; Ditko wrote to me in November 2014, "The ideas could be mine but I had no real right to them when published." For Ditko to leave *Spider-Man*, which translated as regular employment and increasing accolades just as Marvel was beginning to gain a market presence as the feisty, brash, new-kid-on-the-block publisher of *Fantastic Four*, *Incredible Hulk*, *Avengers* and *X-Men*, seemed, on the face of it, self-defeating on many levels.

All comic artists were used to tough working schedules but also used to the fact that very few people actually saw their hard laboured work. The opportunity to change this, however briefly, was a dream for the majority of job-to-next-job comic book artists and the most secure assignment would be on a best-selling title. Perhaps there were other factors involved in Ditko's decision to quit. At this time in the middle-1960s, *Spider-Man* and Marvel Comics in general were on the rise. College students began to read deeper meaning in the contrast between the everyday struggles then cosmic clashes of this new breed of clay-footed superheroes; journalists working for magazines covering "today" concerns sought to explain their sudden popularity and artists working on a broader world canvas such as Andy Warhol and Roy Lichtenstein attempted to steal some of their alchemy for their own work.

It was precisely at this time that Steve Ditko drew his final images of the iconic, web-patterned superhero and, according to urban myth, effectively vanished, not only from Spider-Man and Stan Lee's Marvel, but from the gaze of the world itself. He refused, from this point on and for the rest of his long life, to give interviews to anyone on any subject and shunned all publicity and attention. He remained elusive, but of course, Ditko didn't simply disappear or become invisible, continuing to pursue an active career in comic books and later writing essays and comic strips regularly within his own self-published work. But as Marvel rose to dominate the comic book industry from the 1960s to today, and Stan Lee became the celebrated personality presenting it all; as the 21st Century rediscovered these four-colour characters as blockbuster material for cinema audiences, along with the endless merchandising possibilities they offer, Ditko kept his distance from his historic Marvel creations. He continued to create comic books and new characters prolifically, but by now had gained a reputation within the industry as "difficult to deal with" and "highly principled."

After bouncing from publisher to publisher, often facing what he termed as "editorial conspiracies" against him, he would eventually settle into a life of self-appointed epic obscurity, punctuated regularly by self-published work containing both comic strips and essays, exclusively seeped in his own interpretations of Objectivist thinking of individualism, "rational self-interest" and achievement measured by creative production. These works were created over a 25-year period but as they bypassed major comic book publishers, were little-seen and as he said, somewhat cryptically in 2002 to a door-stepping New York Post reporter, "It's all they'll let me do." With the art becoming looser and less embellished with each subsequent release, the constant message — the expression of intellectual views — becomes the central theme of the work, reworked over again and again, becoming a living example of a core characteristic of Objectivism, the expression of the individual. In this regard, Ditko shares a great deal in common with more traditionally fine art, but similarly obsessed artists, who in their older years, also settled on one theme to relentlessly explore: Monet with his water-lilies and Rembrandt with his self-portraits, as examples.

To tell the story of Steve Ditko is no easy task. Outside of his recorded dealings with the comic book industry and the vast body of unique artwork he created over seven decades, very few confirmed details of his personal life are available, due to his reclusive nature and his abiding belief that the work he produced should speak for itself. He wasn't interested in fame, wealth or how/if history would remember him. Some would cite his rigid adherence to the Objectivist philosophy originally articulated by Russian-born writer Ayn Rand, which he adopted in 1965 and retained lifelong, as a prime reason for his frequent butting-of-heads with many collaborators and the reluctance of some editors to employ him over his long career. "Impossibly uptight" was often a description heard leveled at Ditko.

In his last printed interview, appearing in Marvel fanzine *Marvel Main* in 1968, Ditko laid out his table precisely saying, "When I do a job, it's not my personality that I'm offering the readers, it's my artwork. It's not what I'm like that counts but what I did and how well it was done. I produce a product, a comic art story. Steve Ditko is the brand name."

This book respects this while hoping to offer some new insights to help form a more balanced view of the artist in particular and the times he worked through in general. Because much of Ditko's story is also the tale of many other visionary American comic book artists and writers of the 20th Century, who created timeless characters under laborious working conditions and effectively gave their unique dreams away for next to nothing. The list includes Jack Kirby, Jerry Siegel and Joe Shuster, Jerry Robinson, Bill Finger, Wally Wood, Steve Gerber, and this book also includes aspects of some of their own stories and industry experiences. The book is helped immensely by referencing a near decade-long series of correspondence between Steve Ditko and the author, written from 2008 until 2017. The letters, which often ran six to seven pages in length, all written in pencil with a precise and steady hand, reveal a glimpse into the artists' uncompromising nature while also displaying a pragmatic approach to life, retaining in his later years a commendable wide-eyed interest for its natural mysteries. ("And we have some latest news," he excitedly wrote to me in a letter from 2016 — "A HUGE crater in Australia, a fossil of some LARGEST mammal on earth. If so, the earth continues to reveal its incredible history. Archaeologists continue to find, discover new startling facts about man's life along with new findings in outer space — Mars, Pluto etc., in our ever continually changing universe. Mother Nature is always surprising us. But no-one does us, the human race, as much damage as the irrational man.")

Each example taken from our correspondence has been presented as Ditko wrote them and used within appropriate context. On some occasions, quotes on the same subject have been taken from different letters and combined together to concise information. The book has been further aided by interviews I conducted with other comic book creators between 2011 and 2019 and my thanks go to them all for their time and memories, including appreciative farewells to some on the list no longer with us: Neal Adams, Allen Bellman, Frank Brunner, Rich Buckler, Tom DeFalco, Danny Fingeroth, Ramona Fradon, Neil Gaiman, Paul Gulacy, Jack C. Harris, Bob Layton, Paul Levitz, Larry Lieber, David Lloyd, Pablo Marcos, Val Mayerik, David Michelinie, Ralph Reese, Steve Rude, P. Craig Russell, Joe Sinnott, Roy Thomas, Herb Trimpe, Phil Winslade and Marv Wolfman.

I first wrote to Ditko in 2008 with regards to the possibility of including some of his art work in a show of original American comic book art I was curating for the Victoria Art Gallery in Bath, UK. The art show was free to the public and included examples from masters of the medium past and present, including Jack Kirby, Wally Wood, Graham Engels and Mike Mignola. Lacking an example of Ditko's artwork and feeling it important that he be represented in the show, I decided to go directly to the source and enquire if I could buy or loan a piece directly from the artist. For a well-publicized "recluse" he was staggeringly easy to find, listed as he was, in the New York Manhattan phone directory. I wrote him a letter, quickly received a polite but terse reply in the negative and left it there. Sometime later, I was commissioned to write a lengthy series of interviews with comic book greats for UK magazine *Comic Heroes* and, with pre-knowledge that Ditko never gave interviews, nonetheless chanced my arm with a second letter requesting such. Unsurprisingly, an even terser reply from Ditko followed where he pointedly explained his "all-or-none" policy towards such requests but did so in the form of questions. My amused answers to those questions sparked a series of correspondence that developed into a pen friendship across the Atlantic in the best of traditions, exchanging views and information in letter-form, separated by an ocean. It was how Ditko preferred to communicate, as he wrote to me in 2014, "I don't do computers."

We wrote regularly over a nine year period and our conversations covered a wide variety of subjects including comic books (and Spider-Man), world history, philosophy, the universe and how the "anti-Ditko" (as he put it) backlash started with publisher-wide "editorial conspiracies" against him and his work. He often included cuttings from magazines on a point of interest raised in discussion with the letters and copies of the current comic books he was producing through co-publisher and editor Robin Snyder. Ditko's writing style eschewed the general niceties of regular communication with no opening, "How are you," but rather straight into the subject at hand. He wrote directly about whatever subject matter he desired, sometimes in response to a point I may have raised in a previous letter, often just because it was something he wanted to say. And he liked to use the abbreviation "etc." A lot.

Sometimes he skipped commenting on a particular statement or query I may have posed (and not by accident). One example of this is when I asked if there was any truth to the rumour that after leaving Marvel Comics he wrote and drew a *Doctor Strange* story, almost the length of a graphic novel long before such things existed, exclusively for himself. While he was precise in his responses to queries before and after, on this subject he declined to answer. Loud silence and lack of rebuttal etc. At some point, I mentioned to Ditko how his grittily urban depiction of New York was the first version of the city I ever saw as a child reader of his comics and wanted to reciprocate the favour by introducing him to the vastly different Georgian architecture of my own home city of Bath, in the West of England. To this end, I mailed him birthday cards with scenes of the city and eventually a book on the city, which he loved and called, "A delightful treat for the eye." He conceded that Bath, with its over 200-year-old three-storey high Palladian buildings, would be difficult for Spider-Man to feel at home in but would make for an atmospheric setting for Doctor Strange.

The original Celtic settlers, who founded the city of hot springs long before the Romans arrived, certainly considered the area to be magical and the very gateway to the supernatural underworld. They built and dedicated a temple to their god Sulis and believed the ancient, constantly flowing hot waters possessed magical healing powers. I told him openly of my intentions to write a book about him and comic book artists from the same period at the beginning of our correspondence, to which he replied, "Almost everyone has something they want to do or 'need' to tell. What's the history of revealed SECRETS? Other people have their 'something.' And only time will reveal, not the intentions but the actual." That he continued to write to me with regularity, over a long period of time, in-depth and with increasing openness, aware of my literary intentions, is why I believe some of the content of the letters should be published and his story told with the added weight of his own words. He only wrote, "This is not for publication" on one letter and no quotes have been taken from that particular correspondence. I believe the letters reveal a man comfortable in his own skin, resolute in his beliefs, while at the same time disclosing a sensitive side — of past wounds that hadn't quite healed, of a resigned

PRETTY TRICKY, MASKED MAN! BUT NOW LET'S SEE HOW GOOD YOU ARE ON AN OILY, GREASED FLOOR!!
ACCORDING TO THE LATEST SUPER-HERO MANUAL, THE WELL-TRAINED COSTUMED CRIME FIGHTER TURNS EVERY OBSTACLE INTO AN ADVANTAGE! SEE WHAT I MEAN?
HE'S SLIDING ON THE FLOOR--LIKE AN ICE-SKATER! LOOK OUT!
YOU CAN'T DODGE US FOREVER!! RUSH 'IM FROM ALL SIDES, YOU GUYS!
HE'S RIGHT! I CAN'T DODGE THEM FOREVER! BUT I'M SURE GONNA GO DOWN TRYING!
WE'VE GOT HIM NOW!
YOU CHERUBS ARE MADE FOR EACH OTHER-- SO FAR BE IT FROM ME TO KEEP YOU APART!
WHUMP!
BUT, BEFORE SPIDER-MAN CAN REGAIN HIS FOOTING, THE FAST-MOVING FANCY DAN STRIKES AGAIN WITH A SKILLFUL JUDO ATTACK!
OOFF!
I FIGURE THEY WORE YOU DOWN ENOUGH! NOW I'LL FINISH YOU OFF!
A JUDO-TRAINED LITTLE MAN'S ALWAYS MORE THAN A MATCH FOR A GUY TWICE HIS SIZE! EVEN WHEN THE GUY IS SPIDER-MAN!
REMEMBER THOSE WORDS, LITTLE FRIEND! YOU'RE GONNA START REGRETTING THEM REAL SOON!
17

acceptance of the tragedies of the world and with knowledge of the beauty of life as he reflected on it from an older perspective. Ditko quoted from a poem to me in a letter from 2013, extolling the virtues of the singular day, "Yesterday is only a dream, and tomorrow is but a vision. Yet, each day well lived makes every yesterday a dream of happiness and each tomorrow a vision of hope. Look well, therefore, to this one day for it and it alone is life."

Steve Ditko was certainly a singular man. In many ways difficult to understand, stubborn sometimes to the point of incredulity, and to many people who ever worked with him, often at once inspiring and exasperating. But his art and creations brought pleasure and joy to millions of people worldwide and will continue to do so for generations to come. He never sought fame or wealth to reward this, although it was there for the taking and, in the grand tradition of all renowned artists from all periods of history, remained true to his work throughout his life. He never compromised his firmly-held principles, however they were perceived and frequently used against him by some of the people around him. He had his wounds, his towering successes and his ridiculed failures, but he was far from bitter and a long way from defeated. A little like Peter Parker. He remained true to the conclusions he came to as a younger man about the best way for him to live a long, conflict-free and productive life and certainly achieved all of that. In terms of comic book artists and their mythology-making abilities, we may never see his like again.

The thousands of pages of comic book art that Steve Ditko produced in his lifetime was intended by him to serve as his biography by proxy, no further words needed. He never regarded any of them as art produced to be hung in galleries. As he wrote to me in August 2008 in response to my original request, "I'm not interested in having my original art on public display. It isn't made for that purpose." Despite this, today, those original pencil and ink comic art pages produced by Steve Ditko, Jack Kirby and contemporary artists have become far more valuable than the world outside the comics industry could possibly imagine and are often to be seen in exhibitions worldwide. In the past 20 years, a demand for these original art pages have created a buoyant collector market that continues to push prices for desirable pieces ever higher, especially art from the early Marvel years with Ditko drawn *Spider-Man* pages being among the most coveted. These pages are rare to the market and an interior page averages in the $50,000 – $200,000 range while an opening story page (called a "splash page") or the most desirable — a cover — may demand up to one million dollars. But Ditko never benefited from the sale of any of his original *Spider-Man* art pages. He wrote to me in May 2013, "A lot of original art was stolen from the companies by people within the companies. Comic book fandom is willing to ignore that many of the pages available are stolen property and even eager to cash in on it. We live in a society, world, that does not recognize individual or property rights. Comic book companies with their anti-heroes are continually profiting by celebrating anything goes. It's hard to really know what went on, goes on, inside editorial offices in regard to anything. Dishonesties, thefts, crimes etc. is an age-old continuing activity of people — sellers and buyers — who want the unearned and undeserved."

The original *Spider-Man* art pages that Ditko did eventually receive back from Marvel were few, a fraction of the amount he created, and he never sold a single one in his lifetime. But the extraordinary monetary value now placed on this comic art is evidence that these comic book artists from that period — once ignored, derided, or appreciated by the very few — are now finding new ground in being posthumously recognized as major artistic influences on modern popular culture. It all happened originally in a particular period of 20th Century history — from the onset of World War II, when the concept of the superhero was created and sold, primarily as wish-fulfillment for battle-weary soldiers overseas and idealistic children at home. Then to the sweeping social changes of the 1960s and through to the turbulent 1970s and the new-style comic book creators they ushered in. It was over this time when those ink-stained comic art "Slaves of New York," Steve Ditko included, created characters potent enough to be revered by generations to come, attaining the status of cultural icons. As they rubbed shoulders on the sidewalks with the rushing advertising men of Madison Avenue, they were all busy doing their own work to change the face of American culture, while trying also to protect those creations from the ever-present corporate dream stealers. For these efforts and for many of them, the rewards in their lifetimes would often be acrimony, legal battles with publishers, public disputes over character creation and ownership, stolen art and decades of resentment directed towards individuals and corporations. But Steve Ditko never played those games...

Opposite page: Ditko, pencils and inks, original artwork from ***The Amazing Spider-Man*** #10, March, 1964, ©1964 Marvel Characters.

Chapter One
Heroes Are Born in Times of Chaos 1927-1954

Johnstown, Pennsylvania, in Cambria County, situated over 300 miles from New York, is a town dubbed as "Flood City" and once officially the least likely place in the whole of the United States of America to attract newcomers. But back in the late 1920s it was a hard-working, optimistic town that was forged by workers mining steel, iron and coal, providing economic security for families to flourish and communities to develop. It had been this way for many decades, but Johnstown's past was mired with tragedy of national importance. On May 31, 1889, over 2,000 citizens lost their lives as the original prosperous steel town, settled in 1770, comprising homes, churches, saloons and even two opera houses, became buried under debris and mud in just ten minutes. Relentless heavy rain led to the collapse of the South Fork Dam creating a flood and subsequent fire that destroyed Johnstown, becoming known at the time as "The Great Flood" and commemorated in later years in American culture in movies, books and a Bruce Springsteen song. By 1927, some 38 years on from the flood, the feisty town had rebuilt itself proudly, improving the efficiency of the mills, learning from past mistakes and eager to embrace the 20th Century along with its swift rise of consumerism. Johnstown now boasted a population of over 65,000, its own commercial radio station, five major department stores and apparent job-for-life security within the mills. But despite its seemingly stable economic position, it was still finding it hard to shake off the national tag of Flood City, unaware that the Great Depression and further major floods were just around the corner for the town, rendering its future growth restricted.

It was on Wednesday, November 2, 1927 when Stephen John Ditko was born in Johnstown, Pennsylvania — the tough little town with one eye on the future and, at the time, one that seemed a solid place to build your own personal American Dream. Steve, as he later decided to call himself, was born to Anna and Stephen Ditko, first generation Americans of Slovak descent and part of the working-class backbone of the city. Stephen was, by all accounts, a highly-gifted master carpenter whose artistic talents were put to good use in Johnstown's steel mills and Anna, a devoted mother and talented seamstress and homemaker. The family lived centrally in town on Iron Street, in a fairly large house with a barn at the back on Tennessee Avenue. The house backed up against the woods of Brownstown Hill and gave the Ditko children plenty of hillsides to explore and play in.

Steve Ditko was born the second eldest of a group of siblings, joining his sister Anna Marie, who was one year his senior and eventually joined by second sister Elizabeth and brother Patrick. Slightly built and just above average height, it's reported but not confirmed that the young Ditko first discovered comic strips through his father, as they read together weekly installments of Hal Foster's *Prince Valiant* in the "Funnies'" section of the newspaper. In an era of no other visual home entertainment, great attention would be given to the intricate detail found in the lovingly-rendered depictions of medieval landscapes and battlefields and the people who inhabited them. Soon, the young Ditko would be realizing the images that commanded his attention so were created with little more than a pencil, a piece of paper and an active imagination. His interest increased dramatically in 1940 when the 12-year-old Ditko discovered the rich and shadowy artwork of Will Eisner, in *The Spirit* Sunday supplement newspaper strip, savouring its clever designs and immersive textures, studying each illustrated episode with close scrutiny. From newspaper strips to the emerging proliferation of comic book titles, Ditko's true fascination was held by *The Spirit* but also in the recently debuted superhero character, The Batman. Previous writings on Ditko's early life have reported that his mother sewed together a Batman costume for the young artist to wear, but according to his nephew Mark S. Ditko this never happened. "...his mother never made them costumes but Steve and his friend Mike were known as Batman and Robin around the neighbourhood since they loved those characters and imagined themselves as a team like them." Ditko was among the very first generation of comic book readers to discover the character, along with the very concept of the superhero itself, during this nascent period for the industry. "The evolution of comic books has quite a history," he would later write to me in a letter from May 2015.

Back in 1933, publisher Maxwell Gaines invented the American comic book format by taking a Sunday Newspaper

Opposite page clockwise: Steve Ditko as he appeared in 1945 in his Johnstown, Pennsylvania, senior high school year book; (left) in the U.S. Army, 1945, ©2020 Ditkoverse/Mark S. Ditko; and Johnstown, Pennsylvania, circa 1920s.

No. 71
Featuring the BOY COMMANDOS
A SUPERMAN DC PUBLICATION
The BATMAN
Detective
COMICS
JAN. 10¢
BATMAN and ROBIN versus JOKER in "A CRIME A DAY!"
27 FRIDAY
26 THURSDAY
NOVEMBER 21 SATURDAY
NOVEMBER 13

No.62
A SUPERMAN DC PUBLICATION
The BATMAN
Detective
COMICS
POP
from the collection of jerry robinson

COMIC BOOK SECTION
The Sunday Star
ACTION Mystery ADVENTURE
SUNDAY, MARCH 2, 1941
THE SPIRIT
THE SPIRIT, IN REALITY DENNY COLT, WHO WAS BURIED BY MISTAKE IN WILDWOOD CEMETERY NOW USES THE VERY TOMB TO CARRY ON HIS FIGHT AGAINST CRIME...
BY Will Eisner

COMIC BOOK SECTION
THE SUNDAY SUN
BALTIMORE, MD.
3 COMPLETE STORIES
SUNDAY, JANUARY 5, 1941
TO CENTRAL CITY EACH YEAR COME THOUSANDS OF IMMIGRANTS SEEKING REFUGE IN THE MELTING POT THAT IS AMERICA, AND BRINGING WITH THEM THE GOOD AND THE EVIL OF A WORLD IN FLAMES ... FOR EVIL KNOWS NO BOUNDRIES AND TRAVELS SWIFTEST WITH WICKED MEN ... BUT LET THEM BEWARE, FOR TO THE NORTH LIES WILDWOOD CEMETERY WHERE LIVES CRIME'S MIGHTIEST FOE ...
BY Will Eisner
THE SPIRIT
HA-HA-HA! LET THE SPIRIT BEWARE OF THE WRATH OF THE BLACK BOW!!

Funnies Supplement of the time and simply folding it in half. He was working as a salesperson for Eastern Color Printing — the company printing the Sunday newspaper strips — when he saw, in that folded pamphlet in his hand, hitherto untapped promotional and repackaging opportunities. Gaines convinced the company of the benefits of producing such re-presented comic strips in this format as promotional tie-ins with clients, exchanged for clip-out coupons for their products. Eastern Color first produced *Funnies on Parade* a slim, eight-page, saddle-stitched comic book reprinting syndicated comic strips like Ham Fisher's *Joe Palooka* and Al Smith's *Mutt and Jeff* (America's first popular daily comic strip) and mailed out free to those who sent in Proctor and Gamble product coupons. Over the same year, the company produced numerous such promotional publications for other clients and by the end of 1933, Maxwell Gaines worked with the publisher Dell to produce the 36-page giveaway *Famous Funnies: A Carnival of Comics*. The following year, *Famous Funnies* (July 1934) would launch with a monthly distribution to newsstands and a 10-cent price tag. With this title release, the American comic book could be said to have been effectively born. And its birth was instantly popular and eventually highly profitable. Providing cheap entertainment to Great Depression American kids, the title nearly sold out its 200,000-print run and continued to do so monthly as it eventually mixed reprinted newspaper material with original strips like *Buck Rogers*, which begun in its third issue. Over its time, *Famous Funnies* not only helped create the market for comic books, but also re-formatted artwork to better suit the page size and carried early work by names that would later loom large in the industry's development and history including Jack Kirby and Frank Frazetta. But the first comic book to feature completely new material, ultimately giving rise to the first major publisher of such material and the eventual home of Superman and also Batman, the caped crusader that would so entrance young Ditko, was *New Fun: The Big Comic Magazine* in February 1935. Celebrated novelist, pulp writer and retired U.S. cavalry officer Major Malcolm Wheeler-Nicholson had noted the success of *Famous Funnies* and sensed opportunity within this publishing endeavour. In 1934, he formed a company, National Allied Publications, to enter the field but found that all the licences for the popular newspaper strips were already taken. Undaunted, Wheeler-Nicholson decided to launch a publication containing all-new original material and, by also avoiding the excessive reprint fees of the newspaper syndicates, his approach created immediate work for writers and artists who were eager to create new comic strips — even if it was at a much lower page rate than their newspaper counterparts. Wheeler-Nicholson's somewhat forced decision to solicit original material from these writers and artists and publish previously unknown and untested comic strips is the direct root of the American comic book industry known today.

Opposite page clockwise: Early influences on the young Ditko: Jerry Robinson original cover artwork for ***Detective Comics*** #62, April,1942, ©1942 DC Comics; Covers for the Sunday ***Spirit*** sections from January 5, 1941 and March 2, 1941, ©1941 Will Eisner; and the Jerry Robinson cover from ***Detective*** #71, January, 1943, ©1943 DC Comics.

By the end of 1935, from his Fourth Avenue New York office, Wheeler-Nicholson had added a second title *New Comics* (retitled *Adventure Comics* with issue 32) to his line of all-original material comic books and had assembled a staff of creators that included writer Jerry Siegel and artist Joe Shuster. There was something he was chasing he knew to be true, but Wheeler-Nicholson's pioneering vision of a comic book market receptive to new ideas and creations was just slightly ahead of its time, and his titles struggled to make substantial profits, rendering his life a constant round of battles with banks, distributors, printers and unpaid staff complaints. He would launch one more title, *Detective Comics* in 1937 but would be long departed from the company he founded by the time its twenty seventh issue appeared in May 1939 with the debut of the satisfyingly profitable and enduringly popular character The Batman. Financial pressures mounting, Wheeler-Nicholson had reluctantly formed a joint corporation with accountant Jack Liebowitz and publisher Harry Donenfeld in order to publish and distribute the third title and fell heavily into deeper debt as a result. The company he had originally begun was seized by the pair in early 1938, and the Major was side-lined into history. With Liebowitz now at the helm, National Allied Publications, later referred to as just DC Comics by the 1950s (no doubt as a result of the DC "bullet" logo, which had the words "Superman" on the top outside and "National Comics" on the bottom outside of the bullet) when it handed two 21-year-old creators a cheque, dated March 1, 1938, for the grand sum of $130 in exchange for the first story and exclusive rights to a new character named Superman.

The sons of Jewish immigrants, Jerry Siegel and Joe Shuster were childhood friends growing up in Cleveland, Ohio and worked together as teenagers to create comic strips with a view to selling them to newspapers. With Siegel writing and Shuster providing the artwork, Superman had been first realized by the duo back in 1933 when they were both aged just 19. The earlier seed of the iconic character was perhaps born of tragedy, as Siegel originally conceived of a bullet-proof, bad guy punishing, justice-serving superhero just weeks after his father had died during a night-time robbery at his second-hand clothes store in Cleveland on June 2, 1932. The official cause of death was a heart attack, though police reports indicated that gun-shots had been heard, casting a doubt in the family over whether the shop-keeper had died of natural causes or was instead murdered by a thief of the night. From Siegel's original vision, the idea was worked up with Shuster's designs and a first 13-page Superman story was created and pitched, to eventual mass rejection, for newspaper syndication. By the time editor Vincent "Vin" Sullivan was handed the oft-dismissed art pages and said he'd buy them if they reconfigured the panels from newspaper strip format to comic book page, the concept of a perfect saviour hero from a distant dead planet was fully formed. The creative couple were paid $10 a page, split between them, for their first *Superman* story along with an employment agreement contract between the parties that the rights to the character were included within that miniscule payment, an industry-standard agreement for any work to see print. Sullivan was reacting to a command from Liebowitz to swiftly find material for a fourth comic book he wanted to publish and had already titled *Action Comics*, but the editor had emptied inventory of its best adventure strips and was still in need of a lead feature for the book. Sullivan contacted editor/artist Sheldon "Shelly" Mayer over at the McClure Syndicate for help, and Mayer offered up the Siegel and Shuster Superman pages, which he'd previously read and loved, wondering to himself why they had been so routinely rejected. Superman was introduced in *Action Comics* #1 (cover-dated June 1938 but on sale in April of that year) and was an immediate 10-cent sell-out, whose popularity increased with subsequent appearances ensuring the title was regularly selling over a million copies during the initial height of its success. In his primary-coloured, red-blue-yellow costume and cape, and with his kiss-curled matinee idol looks and astonishing super-human feats, Superman set the template for all costumed super-adventurers to come, transcending the approaching pack by eventually becoming a benign omnipresence of wisely-wielded immense power. Regarded as the comic book title that introduced not only Superman, but also the entire genre of superheroes, *Action Comics* #1 is today one of the world's most valuable comics, with only an estimated 50-100 copies, in varying condition, in existence. In 2014, a recently-discovered high-grade copy sold at auction for over $3 million, becoming the only single comic book to have sold for such a princely amount. From its initial print run of 200,000 to less than a hundred left, it's worth noting here that the paper-drives of the coming years, encouraging citizens to collect paper for the war effort, was a major contributory factor to the scarcity of comic books from this era and the value placed on them today. It was a throwaway entertainment, after all, and little worth was seen in them at the time. But as intellectual properties of the publishers, there were many rewards scooped up by the sale of hundreds of thousands of cheaply-produced pamphlets, if they proved popular, and Superman, with his strident manifesto of "Truth, Justice and the American Way" and eventual family of spin-off characters, including Superboy and later Supergirl, made Donenfeld a rich man and set a solid cornerstone in the building of a corporate publishing giant. In September 1938, just a few months after the superhero's debut and bolstered by the apparently endless financial super-power of their creation, Siegel and Shuster attempted to renegotiate terms with that publisher for the rights to a character they now regretted signing away so blithely and cheaply. The attempt failed dramatically, with their current employment emerging to be at risk if they continued. The rights had been signed away, the publisher asserted, and as freelancers they could be replaced on Superman at any given moment. Against this soundtrack, and fearful of losing their income completely, the duo relented and instead signed 10-year contracts with National/ DC Comics with a condition that gave the publisher first refusal on all new stories they created, including any Superman ones, at a locked-in and only slightly enhanced freelancer payment rate. But as the "faster than a speeding bullet" success of Superman continued, extending very soon to merchandising, radio and film rights, Siegel and Shuster's resentment at no profit shares grew steadily and before the 10-year contracts were up would be staging the first in a series of increasingly desperate attempts to reclaim legal ownership of the lucrative character from the publishing house.

Meanwhile....

Martin Goodman was a resourceful and astute entrepreneur who, after traveling around America seeking work during the Great Depression while staying in Hobo encampments, returned to his native New York by 1929 to eventually flourish within the Manhattan publishing industry. Becoming an investor and part owner of Mutual Magazine Distributors, Goodman was appointed editor of an affiliated new company Newsstand Publications Inc. to produce prose Pulp Magazines for the popular men's market of the time. From 1933 Goodman published a variety of pulps titles including *Complete Western Book*, *Real Sports*, *Mystery Tales* and the fantasy magazine that would make first use of an important word in its title, *Marvel Science Stories* (August 1938). In 1937, aged just 29, Goodman was an increasingly successful businessman and a newly-married one as well. He narrowly escaped death, his current good fortune extending even further, when returning from Europe with his honeymoon bride. The tickets he had previously booked on a passenger airship bound for America did not provide seats together for Goodman and his wife, so the couple decided to take a plane instead. By avoiding the flight of the Hindenburg on May 6, 1937, Goodman secured the future of comic book history by escaping a disaster that claimed 36 lives.

From his New York offices at the McGraw-Hill building at 330 West 42nd Street, the sharp-featured and prematurely grey-haired Goodman had observed the astonishing success of National's Superman and formed an opportunistic idea. He contracted original material in a similar vein from comic strip packager Funnies Inc. to rush out his very first comic book publication in a bold attempt to gate-crash the current powered hero popularity party. This business model of the early spotting of trends in order to act quickly enough to hitch a ride on them, is one that Goodman would utilize, with varying degrees of success, for the rest of his publishing career. *Marvel Comics* #1 (October 1939) introduced among other strips, Carl Burgos' *The* Human Torch — a scientist-created android character who bursts into flame while acquiring the power of flight and ability to throw fireballs and Bill Everett's aquatic angry-young-man The Sub-Mariner. Despite the oceans being his natural habitat, Namor, his real name, can also fly, thanks to his ankle wings, but — in a reversal of the Superman model — will use all powers at his disposal in attempts to destroy the human race, rather than protect it. Holding "surface-dwellers" responsible for damage to his underwater home and general disregard for the health of the oceans and its inhabitants, Sub-Mariner wages regular campaigns to terrorize New York in subsequent appearances. He starts as he means to continue in his first comic strip appearance by strangling a deep-sea diver, who happened to stray into his seabed territory, with his own oxygen cord. The story, in actual fact a reprint as it first appeared in *Motion Pictures Funnies*, a promotional giveaway, some months prior, ends with a front-facing Namor, dagger in hand, standing resolute beneath a caption which read, "And so Namor, the Avenging Son, faces the surface men of the world, in what promises to be mortal combat!" The 10-cent comic, regarded today as the world's first Marvel comic book (with the most recent sale recorded at $300,000 for a copy not in its highest grade) sold out its 80,000-print run within a month, and Goodman swiftly sent it back to press for a second edition (cover dated November 1939). This edition also sold out its more ambitious 800,000 print run, and the 31-year-old publisher realized he had an additional, and highly profitable, subsidiary product to add to his current range of pulps and men's magazines.

Deciding to bring the creative element in-house, Goodman offered writer/artist Joe Simon an editorial position to head up and gather the necessary talents to produce more comic books under the Timely banner. Simon brought with him Jack Kirby, his collaborator at Fox Feature Syndicate, and began assembling other artists, led by Syd Shores, for the newly-required team. With *Marvel Comics* (now retitled *Marvel Mystery Comics*) as its flagship title, Timely rapidly created and published a succession of new comic books for the emerging market: *Daring Mystery Comics* #1 (January 1940); *Mystic Comics* #1 (March 1940), *Red Raven Comics* #1 (August 1940) and continued with ever-derivative additions in a fine example of Goodman's own oft-quoted business edict, "If one sells, add another ten."

In 1940, it was a fierce and crowded market that Goodman was battling in, with the success of *Superman* igniting visions of dollar signs in a multitude of publisher's eyes ensuring an endless parade of new comic book titles from both established and hastily-formed companies. With National adding to their own range of costumed heroes with the debuts of The Flash, Green Lantern, The Spectre, Doctor Fate and Wonder Woman — resulting in the first superhero team The Justice Society — and Fawcett Publications enjoying comparable sales figures to *Superman* with its original *Captain Marvel*, created by artist C.C. Beck, Timely Comics fought for newsstand attention, and those hard-earned dimes, with all of its titles. But Goodman's first big hit, the one that would sell a million copies and provide the company's first real competitor to *Superman*, would debut on American newsstand racks in December of 1940 with all the visceral impact of a fist to the jaw.

Captain America Comics #1 (cover-dated March 1941) introduced Simon and Kirby's patriotic, red-white-and-blue superhero to a country that was anxiously reading the daily newspaper headlines, displayed on those same newsstands, of the insidious rise of Adolf Hitler's Third Reich in Europe. On the comic book's cover, on sale a year before the bombing of Pearl Harbour and America's entry into World War II, Captain America is seen smashing into a Nazi bunker and punching Hitler squarely in the face. It may have taken another twelve months for events and politicians to decide in the real world, but in the four-colour realm the superheroes, and their readers, had already marched boldly into the battle against oppression. With its first issue, and set to continue for almost a year, *Captain America* would not only outsell the majority of its comic book competitors but outsell, for a time, even *Life* magazine with its instant acceptance into the popular psyche. It would elevate Timely and Goodman's financial status to a great degree, and also that of its creators, to a far lesser degree.

Jack Kirby, then aged 23, was producing astonishingly original, dynamic pencilled comic art, that captured the eye with its panel-exploding fight scenes, maverick approach to layout structuring and crystal-clear clarity of story-telling. While most other comic book artists of the time were portraying action in traditional, stiffly-rendered poses, Kirby's art captured the fluidity of the human form in motion with captivating, page-turning results. Combined with Simon's story plot input and sympathetic inks to Kirby's trend-setting pencils, "Captain America Comics" was nothing less than a publishing sensation. Born and raised on the Lower East Side of Manhattan, Jacob Kurtzberg, the son of Jewish immigrants, was a scrappy, street-wise, self-taught artist who first entered the field in 1936 as a 19-year-old newspaper strip and one-panel gag artist. He then worked briefly in animation at Fleischer Studios as an inbetweener artist (working on the required number of drawings in order to convey the illusion of movement) on *Popeye* and *Betty Boop* cartoons before working for comic book strip packager Eisner and Iger. Now signing his work with the pen-name Jack Kirby, the artist then moved to work for Fox Features in early 1940, where he was given a drawing board in a studio sat next to Sub-

Mariner's creator Bill Everett, and a respectable $15-a-week salary to work, among other things, on a newspaper strip version of Fox's own superhero success *The Blue Beetle*. This was Kirby's first work in the superhero idiom, and it was also at Fox where the rapidly-learning, innately-gifted artist would first meet editor Joe Simon and begin a long and fruitful creative partnership together, beginning with the creation of Blue Bolt and *Red Raven Comics* for Timely. Just a few months from that initial meeting, Martin Goodman would be luring the duo over from Fox to enlist their burgeoning talents for the benefit of his own empire-building plans.

Joe Simon created Captain America in an undated sketch naming the character "Super American" before settling on his final and soon-to-be-famous name. Written in pencil by Simon on the sketch is also the message, "Martin, here's the character. I think he should have a kid buddy or he'll be talking to himself all the time."

In a 2011 interview for online news site nj.com, Joe Simon recalled of the creation of Captain America and his teenage sidekick, who Simon named Bucky after a schoolfriend, "Both Jack and I read the newspapers and knew what was going on over in Europe. World events gave us the perfect comic-book villain, Adolf Hitler, with his ranting, goose-stepping and ridiculous moustache. So, we decided to create the perfect hero who would be his foil. I did that first sketch of Captain America, and Jack and I did the entire first issue before showing it to Martin Goodman at Timely Comics. He loved it immediately. But when Captain America came out, America wasn't yet in the war, so the American Nazis weren't happy with what we did to their beloved Fuhrer. We had a couple of personal encounters with the Bund (an American Nazi-sympathizer group). But that didn't stop us. If anything, it added fuel to the fire."

The encounters that Simon referred to took the form of threatening telephone calls to the Timely office from members of the American Bund, unhappy with what they saw as a propogandist character, contrary to their own beliefs. For a time, the calls, and occasional letter, continued until one day when the caller said they were waiting in the downstairs lobby to see Simon and Kirby. Fired up, Kirby told them he was on his way and stormed down ready to tussle with the thugs, only to find them long gone. It wasn't the Bund that forced Simon and Kirby away from Timely Comics and *Captain America* — it was a combination of a caught-in-the-act-while-moonlighting drama and a broken financial promise made by Goodman that saw the final parting of the ways. Convinced of the appeal of their creation, Simon and Kirby had originally negotiated a 25 percent profit sharing deal with Goodman before the character's first appearance. They had both received some pretty healthy pay packets when Ca*ptain America* proved a success, but Simon later revealed in his memoir that the publisher's accountant had informed him of the "creative" bookkeeping methods Goodman was using to financially short-change the pair out of their true share of the star-spangled profits the popular comic book was generating. Resentful and now highly suspicious of Goodman, the team secretly signed a tempting, $500-a-week year-long contract to create new characters and titles for Jack Liebowitz's DC Comics under a "do what you want" edict, while continuing to accept Goodman's money for work they would rush through at Timely, now seen as little more than pre-agreed, contractual chores.

Simon and Kirby set up drawing boards in a tiny hotel room located near the Timely office they worked in by day, to meet up there evenings and weekends to plan and create their next big idea which they would be delivering to Goodman's main business competitor. In some way, either through being informed by a National employee jealous of Simon and Kirby's sweetheart deal or by a member of Timely's own staff (suspicion would fall on one individual in particular) Goodman discovered their two-timing machinations, confronted the duo and angrily dismissed them from his employment. But the collaborators, whose combined names were now seen as a mark of quality and success in the industry, would not miss a step and repeated their golden streak over at National creating the original Sandman and Manhunter characters then achieving a *Captain America*-sized success with *Boy Commandos* (July 1942), another million-seller which became National's third best-selling title for a time.

With a home front version of the kid-gang adventures model *The Newsboy Legion* quickly following, the pair were kept very busy creating new titles and new profits for their equally new employer. Simon and Kirby's sudden departure from Timely necessitated fast replacements to ensure publishing schedules on top-selling titles in Goodman's ever-growing roster were met, but the company was still seeking new recruits for some time after they had left. Allen Bellman joined Timely Comics as a 17-year-old boy when responding to a recruitment advert in the New York Times from the company seeking artists. He would later emerge as the last surviving person to have worked for Marvel's earliest incarnation during its first three years when the 95-year-old artist recalled to me in November 2018, "I saw the ad on Columbus Day in October 1942, my father first pointed it out to me. I told him that I would go tomorrow after the holiday. I was afraid of rejection really, but I listened to him and went that day to the McGraw-Hill building in New York, a city that was a different and safer place back then. It took about ten minutes and then Don Rico, who was then the artist on *Young Allies*, returned with my art samples and said I was hired, report Monday."

Bellman continued, "Simon and Kirby already left for DC Comics and that's how I got my job. When I came in on Monday, Don Rico introduced me to the staff. Syd Shores was now the artist doing *Captain America* with his inker, Vince Alascia sitting behind him. I sensed there was some kind of discord in the air. It seemed to me that Don with his friends were mad at Syd for getting the top assignment."

Syd Shores became Timely's Art Director soon after, before passing on the coveted *Captain America* pencilling task to Al Avison when the artist returned from World War II military service. Avison had previously inked a couple of earlier issues over Kirby's dynamic pencils and had also drawn the character in *All-Winners Comics*. Now with a line-up of almost a dozen comic book titles under the Timely banner to coordinate, including *Mystic Comics*, *Young Allies*, *The Human Torch*, *The Sub-Mariner* and *Marvel Mystery Comics*, Shores' time for pencilling in the office was becoming increasingly reduced. But the sheer volume of material needed for the various monthly titles meant that most artists who worked in Timely's cramped, one-window office, could also take work home and earn the average freelance rate of $15 per page for completed pencils and inks, to supplement their income. But with staff changes and internal squabbling rampant, and Joe Simon's departure still leaving a yawning chasm in editorial control, the scene was set for the return of someone who would eventually prove to be the company's prodigal son.

"Stan Lee was still in the army when I first joined Timely Comics but returned after I was in the job for about two weeks," Allen Bellman wrote to me in December 2018, continuing, "He originally started as an office boy, as I was told, but was now quickly being instructed for the editorship by his Uncle Robby Solomon, who everyone called 'Uncle Robby.' Actually, Robby was not liked by the staff, as everyone thought he was a spy for Goodman. He was a former ladies hat salesman, who made every artist on staff miserable with his criticism, pretending he was an art editor. Robby was brother-in-law to the publisher Martin Goodman and he was breaking Stan in, and Stan walked behind him like a little puppy dog at first. I was 17 when I joined Timely and Stan was about 19 or so at the same time. He was as green as I was but successfully got through being unsure of himself in a very short time. Robby passed away soon after at an early age and Stan Lee never walked behind anyone else ever again!"

Stanley Martin Lieber was indeed a returning employee, having first joined Timely two years prior with the help of Uncle Robby working as a general assistant to Simon and Kirby, fetching coffee, running errands, checking for errors on pages, all the while observing and learning as he did. He signed his first published comic book work — a prose serial that ran for eight issues starting in *Captain America Comics* #3 (May 1941) and titled "Headline Hunter, Foreign Correspondent" — with the name "Stan Lee," reserving his full name for the great American novel he intended to one day write, not wishing to tarnish it with any comic book writing associations.

Conversely, if there were any accolades to be had for the writing on offer, Stan Lee was the man who would receive it, as it was uncommon at the time for any comic book writer to receive, or ask for, any published credit for the mountain of monthly stories they were expected to routinely hack out. But Stan signed his name to practically every script he produced, secure in his youthful conviction that his writing skills would one day bring him great success and security in a reversal of the memory of grinding poverty he had experienced growing up in 1920s/30s New York, the first son of his Romanian-born Jewish immigrant working-class parents. Lee was back at Timely after serving in the US Army, assigned to the Signal Corps Division where he was initially trained to install telephone lines before his comic book writing credentials were brought to someone's attention and then became one of only nine individuals in the Army at the time to be attributed the official job title of "playwright" — a fine company of worthies to be in, including the film director Frank Capra, *The Addams Family* cartoonist creator Charles Addams, and Theodor Geisel, acclaimed children's author, more famously known as Dr. Seuss. Glamorous as it may sound, the reality was that the teenage Lee's skills were put to use writing training and advice manuals, where he excelled at writing snappy copy for posters warning of the dangers of venereal diseases for lonely overseas servicemen.

Duties delivered, Stan Lee was happy to be back at work at Timely Comics but, at an incredibly young age, now had the great responsibility — and the power that came with it — of overseeing Goodman's entire comic book publishing division. By the end of 1942, the Timely offices had moved to Suite 1401, 14th floor of the Empire State Building on Fifth Avenue, a New York landmark which had only opened eleven years earlier and was still offering affordable rental rates for businesses in an attempt to fill its many still-empty office spaces. Opening in 1931 on the cusp of the Great Depression had meant that the building earned the mocking title of the "Empty State Building" during its first decade, although canny marketing and promotion had created a profitable tourist attraction of its observatory deck — helped in no small degree by the success of the 1933 release of the original and truly iconic *King Kong* movie.

When Willis O'Brien's seminal, stop-motion animated Kong swatted away lead-spitting, bi-planes, while protecting Ann, before making his tragic fall from the top of the building, along with the revelatory final line ("It wasn't the planes, it was Beauty killed the Beast") a cinematic legend and adoptive son of New York was born. The protagonists were fictional, but the drama-infused location was real and was only an elevator ride and a few dollars away. Settled into its new grand address, many floors beneath the tourist attraction, Goodman's publishing empire continued its steady progress, with Stan Lee confidently heading up the comic book division and now receiving more autonomy and less supervision from his superior.

"The Timely office at the Empire State Building was no different than thousands of other offices in New York at that time," artist Joe Sinnott recalled to me in 2013, adding, "It had a little waiting room where all the artists sat and waited their turn to see Stan. I met other artists waiting there like Bob Powell, Gene Colan and others."

"Stan had his own office and I got along with him fine but he was all business and was probably told by Goodman not to get too friendly with the staff," Allen Bellman wrote to me in 2018, adding, "Martin Goodman was aloof with the staff and kept to himself, locked away in his own office." With the office day running 9am to 5pm, five days a week, the regular staff were kept busy by the now 20-year-old fresh-faced editor with his energetic approach and exuberant style. It was during this initial taste of being in charge when Stan Lee first used the phrase "Excelsior" to staff, as Bellmen recalled to me, adding that there was "respect at once" for Lee's leadership, despite his young age. Power-walking in and out of the office constantly, Lee would encourage writers and artists to deliver more by stretching their creativity and become infected with his own enthusiasm for the scripts he was giving them. From leaping on desks and filing cabinets making office-wide declarations, to wearing a beanie hat with propeller on top for no discernible reason, the gently-humoured zaniness of Lee's style entertained many. And for those members of staff who may have found his approach more of an irritant — well, he was a relative of the real boss, after all. And there were also rumours, later confirmed by Simon though denied by Lee, that the young editor was the person who followed Simon and Kirby to their secret work-place one day and informed on them to Goodman, resulting in their ignoble departure. The suspicion would linger, especially with Kirby, for many years to come.

Lee was a prolific writer of five to eight-page comic tales and was paid in addition to his editorial salary for every story he wrote, an average of three to five a week. He would write full scripts for artists in a required variety of genres — superheroes, westerns, crime stories, romance, horror and fantasy — hammering them out on sheets of paper, accompanied by the clatter of typewriter keys, learning and honing his craft as he did.

"I started at Timely doing backgrounds on *Captain America* but later on Stan gave me scripts to pencil and ink," Allen Bellman wrote to me, confirming the existence of early Lee scripts and adding, "During this time, I did whatever Stan threw at me, *Human Torch*, *Sub-Mariner*, *The Patriot*, *The Destroyer* (introduced in the sixth issue of *Mystic Comics* and Stan Lee's first co-creation for the company), crime stories, war stories, westerns and so much more. I created a back-up feature called *Let's Play Detective.* Many of my stories have been reprinted by Marvel today. I still have memories of the people I worked with back then but all are gone now. Gene Colan, Mike Sekowsky who was a great artist but with a bad attitude, Sol Brodsky, Syd Shores — we became very good friends and there were so many more."

During this time and at the height of his success with Joe Simon, Jack Kirby was drafted into the US Army Infantry in June of 1943, eventually joining General George S. Patton's platoon on its eastward offensive across France. His fast drawing skills were put to valuable use creating detailed reconnaissance maps of enemy territories that the young solider would perilously scout under the cover of night. Kirby took part in many theatres of battle during World War II and received an honourable discharge, together with honours including the Bronze Battle Star, in July of 1945. The savage and violent experiences that Kirby endured during his military service, combined with the human heroism also on display, would inform and influence his still-developing comic book stories and art in the coming decades. In the same month that Kirby left the Army, the Timely offices were closed on the Saturday of July 28, 1945 when a B-25 Mitchell Bomber airplane, flying in thick fog, hit the building in fatal error, crashing between the 78th and 80th floors. The air disaster claimed 14 lives, but the resultant blaze was quickly contained by fire fighters from the local ladder and despite the shocking event, the building was open again for business the following Monday.

Allen Bellman recalled, "A plane hit the Empire State Building on a stormy weekend day and I remember going to work at Timely on Monday morning and seeing glass and debris which was still littered all over the streets." Now firmly established as industry leader, DC Comics, known as National, continued to mine the successes of Batman and Superman, adding constantly to their line-up of comic book characters and titles, but the publisher was suddenly hit by a lawsuit from Siegel and Shuster in late 1947 — just before the creators' 10-year contracts came to an end.

It marked the first attempt by comic book creators to legally challenge a publisher for ownership of a successful character, and it was a case that lasted well into 1948. Asking for the rights to *Superman* and *Superboy*, along with what the duo termed a "just share" of profits generated from licensing deals, they made their case before the Supreme Court of New York, who eventually ruled that their original payment and signed employment contracts gave clear ownership of the rights to *Superman* to National. But with the character of Superboy it was an entirely different story altogether. Siegel had repeatedly pitched the idea — stories about a younger version of the hero, name of Superboy — to National only for it to be consistently flatly refused or ignored.

The first story to feature the character was published in *More Fun Comics* #101 (January 1945) and though drawn by Joe Shuster and based heavily on Siegel's un-sold proposal script, was actioned when the writer was away in Hawaii on military duty for the US Army and without his further input. This incensed Seigel at the time, but during the lawsuit case it proved to be a distinct advantage. In support of its claim to *Superboy* rights, National insisted the character was created as "work-for-hire" referring to the 10-year contracts the pair had signed back in 1938. But that self-same contract contained the "right of first refusal" clause and as Seigel had offered *Superboy* on numerous occasions and had not been taken up on the offer within a six-week window each time, the judge ruled that *Superboy* did not fall under work-for-hire and the rights belonged to the creators.

Swiftly, National settled the entire case out of court and paid the creative duo just over $94,000 between them for the exclusive rights to both *Superman* and *Superboy* and promptly ceased any existing employment agreement with them. In the same day, Seigel and Shuster had been paid off, fired from their jobs and lost the rights to create any more Superman stories. But the income generated from the *Superman* properties would continue to rise in scale over the ensuing decades — with television and eventually motion pictures success enabling heightened merchandising opportunities — and Siegel and Shuster's battles for creator-recognition and "just share" were far from over.

Oblivious, as a reader, to all the office dramas and intrigues already prevalent behind the production of comic books, this embryonic period — when the superhero was first conceptualized and explored, along with a multitude of other story genres — was held in the greatest affection by Steve Ditko for the whole of his life. As a young enthralled reader back in Johnstown, his exposure to them would soon form the influence and impetus for him to master the skills necessary to create his own versions. While historians may pin labels to mark the industry's boom periods in sales and development, the true Golden Age of an individual reader is commonly when the impact of their simple yet effective stories is first felt. As Ditko wrote to me in 2015, "The start, origins are usually the most interesting. The greatest creative period for comics was the 1940s, starting the comic book industry. (They were) 68-page comic books for ten cents (now 20 pages or less). Eight to ten different stories, etc. Imagine a character called The Green Turtle or The Clock. A comic with a wide variety of stories, characters and styles. There were two text pages which were a post office requirement. Comic companies (eventually) kept the comic book cost down by reducing page count – 68 – 56 – 48 – etc. The lower number of pages meant the less creativity, exploring potentials, off-beat ideas."

The young Ditko would discover his life-long calling in the cheap paper pages of this newly invented disposable entertainment, and he read as many different comic books as he could buy or borrow. Despite the wide variety of different characters on offer, increasingly within the superhero genre, Ditko's firm favourites remained *Batman* and *The Spirit*. Each of these were archetypal, granite-jawed, no-nonsense heroes of the age who bravely battled for justice and expressed little regard for the fate of the villains they fought, often including any collateral damage. There was no political correctness, remorse or self-doubt in these self-assured costumed brawlers that so captivated Ditko.

With Europe, and eventually America, poised on the brink of a devastating world war, the distinctions between good and evil were being succinctly drawn in society, in politics, in comic books. It was becoming a world of sharp-edged black and white, with suspicion coloured grey. "You may have heard the expression, 'There is NO black and white, NO extremes, everything is grey.' So, NO truth or lie? NO good or bad/evil? Who's to judge, to say," Ditko would write to me in February 2013, adding, "So, it's compromise on everything. There's a very long, terrible history of the destruction of human knowledge, achievement — like an Islam war leader ordering the destruction of the Library of Alexandria, Moguls destroying the libraries of Baghdad, religious leaders destroying pagan art and writings, 'book burnings,' etc. Aristotle, 4BC, defined 'man is a rational animal.' But rationality is a choice — to be rational or irrational. Most minds throughout history chose to be irrational, destructive to self and human life."

Ditko — a war veteran himself — wrote to me in December 2012, expanding on his views of how the times he lived through informed his mindset, saying, "Before World War I, in the USA, it was written and believed by many, how benevolent the country, society was, the goodwill among people — a recovery after the brutal Civil War. Certainly, there was prejudices, corruptions, crimes etc. but the culture as a whole had more good will, a sense of a benevolent universe. Then came WWI, the horrors of trench warfare, poison gas victims, years of ongoing misery etc. The world never really had a chance to recover and then followed the birth of the worse horrors of fascism, Nazism."

Ditko continued in the same letter, "My generation had a saying 'I pay my own way.' People were ashamed to need, take charity. Yet, in emergencies, fires, etc, people were generous. Today, affairs are more international, global so there is far less chance of 'peace' or sanity 'in our time.' More and more the individual needs to positively fuel one's spirit. Fables, poems etc. are good sources. Even today, too many now don't care about the difficult lessons learned in the past or the truths right today. A big problem is that too much is done by too many to protect, excuse the wrong, bad, even the evil, 'To get along,' 'don't make trouble' etc. Veterans of war are often silent about their honourable experience, others don't really want to hear about such tense, frightening horrible conditions, hourly, daily faced by the military men. With most individuals it's 'I don't really want to know, don't want to face it, it's too upsetting' as seen today with communities, society's problems, troubles, until it escalates to dangerous situations like national debt etc."

The comic books that saw the birth of the superhero were spawned during this era of global conflict, offering inexpensive escapism to millions of readers, Ditko included, in a parade of seemingly inexhaustible brightly-coloured home-grown heroes. Labelled The Golden Age by comic book historians from this explosion of creativity emerged Superman, Batman, Green Lantern, Captain America, Wonder Woman, The Flash, Hawkman, the original Captain Marvel and many more. Their influence was widely felt — Elvis Presley's hair-style and stage costumes were derived from the appearance of Fawcett's Captain Marvel Jr. created by writer Ed Herron and artist Mac Raboy, a comic book character the future king of rock and roll adored. He based his corporate "taking care of business" lightning bolt design on the Captain Marvel insignia — and would soon extend far beyond their paper pages to merchandising deals and media adaptations.

As a hero reflecting the sensibilities of the age, Batman's vow to never use a gun or take a life, expressed in later versions of the character, was wildly absent from his earliest appearances. Frequently, the Dark Knight would use guns with abandon, allow villains to die through inaction or even directly murder them. Often a rogue would fall to their death after being soundly round-housed by the caped crusader — a precedent set in Batman's very first appearance in *Detective Comics* #27 (May 1939). In "The Case of the Chemical Syndicate" — Batman's first story by Bill Finger and Bob Kane — the hero tracks down a killer of business rivals and a climatic fight ensues on a catwalk suspended above a vat of acid. Batman happily knocks the villain straight into the flesh-eating acid with the equally acerbic comment, "A fitting end for his kind."

The first issue of *Batman* (Spring 1940), as well as introducing The Joker and Catwoman, includes a story with villain Hugo Strange, where Batman even murders an unwilling participant in the drama in a decidedly grotesque manner that makes you look at his "wonderful toys" in a darker light. In "The Giants of Hugo Strange," the evil scientist has created a serum that turns ordinary, innocent people into slavering, Frankenstein-like monsters that he intends to use as battering rams during bank raids. One such unfortunate is being transported in a van until Batman comes swooping in flying the Batplane with a machine-gun mounted on the front. ("But out of the sky, spitting death, The Batman") The driver is gunned down and the van crashes, leaving the monster exposed in a tangle of metal. Rather than use the antidote he'd only just created and used on himself to avoid becoming infected, Batman decides instead to lower a noose around the monster's neck and nonchalantly hang him from the Batplane, with the reassuring comment to himself that "He's probably better off this way."

The black-and-white view of heroes that Ditko would create and adhere to throughout his career may possibly have their roots far deeper than the Objectivism beliefs he would later articulate as an adult and originate with his fascination for the superheroes he read as a child who were all in their most primally raw, uninhibited forms. Inspired, he began to teach himself the rudimentary skills of comic art, filling up countless sketchbooks with doodles, shapes and costumed heroes, copying the style and structures of the artists he admired. And it wasn't just characters that flowed from his pencil; his brother Patrick recalled that he "sketched and wrote about a lot of things," adding that he "specifically remembered sketches of chemistry experiments with test tubes and burners." Gaining a sense of creative achievement along with the comforting familiarity of a pencil in his hand, Ditko would spend most of his spare time drawing. Another relative once remarked that the young Ditko was notably "good with his hands."

A photograph of a slim-faced teenage Ditko in his high school senior year book in 1945 showed him wearing glasses and looking every inch the studious model for his later comic book creation, Peter Parker. After leaving school, Ditko, now 18, joined the US military during the last months of World War II and was posted for a time to Germany. He helped out with the military base newspaper while there, creating editorial gag cartoons along with general office duties. When he returned home after army discharge in the late 1940s, his desire to pursue a career in the somewhat derided field of comic books remained as fierce as ever, and he continued to draw comic strips with the firmly held conviction that the industry held a future for him. Previous reports that Ditko enrolled on a sign writing course, a more reliable vocation perhaps, to placate his father's concerns proved to be false as Mark S. Ditko confirmed to me saying, "His dad loved comics. He took vacations and sat in his favourite chair and read comics. He would have been proud to have his son pursue that career path." With a supportive family behind him, Ditko enrolled in a local commercial art school, but when he saw an advertisement that offered the opportunity to be trained to draw professional comic book art in New York by the very artist who had drawn all the *Batman* comics that Ditko had spent many hours studying and copying — his path was finally clear.

In 1950, with funding gained through the G I Bill — a recent law providing benefits for returning war veterans, including tuition and living expenses, to attend further education — Ditko, then aged 23, moved from the family home in Johnstown to live for the first time in New York City and attend classes at the Cartoonists and Illustrators School at 209 East 23rd Street. At this time, New York was sparking bravado optimism, creativity and confidence in all directions, populated with individuals reflecting writer Jack Kerouac's preference for people "who are mad to live, mad to talk, mad to be saved, desirous of everything at the same, the ones who never yawn or say a commonplace thing, but burn, burn, burn like fabulous yellow roman candles exploding like spiders across the stars."

Opposite page: Ditko reminisces about the comic books of his youth in this letter to the author from May, 2015.

1650 Broadway #715
New York, NY 10019-6833
May 9, 2015

Dear David,

the pre-comic code period.

the evolution of comic books has quite a history.

the first comic books were just reprints of the daily, sunday comics.

I have a vague memory of some comic books from Canada.

A fan, from Denmark sent me a reprint of a Daredevil comic - Black and white with a 5 page story I did. the printing clear, paper okay.

So marvel material was reprinted, I don't know how early or where.

With marvels growing success, reprints potential had to increase.

I've seen philiphine comics - well done and Australian comics. they seem to have done a lot of good original comic book material.

Oh, yes, the early 68/64 pages for ten cents, the comic with a wide variety of stories, characters and styles.

Yes, the 2 text pages were a post office requirement.

Comic companies kept the comic book cost down by reducing page count - 68 - 56 - 48, etc.

The lower number of pages, the less creativity, exploring potentials, off beat ideas, etc.

With superheroes, U.S. comic fans didn't want the 5 pagers, ALL superhero.

So killing creative imagination, exploration,

In *On the Road*, which Kerouac would complete writing in Manhattan in 1951, he was describing the people he met and inspired him on his travels across America, but it could also adequately describe the city of New York's own "Empire State of Mind" throughout the decade of the 1950s. America itself would emerge for the first time as a global superpower, as the political deck of cards was reshuffled over the same period. At the top of the curve of a post-war economic boom, New York's appearance to the world as the centre of the universe was convincingly formed, with the 1952 completion of the United Nation headquarters in the city, confirming its global neo-influence, both economically and politically.

Ditko would later dismiss this development in a 2013 letter to me, "The U.N. is made up of all kinds of corrupt leaders and dedicated to a one-world government that will decide policy for every country, every individual." Within the arts, the rise of the Abstract Expressionism movement in the city, spear-headed by the drip style paintings of Jackson Pollock, the oil wash, atmospheric, horizontal matte expanses of minimal colour distilled into the paintings of Mark Rothko, and the frenetic portraits of Willem de Kooning, eventually saw New York replace Paris as zeitgeist central for the art world. The emergence of this new art genre taking place around him, while he was learning his own disciplines and techniques, had no influence on Ditko, however, despite the wonderfully surrealistic and decidedly abstract qualities he would apply to some of his later work.

In a 2013 letter to me, Ditko scathingly remarked, "Modern abstract art is a deliberate distortion of man/(and his) mind's proper means of comprehending life, the world. I don't get involved in trying to understand someone's nonsense. It's not a valid mystery." The young Ditko would perhaps have found more inspiration in the movie theatres of Times Square as Hollywood, now competing with television, produced films of increasingly greater spectacle as they tempted in audiences with the promise of enhanced viewing experiences in Cinemascope or VistaVision or later 3-D. While he trained his hand to perfect drawing techniques, future movie classics would help train his mind's eye to recall details of camera angle shots to convincingly tell a story, using dramatic lighting and shifting perspectives to inform or build suspense in a visual narrative.

For fantasy imagery Ditko would have been spoiled for choice as science fiction movies were enjoying their first heyday with a variety of alien invasion blockbusters including *The Day the Earth Stood Still* (1951) and *War of the Worlds* (1953) to films with a subtler alien presence in *This Island Earth* (1955) and the undisputed classic of the era *Forbidden Planet* (1956). A notable precursor to *Star Trek*, *Lost in Space* and *Star Wars* with its human space crew, robot supporting character and bolder attempts to visualize alien landscapes by combining sets with animation and matte background paintings.

In a different flavour were the Cold War-induced, Atomic Bomb paranoia sensibilities of movies such as *Them!* (1954) and *Invasion of the Body Snatchers* (1956) or the apocalyptic visions on offer in end-of-days movies like *When Worlds Collide* (1951). During any down time between work and art school, Ditko would enjoy time in front of the silver screen, with a selection of different cinema theatres to choose from showing a wide variety of film genres in Times Square. A district of the city he would become very familiar with over the whole of his life, the Times Square the young Ditko would have first experienced in 1950 was a heady mix of brightly-lit cinemas, amusement centres, cocktail lounges and a burgeoning sex-business presence. As ever-higher advertising billboards jostled for attention selling Planters Peanuts or *Life Magazine* or Admiral Television Appliances or Canadian Club Imported Whisky, the streets below were filled with starry-eyed visitors, intoxicated already by the sheer speed of life on display before them. Back then, and for some time to come, New York, and an artists' proximity to it, was intrinsic to any developing freelance career in the comic book industry. If you didn't live in or were close enough to Manhattan to able to economically travel in and walk into the publishers to pick up and drop off work, the reality was you would never be offered a single assignment.

Allen Bellman wrote to me in 2018, "At Timely Comics, all the artists lived locally in New York, meaning we could drive or take the Subway to work," and this hadn't changed when Ditko first attempted to break into the industry in the early 1950s. By the time Ditko arrived in the city to attend classes at the Cartoonists and Illustrators School (later named in 1956 School of Visual Arts), superheroes were viewed as a fad gone out of style as readers' interest rapidly waned in them following the end of World War II. The Manhattan-based school was originally founded in 1947 by *Tarzan* newspaper strip artist Burne Hogarth and philologist Silas H. Rhodes and is today ranked #18 of all US art graduate schools. His career-shaping decision to enroll was encouraged by the teacher Jerry Robinson, whose artwork in comic books, particularly *Batman*, Ditko had long admired and would have been eager to directly learn from.

Robinson was at the school giving lessons almost by default as he was there at the request of fellow artist Mort Meskin. Painfully shy together with artistically brilliant, Meskin had been hired to give lessons at the school but decided instead to split the fees with Robinson in order to gain an accomplice teacher. There were many lessons to be learned from Robinson's Golden Age career and not all of them were simply techniques you could apply to producing better comic art. In reference to Robinson's experiences with *Batman* and his well-publicised creator Bob Kane, there were cautionary tales aplenty for any budding creator of comic books. Born and raised in Manhattan, Kane already had four years' experience in the fledgling comic book industry when he pitched "The Batman," early in 1939, to National, a publisher then eager for fresh ideas to compliment and replicate the runaway success of Superman.

The 24-year-old Kane had the name and a sketch of a domino-masked, red-suited, blonde-haired character with bat-wings when he first approached writer Bill Finger for help in working up the idea. The artist had previously worked with Finger, who had ghost-written earlier strips for him, and Kane trusted his artistic input. Finger suggested changes to the costume, adding the cowl, cape and gauntlets, altering its colour scheme from red to black, and wrote an origin story containing essential elements of Batman lore — the naming of Bruce Wayne, Gotham City, The Batmobile, the motivational death of his parents by a criminal, his detective skills without superpowers to rely on and a great deal more. Kane then took the revised idea, without Finger, to Vin Sullivan at National with a view to the company publishing his now pre-copyrighted character — an astute and unusual-for-the-time move, responding to the financial bonanza *Superman* was generating.

As Ditko wrote to me in February 2015, "Bob Kane took his Batman idea to National as his copyrighted creation — he legally, morally, owned Batman. It's a big difference with Seigel/Shuster and Superman. They may be creators of Superman morally, but not legally." The agreement Kane reached with National included the proviso that the artist would receive sole credit for the creation of Batman in all published appearances, no matter who the actual writers and artists of the strips were.

For many future creators on the strip this would have an irritating effect but for Bill Finger, who would also co-create The Joker, along with Jerry Robinson, it would be the catalyst for an eventually fruitless quest for creator recognition decades later, that would be brusquely dismissed by Kane as "hallucinations of grandeur."

"Many writers of novels have, use, ghostwriters but it's the original name that sells," Ditko wrote to me in February 2015, continuing, "So whatever Kane's true personality in dealing with the actual writer/artist on Batman, Kane protected his idea from the start. Inventors, etc, in all businesses have problems of copyright, ownership. And it's common with all originators, creators, that there will be voices that claim the idea was stolen from some assistant, or someone prior." Kane had already shown allegiance to his corporate benefactor through his actions around the time of Siegel and Shuster's first lawsuit against the company, when he effectively ratted-out the duo's plans to Liebowitz.

In seeking Kane's collaboration in creating a joint suit against National, unaware of the bargain he'd originally struck, Siegel had outlined their own case in detail to Kane. Not only had the manipulative artist forewarned the publisher of the impending legal action, he had also renegotiated his own contract renewal with enhanced rates, a share of subsidiary rights to Batman and a continuation of the exclusive creator credit in the process. Robinson himself, who first suggested the name Robin for Batman's teenage sidekick, would later claim first rights to the creation of The Joker, contested by both Kane and Finger. From playing cards to original clown-like sketches to modeled on the appearance of German actor Conrad Viedt in the 1928 movie *The Man Who Laughs*, the creative origins of the arch-villain will always be clouded in doubt and remain unconfirmed, as Ditko wrote to me in a letter from February 2015, "The Joker is an unresolved issue." The young artist would spend the next two years of his life studying at the school, among a group of other hopeful artists including Joe Sinnott, Don Perlin and Eric Stanton, the latter of which would become a friend and collaborator as the two would later setup a shared studio space from which to launch their careers.

Above: Jerry Robinson, 1941, in his studio at his drafting board; in the background is a splash page featuring Batman.

It was Robinson who pushed for Ditko to be awarded a grant enabling him to attend a second year at the school, a course that demanded five hours a day for five days a week over its duration. "I was working during the day (non-art job) and going to the school at night. Periodically, I made the rounds of all the comic publishers and was turned down by all," Ditko said in a 1964 interview for the sixth issue of comics fanzine *Komik Heroes of the Future*. Despite his initial rejections, Ditko was a fast learner under Robinson's tutelage, learning how to tell a story with inventive layouts, experimenting with different inking techniques and rapidly absorbing his chosen craft. In one of his last ever interviews in 1966 for comics fanzine *Rapport* #2, Ditko offered this extensive advice to future comic book artists, reproduced here in full due to the rarity of such instruction from the master artist, "You must really understand the basics of art — perspective, composition, anatomy, drapery, light and shade, storytelling, etc. You need a solid foundation of what is right and good to build on. You can't really draw anything well unless you understand the purpose of that drawing (storytelling), the best way to get the drawing across (individual point of view — composition), and convincingly (perspective, anatomy, light and shade). Until I came under the influence of Jerry Robinson, I was self-taught, and you'd be amazed at the hours, months, and years one can spend practicing bad drawing habits. Jerry gave me a good foundation, but I have to constantly watch out; bad drawing habits are hard to kill. Practicing on a solid, proper foundation, you train your hand and mind to work like a unit while correctly broadening your knowledge and ability. Spend more time practicing the things you find most difficult to do, not what is easy or what you like. Keep eliminating the problems. Study, draw life around you - people, drapery, and reality. Study other artists to see how they interpret reality to art. Study and compare your art to others and reality - not copying, either, but interpreting it the way you think best. No one is an original artist; no living artist today or yesterday invented or discovered art, brushes, ink, paper, or comics. Everyone builds on what was done before or is being done (whether it's a shoe, a light bulb, an airplane, or a drawing). In art, the artist interprets in his own individual way; he plays up more of or less of: uses more or less of what others have built. He can stress constant over natural action. A comical approach or a serious one? A lot of fine lines or bold lines? Detailed or plain? Use line-pattern textures or solid and straight black and white. Any mixture of all there is. His style or 'originality' is just his individual interpretation. If you draw a scene the way you personally think it should be, rather what this or that artist did with a similar scene or might do, you will have your own 'original' style. After all, there's really no one else in the world just like you."

Jerry Robinson recalled of teaching Ditko when interviewed on camera by English chat show host and known comic book buff Jonathan Ross for his 2007 BBC television documentary *In Search of Steve Ditko*, "He was serious about the art, serious and dedicated about learning and becoming a story-teller." While Ditko was head down at art school, the comic book industry rolled on, and, despite the downturn in popularity in superheroes, its current scattergun approach to genres yielded other profitable gains as publishers explored everything from westerns and crime thrillers to horror and science fiction yarns in order to keep the readers coming back for more. Over at Timely, keeping all this required material churning out at necessary speed meant that more office employees and freelancer creators were needed to keep pace with it all.

Larry Lieber was among the new recruits on Goodman's payroll at the time. He was Stan Lee's younger brother by nine years ("We had different friends and so did not play together but I guess that he was someone I always looked up to") and the writer/artist first started work there as a production assistant. "I was about 18 or 19 years old when I first joined the company around 1949 and not directly through Stan," he wrote to me in 2013. "I did not work for Timely Comics exactly, I worked in an adjoining room for their parent company, Magazine Management in the layout department. I did paste-ups on movie, romance, and men's books until 1951 when I left to join the US Air Force for the next four years, during the Korean War. I met publisher Martin Goodman at that time, and I considered him an intelligent and ethical businessman."

It was in the latter part of that same year, November 1951, when Timely changed its name and branding to "Atlas News Company," referred to as Atlas Comics for a time thereafter, following Goodman's acquisition of a distribution company in an attempt to gain more leverage in the monopoly game of comic book publishing. The strategic move would eventually backfire on Goodman but for now carried an optimism and further reason for Stan Lee to solicit more work from the increasing number of freelance artists on his rolodex. Artist Joe Sinnott wrote to the author in 2013, "I first met Stan Lee in 1951 when Marvel was still known as Timely Comics — even before Atlas. After working with Tom Gill for about nine months while at school, I went over to see Stan for the first time. He liked my work and gave me a 3-page western story to pencil and ink called 'The Man Who Wouldn't Die' in *Apache Kid* #8. I loved the stuff we did in the 1950's at Timely/Atlas such as the westerns, war, sci-fi and mystery titles, among others. You never got bored!"

Sinnott would later carve his niche in comic book history with his lusciously sleek and highly complementary inking of Jack Kirby's 1960s *Fantastic Four* and follow a career as primarily an inker thereafter. As a first-generation reader of comic books, enjoying the newly invented medium he observed, "I read right from the early *Tip Top Comics* with the reprints of the syndicated strips." Sinnott recalled to me, "Then *Action Comics* (my favourite feature inside was *Congo Bill*), *Batman*, *Captain America* — I read them all. And like everyone else, we threw them away after we were finished with them or passed them around to the kids in the neighbourhood. Like most comic fans, my hero cartoonists were Milton Caniff and Alex Raymond of *Terry and the Pirates* and *Flash Gordon* fame."

Sinnott had a crayon in his drawing hand since the age of two and further recalled, "We moved from one part of town to another when I was two and I can remember sitting in a stuffed chair in the back of my father's truck on the way to our new house. My father had cut the back end off of an old car to make a truck and this is how we moved our belongings and furniture. Around the same time, I started drawing." Sinnott continued, "I was at the Cartoonists and

Opposite page: Original art from ***Captain 3-D*** #1, December, 1953, ©1953 Harvey. This page was inked by Mort Meskin and Ditko.

BUT THE GUARDIANS WERE CLEVER, TOO! THE CAT PEOPLE NEVER FOUND THE BOOK!
UNTIL TODAY?
WHEN THEY KILLED THE GUARDIAN!..SAY, I GUESS THAT MAKES ME...
...THE NEW GUARDIAN, DANNY!
GOSH! DOES THAT MEAN THE CAT PEOPLE WILL BE AFTER ME!
NO...US, DANNY! FOR I'LL BE WITH YOU!
BLUE
CAPTAIN 3D VANISHES, AND IN HIS PLACE IS HIS PICTURE IN THE BOOK OF D!
GOSH! HE'S A PICTURE AGAIN!
HE WENT BACK INTO THE BOOK! I WONDER WHY?
THIS MOST AMAZING SECRET WILL BE REVEALED AS CAPTAIN 3D COMES TO LIFE IN A WHIRLWIND OF TWO-FISTED ACTION!
CAPT. 3-D #1 PG 12

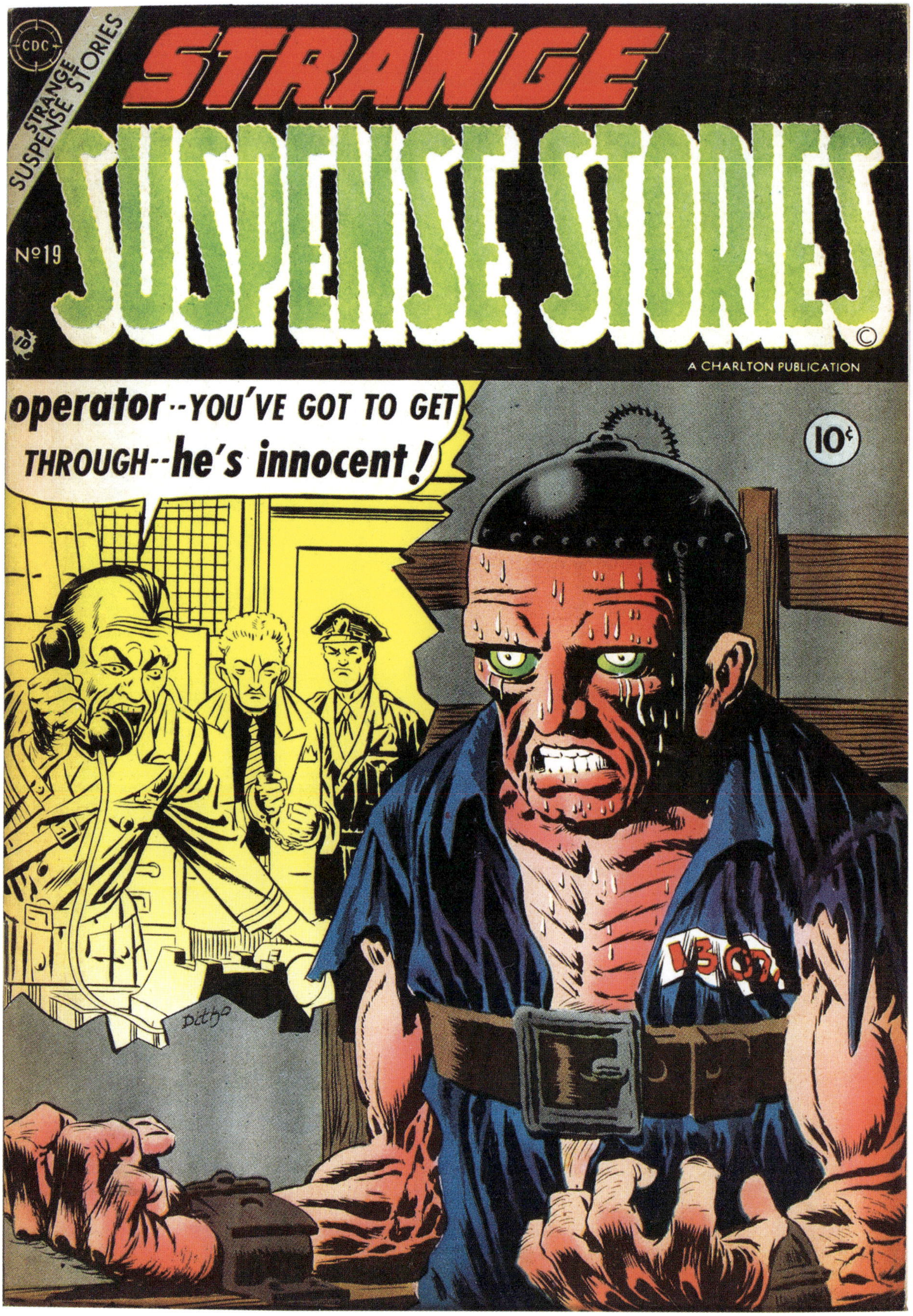
CDC
STRANGE SUSPENSE STORIES
STRANGE
SUSPENSE STORIES
No19
©
A CHARLTON PUBLICATION
operator--YOU'VE GOT TO GET THROUGH--he's innocent!
10¢
Ditko

Illustrators School in New York, and one of my instructors, Tom Gill, liked my potential and asked me to be his assistant. Tom, of course, was a famed artist who notably had an 11-year run drawing *The Lone Ranger* for Dell Comics. This was my big break and I owe my success to Tom. He was a great talent and a great guy. Working on Timely books for Stan Lee such as *Red Warrior*, *Kent Blake*, and others for Dell, Western etc. really advanced my career. Of course, after Tom, I went over to Stan at Timely and he gave me work right away."

Ramona Fradon was one of only two female comic book artists (the other being Marie Severin) working in the male-dominated industry of the 1950s — a hard-boiled period with urban-legendary tales of artists working together in over-crowded studios embarking on 48-hour marathon stints drawing comic strips against merciless deadlines, often driven by copious amounts of cheap liquor and cigarettes.

Luckily, Fradon lived outside of the city and was a mail-in freelancer. "Even though I loved to read the funnies, I never thought of being a cartoonist until I married Dana Fradon who was an aspiring *New Yorker* cartoonist when I met him in art school," she wrote to me in 2012. "He and I worked on a couple of strips together; he wrote them and I did the art, but we never submitted them. We were quite broke and a friend of ours who was lettering comic books suggested I make up some samples and take them around. I bought some comic books and immersed myself in them for a couple of weeks, then made up a page of western vignettes because I liked drawing horses. I took it to a place called Fox Features and they gave me a 12-page script which I returned because I heard they didn't pay and I was actually terrified because I didn't think I had the ability then to draw it."

Fradon continued, "Driven by the prospect of starvation I went to Stan Lee's Timely Comics and they gave me a couple of war stories to draw. Then I went to DC Comics where I was given a *Shining Knight* script and I really worked for them for the rest of my comic book career. Because I was so inexperienced and it had been so easy to get jobs, I thought there must be something wrong with the comic book industry — kind of like you wouldn't want to go to any party that invited you to it — and I have never really gotten over that feeling."

Despite being in a distinct minority in her chosen field, Fradon would go on to enjoy a long career as a comic book artist, notably at DC Comics in the 1960s where she produced memorable work on *Aquaman* and co-created the characters Aquaboy ("He appeared in a script and I had to decide what he looked like and what his costume should be, as I did any other character. I'm not sure I appreciated that he would be a permanent character or one who would have a place of his own in the comic universe but I have developed a kind of maternal fondness for him") and Metamorpho, the Elemental Man ("I experimented with a few conventional ideas for his costume — you know, capes, tights, masks, etc. — but finally decided that since he had been fried by the intense rays in that pyramid, he would have a mangled face and a weird body. And since his thing was to transform the elements in his body into different chemical compounds, clothes would get in the way. So, I put him in shorts and divided his otherwise-naked body into four colors and textures to represent the four elements. In comics, things are so because you say they are and Metamorpho emerged from the pyramid wearing black shorts with an 'M' on his belt and that's just the way it was!").

"I never experienced discrimination," Fradon wrote to me in 2012, continuing, "I know women complain that they can't break into the male-dominated mainstream houses and I think that's because the things they are interested in drawing and writing about aren't what the editors are looking for. In general, I think women are tuned in to relationships and the action that flows from them, while men are fond of action and the violent, never-ending battle against evil. I don't share male fantasies but lacking any desire to express myself in any other particular way, I drew superheroes. I don't know if I got paid the same as men. I worked at home and didn't know much about the business. I knew only a few people at DC, mostly the editors I worked with. From the time I started doing comics, people would ask me if I knew Marie Severin, the only other woman drawing comics at the time. I didn't meet her until 1995 at a convention where we were seated next to each other. I'm sorry I didn't meet her sooner. We could have stood together against the male tide!"

For a time, the comic book industry profitably turned to "the action that flows from relationships" that Fradon mentions, as Simon and Kirby's *Young Romance* #1 (October 1947) for Crestwood Publications had heralded the invention and sudden popularity of romance genre comic books, successfully targeting a female demographic along with a male one that perhaps wanted to pick up a few handy tips. Soon the racks were filled with imitations of romance comic books and their covers of teary-eyed, lovestruck or dejected American girls, whose laments would later influence, very directly, a number of paintings created by American artist Roy Lichtenstein in the early 1960s, including one of his more celebrated works "Drowning Girl" (1963) — on display today at the Museum of Modern Art in New York. Surrounded by swirling seas threatening to engulf her, a sobbing girl seems resigned to her watery fate with the thought, "I don't care! I'd rather sink than call Brad for help!" in a precise example of the melodrama associated with the comic book genre that would prove to be popular for a couple more decades.

Such a precise example, in fact, when you consider that Lichtenstein created "Drowning Girl" by literally enlarging a detail from the opening page of a story called

Opposite page: Ditko artwork for the over from ***Strange Suspense Stories*** #19, July, 1954, ©1954 Charlton Comics. This is one of many horror covers created by Ditko in 1954.

science fiction SPACE ADVENTURES
CDC
No 12
SCIENCE FICTION SPACE
ADVENTURES
A CHARLTON PUBLICATION
10¢
HELLO, EARTH... I'VE LANDED SAFELY... NO SIGN OF LIFE HERE...
Ditko

"Run for Love!" published in DC Comics' *Secret Hearts* #83 (November 1962). The comic book image was drawn by artist Tony Abruzzo, and Lichtenstein made only minor tweaks to the composition and rendering of the original, added Ben-Day dots to his oil and magna painting to mimic the appearance of the cheap printing process and changed the name of "Max" to Brad in the thought-bubble text, a name which would feature in several other works by the artist in a similarly influenced style.

Employing this same technique, Lichtenstein would raid further comic book art to produce his isolated panel image paintings and emerge as a founding member of the pop-art movement of the early 1960s to global fame. By placing the powerful immediacy and flat, bright colours of a single comic book art printed image in an exhibition-sized frame, Lichtenstein highlighted its unique aspects and the work he produced would eventually serve as a conduit between the artform itself and society's perception of it. As publishers searched for the next big hit with a wide variety of different genres, William Gaines, son of the comic book format inventor and publisher Maxwell Gaines, began to build his EC ("Entertaining Comics") line of books, taking over the imprint from his father who had died in a boating accident in 1947. Under the editorial and artistic skills of Harvey Kurztman and Al Feldstein, Bill Gaines had transformed the imprint previously aimed at younger children that he'd inherited from his father into an attention-grabbing, high-quality line of ground-breaking horror, war, crime, western and science-fiction comic books.

Aimed at a more mature audience, the stories revelled in twist-and-turn plots with shock endings, and the entire group of titles placed an emphasis on the superior quality of its scripts and the craftsmanship of the art. From the gory thrills of *Tales from the Crypt*, the futuristic fantasies of *Weird Science*, to the gritty realism of war in *Frontline Combat*, EC Comics utilized the talents of some of the best comic books artists from the period including Frank Frazetta, Bernie Krigstein, Johnny Craig, Graham Engels and Wally Wood, to produce work offering more sophisticated narratives. Unlike other publishers of the time, EC Comics credited all writers and artists on their strips, promoting individuals and their own distinctive styles and making readers aware of the creators behind the stories.

It was still work-for-hire, but the creators of EC comic books were beginning at least to receive a by-line and some recognition for the work they created. Bill Gaines' comic books invited audience reaction and participation with lively, engaging editorial and letters pages and promotions, like the "EC Fan Addict" mail-in fan club, and successfully formed a core identity for their group of titles with methods that Timely's editor Stan Lee may have paid close attention to when attempting to understand the reasons for their growing popularity. At his own recently sourced office, Ditko was focusing his hard-won knowledge into creating saleable comic strips, building a portfolio of readily available work to tout around the New York comic publishers in the hope of opening doors and gaining paid assignments. Ditko's first published comic art work appeared in Gilmor Magazines' (an imprint of Key Publications) *Daring Love* #1 (September-October 1953), where he provided both pencils and inks (from a script by an unknown writer) for a six-page romance genre comic strip titled "Paper Romance!"

It told the somewhat steamy pre-comics code tale of oversexed farm girl Liza, who solicits letters from male admirers through the local newspaper and her dutiful boyfriend Seth, who is aware of this and nonetheless still keen. Ditko's youthful art, seeking different forms in each panel, from the precise lines of Robinson to the shadowy depths of Eisner, is heavy with sexual innuendo. Liza is

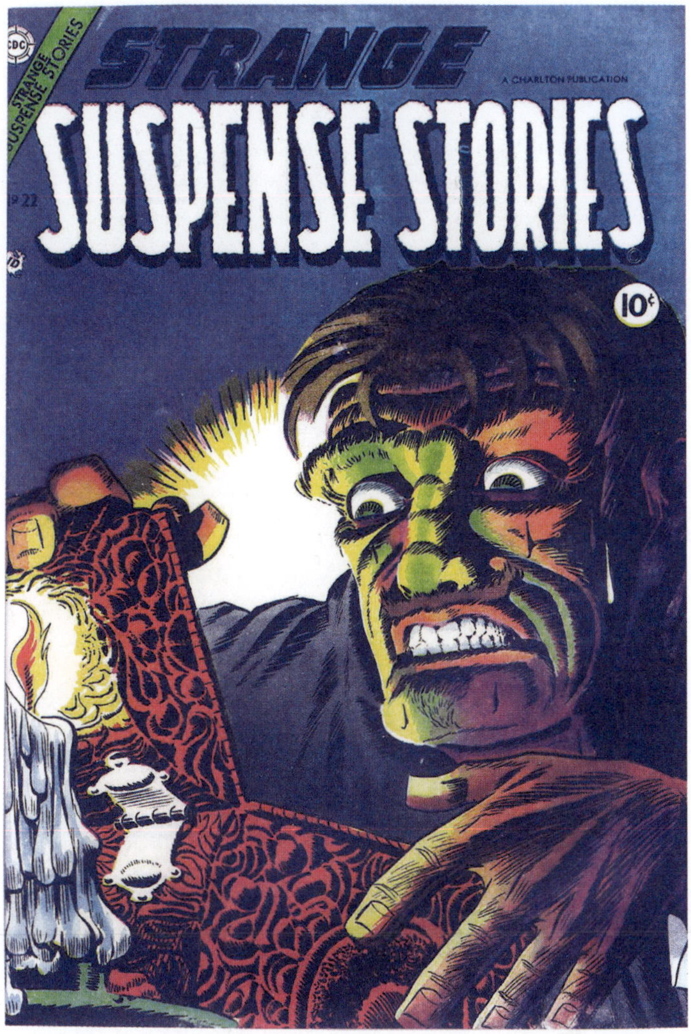

Opposite page: Ditko cover artwork for ***Science Fiction Space Adventure*** #12, August, 1954, ©1954 Charlton Comics. Right: Ditko cover artwork for ***Strange Suspense Stories*** #22, November, 1954, ©1954 Charlton Comics. These covers are clearly more creative than most of the pre-code fare being produced at the time.

A CHARLTON PUBLICATION
WEIRD TALES OF SUSPENSE AND HORROR
CDC
THE THING
Nº12
THE
THING!
10¢
S.J. Ditko

depicted grasping pitchforks below her ample bust, drawn spilling out of her low-cut top, nipples accentuated, or dreaming of love from strangers as she lies open-legged on her bed or posing nonchalantly by a window with the moonlight making her nightgown transparent. This is not unusual for the time, when many creators were producing work for publishers — led by EC Comics — that was edging up to an invisible line in visual depictions of implicit sexuality, along with less-implicit images of war and increasingly explicit, blood-spattered horror.

Eventually, it would all not go unnoticed by the general public. Though the romance comic strip was the first of Ditko's work to ever see print, it was not the first comic strip of his to be commissioned by a publisher. "Stretching Things," scripted by Bruce Hamilton was more indicative of what would later come from the young artist. The horror yarn, complete with atmospheric lighting, ghoulish faces and well-staged camera angles, was originally sold to low-paying Stanmor Publications, who then sold it on to another publisher, Ajax, where it finally saw print in *Fantastic Fears* the following year. It was Jerry Robinson who first introduced Ditko to Joe Simon and Jack Kirby during a visit from the pair to the school, and they were impressed with his developing art style and driving ambition. In the summer of 1953, they hired Ditko to join a pool of artists drafted in to ink backgrounds for an assignment on Harvey Comics' *Captain 3-D* #1 (December 1953), a one-off project designed to hitch aboard the current popularity wave of 3-D movies like *It Came from Outer Space* (1953) and *House of Wax* (1953).

Robinson, along with Mort Meskin, shared a studio space with Simon and Kirby and they all pitched in to help finish the book, resulting in the first time Ditko would ever work with Kirby — his future Marvel Comics colleague and fellow architect of amazing mythologies.

Ditko wrote to the author in 2015, "I had my own office, studio at the time. Simon and Kirby were involved in their *Captain 3-D* project. They needed artists to work on the different acetate sheets for the 3-D to work in the comic book with the glasses. So, they rented a room for all they needed and called artists for help in putting out the 3-D issue. I was lucky to be sitting next to Mort Meskin, whose work I always liked. So, it was a short, one-term deal. I did do a couple of freelance stories for them later."

Towards the end of 1953, Ditko received his first work from the company he would learn to rely on for regular assignments for most of his career, Charlton Comics, where his early artwork was now published in titles like *Tales of the Mysterious Traveler*, *Space Adventures*, *This Mag is Haunted* and *The Thing!* — the 12th issue of which, cover dated February 1954, sported the artist's first-ever published comic book cover. To the Connecticut-based publishers' small, satellite office in Manhattan, Ditko handed in just under 200 pages of stories and nearly 20 covers in a less than nine-month period. He was working at low rates, producing many pages of artwork monthly in order to build a livable wage along with his other "non-comic jobs," but Steve Ditko had effectively arrived as a professional comic book artist and gigging freelancer around the New York publishing houses — from hopeful student to paid practitioner in three long years, achieved with a lot of commitment and with a little help from his friends.

Ditko wrote to the author in February 2015, "Meeting Jerry Robinson, Mort Meskin, Simon and Kirby, made it possible for me to break into a very difficult, competitive field with so many good comic book artists. The best provides some kind of edge that adds something visually special and not seen in the usual competent artists. It was a very competitive business before the Comics Code ruined the industry." Just before this cataclysmic event occurred, Ditko's own career was suddenly halted in the spring of 1954 when he contracted tuberculosis, and fell so ill that his mother traveled into New York to accompany him back to Johnstown, where his slow recovery from the infection would take well over a year. A colleague who saw him struggling while working at a drawing table in Charlton's office reportedly remarked at the time, "He's not long for this world."

While that was an exaggerated attempt at fortune-telling, the young artist was certainly exhausted, working what he labeled as non-comic jobs by day and drawing comic strips to deadlines by night. Ditko wasn't alone in his misfortune, as, despite being on the decline by this decade, the airborne infectious disease was still very much a city-wide problem with over 1,000 New York residents dying of TB each year out of the over 20,000 who annually contracted it. As devastating health issues forced Ditko to leave the city and his fledgling comic book artist career behind, that very same year would see the industry itself face a deadly adversary, armed with the super-powers to destroy, disrupt and eventually force down its own particular change. A sensationalistic book, written by a campaigning psychologist, would be the harbinger of the coming of the game-changing Comics Code Authority.

Opposite page: Dtko cover artwork for ***The Thing!*** #12, February, 1954, ©1954 Charlton Comics. The first comic book cover created by DItko. The cover signed, "S.J. Ditko" is clearly in tune with horror fare of the era and shows the influence of Jerry Robinson in its layout and composition.

Astonish-13 p18
MY FRIEND IS....
NOT QUITE HUMAN!
IT IS THE YEAR 1799, AND I AM HARD AT WORK IN MY LITTLE COTTAGE AT THE CROSSROADS IN AMIENS, FRANCE...
BEHIND ME ARE SHUTTERS AND LOCKED DOORS THAT HIDE THE OUTSIDE WORLD AS I SIT HUNCHED OVER MY WORK...
AND AS I WORK -- MY THOUGHTS ARE FILLED -- WITH BEAUTIFUL MAIDENS...
...WHILE MY GNARLED HANDS CREATE THE WOODEN FIGURES FOR WHICH I AM SO FAMOUS!
HA! IT IS FINISHED! A SHIP'S FIGUREHEAD WORTHY OF THE PIRATE'S BOW IT WILL PERCH UPON! IT WILL TRULY HAUNT THE SEVEN SEAS!
S. Ditko
1
18

Chapter Two
From the Debris, a "House of Ideas" 1955-1961

In late 1955, a recovered but weakened Steve Ditko returned to New York to seek work in a shambolic comic book industry at the exact same time the majority of seasoned veterans were either abandoning it or being abandoned by it. With many publishers facing bankruptcy, laying off staff to a skeleton crew and completely unsure of what products to offer in which genres, it was the worst of times to pursue such ambitions in a field that many believed would soon disappear altogether. "I remember the time in the 1950s when the industry almost collapsed and lots of artists were out of work," artist Joe Sinnott wrote to me in 2013, continuing, "Our page rates had been cut over the preceding years but then things stopped completely. Many of the guys, like Johnny Craig, left the business altogether. It was about six months before things recovered a little and Stan Lee started up again at Atlas Comics when we began doing the "Monster" comic books." With barely a years' previous experience to offer and the memory of a prolonged serious illness, Ditko was nonetheless an individual who embodied a core characteristic of his later creation Spider-Man, one of resolute determination. He simply didn't know how to quit on something that was deemed to be important to him. There were many indications of this in quotes from sayings or poems that Ditko chose to include in his correspondence to me, like this one from February 2013, "Your Winston Churchill voiced it in a critical time during WWII 'never give up, never, never give up.' Never QUIT when you're in the fight. When your feet are so tired that you can hardly lift your hands to come on guard, FIGHT ONE MORE ROUND! When your nose is bleeding and your eyes are black and you're so tired you wish your opponent would crack you one on the jaw and put you to sleep, DON'T QUIT — FIGHT ONE MORE ROUND." Or this one from a letter written the same year, "When things go wrong as they sometimes will, when the road you're trudging seems all uphill. When the funds are low and the debts are high. And you want to smile but you have to sigh. When care is pressing you down a bit. Rest! If you must — but never quit."

Opposite page: Ditko, pencils and inks, original artwork for the splash page from ***Tales to Astonish*** #13 from the five page story "My Friend is Not Quite Human," November, 1960, ©1960 Marvel Characters.

Perhaps a similar message echoing in his mind would have informed Ditko's reluctance to give up on his chosen career, despite the fact that the industry that held it was seemingly in its final death-throes at this time.

While Ditko had been fighting for his own life back in Johnstown, comic books had been making news headlines across America for all the wrong reasons as the industry itself came under intense media attack and condemnation — propelled by the apparent gravitas delivered in the line "according to a best-selling book written by a doctor." Allen Bellmen recalled to me in 2018, "Dr. Frederic Wertham was a fraud when he wrote *Seduction of the Innocent*. He threw the whole comic book world into a tizzy. Stan Lee was packing up to become a salesman, and the whole industry was in a lock-down. I survived doing art and layout work for different publications. A few artists went to California to do animation work." Frederic Wertham was a German-born psychiatrist/author whose 1954 best-selling book *Seduction of the Innocent* unleashed a remarkable flood of public damnation down upon the industry, demanding the publishers and creators be held to account for their "lurid" products that were, as the book asserted, a prime cause of the rise in juvenile delinquency plaguing the country at the time. In the decade the word "teenager" first came into usage, Wertham's book made spectacular, and largely unsubstantiated, claims about the content of seemingly innocent 10-cent comic books of the time — from subliminal sexual imagery hidden in the artwork to far more graphic images of crime and murder the book claimed were influencing and reinforcing negative behavioural patterns in the developing minds of the children who read them. Searching for examples to back up his theory, Wertham's book took increasingly bizarre turns in its attempts to validate his claims, and even DC's cosy superheroes came into question with Wertham famously asserting that Batman and Robin shared a gay relationship, Wonder Woman brazenly displayed an overt bondage sub-text and even the advertisements for air rifles and pocket knives within the comic books incited further thoughts of violence. Coupled with examples of comic art panels delighting in gore and horror, especially from EC's well-illustrated line, Wertham's book, and its subsequent media attention and public reaction, prompted a McCarthy-like interrogative period for the comic book industry. A U.S. Senate Subcommittee inquiry was launched to determine if comic books were potentially harmful literature with Dr. Wertham appearing as the prime witness for the prosecution. The hearings took place, to great public attention, on April 21, 22 and June 4, 1954 with EC publisher Bill Gaines appearing before the Subcommittee following Wertham to defend his own line of accused comic books. Following the hearings, many US towns held mass comic burnings and some states, including Texas and Oklahoma, had already passed laws banning the sale of horror and crime comics altogether. An example of one such organized burning was documented in an article in the Mansfield (Ohio) Journal on November 4, 1954. Under the headline "Civics Club Burns Comics" it read, "Concerned by the 'horror, the brutality, the undisguised sex' found in many comic books, the seventh and eighth graders of St. Mary's School Civics Club — at the suggestion of principal Sister Mary Josepha — decided to take action." Along with a photo of the children gleefully placing comic books in a trash can, ready for burning, it continued, "First, they set up an exchange, where students could trade one disreputable comic — those featuring horror, crime, war, and romance primarily — for two 'good' comics, featuring the likes of Mickey Mouse, Little Lulu, Blondie and Bugs Bunny. Then they took the sordid ones out and burned them."

The article included some comments from the children where one said of comic books "They put bad thoughts in your mind and you start doing what you read in them" and another stated unreservedly, "I think they are a disgrace to the human race." The Committee's final report found no direct cause between comic books and crime but nonetheless concluded with a recommendation that the industry should effectively clean up its act. This sparked a time when many publishers folded, the majority of creators were suddenly thrown out of work all at once, and the sanitizing Comics Code Authority (CCA) emerged from the resultant chaos. A voluntary code of specified standards, the CCA was established by the combined publishers themselves, to self-censor their own comics in an attempt to placate the rising intolerance towards the industry. The Code held many restrictions for future comics: banned outright were "lurid, unsavoury or gruesome" images; any depictions of vampires, werewolves, zombies or ghouls; no stories showing disrespect for police, judges and government, adding that all stories must "in every instance show good triumph over evil" and any scene of passion staged as to "avoid stimulating lower and baser emotions." For comic book titles, the word "crime" was subject to many restrictions in its usage and banned completely were the words "horror" and "terror."

The collective independent scrutiny body was set-up under the title of the Comics Magazine Association of America and, operating from an office at 300 Park Avenue South, examined every single page of original comic book art from all publishers before the issue saw print. To be cleared for publication, the artwork would need to be blue-stamped "approved" on its back. The iconic CCA approval seal appeared on the cover of every comic book published in North America from September 1954 until its demise as recently as January 2011 — eventually rendered obsolete by the publishers as they decided one-by-one to silently ignore it, reflecting the social changes that took place over its 57-year-long history.

Between early 1954 to late 1955, from his convalescent bed at home in Johnstown, Ditko would read or hear of these events unfolding at a distance, but the ramifications of them would make an indelible impression on him and his own creative freedoms for some years to come. Ditko wrote to the author in March 2015, "The Comic Book Code killed many comic book companies. It drove editors, writers, artists out of the business. Yet, it had no effect on all the other publications publishing 'worse' material. The driven-out were eventually replaced with comic book fans without the needed professional qualities, understanding. The fan editors wanted their own kind of ideas, material, not demanding actual high standards. I had a wide experience with the pre-code, with comic book publishers, editors, writers and artists, with the incredible variety of titles, features, characters, story ideas in comic books of 64–54–48 pages. So many different art-styles, story ideas, etc. The comics code material in comparison was bland beyond belief. I wanted to do comics so I stuck with it. I knew artists who could draw far better than I could, who, for some reason, lost interest in comics. It's not always the best, but the ones willing to put up with negative conditions. The comic book publishers had no choice. No comic book could be printed without the code's seal of approval — it had the law behind them (from) 1953/4-2011 (when) the code was abandoned or became irrelevant but the damage was done."

In his later years, Wertham attempted to reconcile his relationship with the industry he nearly destroyed with his final book in 1973 titled *The World of Fanzines*, in which he praises such publications as "healthy exercises of creative drives" and explains that he really had nothing against comic books in principle all along.

That same year he accepted an invitation to hold a talk at the New York Comic Art Convention (founded by Phil Seuling) but was greeted by an air of hostility and crowd-jeering. Wertham left the stage and never wrote about comic books ever again. With more recent findings revealing that he had greatly exaggerated and manipulated his research to substantiate his claims in *Seduction of the Innocent*, Wertham remains the archetypal pantomime villain of the comic book industry — a larger-than-life plunderer of houses and a malignant presence that no-one ever knew was behind them until it was far too late and the curtain swiftly fell. In the intermission, however, returning players would soon take to the stage...

As Ditko found a rapidly-changing and now somewhat reduced and stifled industry, he also found work opportunities were made even scarcer due to his previously dependable employer, Charlton, offering no current assignments after a natural disaster that flooded its 72-acre production plant in Derby, Connecticut on August 18, 1955. Operating an "all-under-one-roof" facility, including offices for creatives, printing presses and distribution, the extensive flooding — caused by heavy rainfall following Hurricane Diane — rendered the publishers' operations crippled for several months thereafter.

When back in business following the flood, and despite the government-aid dollars received, Charlton co-owner and publisher John Santangelo informed staff that he could no longer afford the same pages rates as before and promptly halved the payment from $13 (already well under the industry standard) to $6.50 a page for artists. When Ditko resumed regular work for the company, he would now be paid exactly half for the same amount of work delivered. "Charlton Comics were low-paying but I got more out of working for them in developing my own art style, etc. than I got at Marvel, DC, with their picky editor's 'corrections,' etc.," Ditko wrote to me in July 2015, adding, "An actual editor once said to me, 'The editor is always right. Case closed.' Whoever has the power sets the terms."

Originally established in 1944, Charlton was the brainchild of two men who first met while both serving time in a New Haven County Jail back in the early 1930s. Italian immigrant Santangelo was there for copyright violation after profitably selling unlicensed song lyric sheets, and Edward Levi was a disbarred attorney, imprisoned due to his role in a political scandal. Committing with a handshake, the two set up a company on their release to legitimately produce song lyric magazines and in 1945 added comic books to their profitable range. By 1951, when Al Fago, brother to Vince, an editor at Timely Comics, was hired as Managing Editor of the on-site comics division Charlton had developed within their sprawling production plant, the company was churning out a sizable number of horror, western and crime titles, including one that gave Ditko early assignments but was also cited as an prime example of a comic "with excessive violence" during the subcommittee hearings, *The Thing!*

With Charlton joining the majority of other comic publishers currently out of action, Ditko's path would very soon cross again with a young but experienced editor who was still, surprisingly, handing out work at that very specific time. Stan Lee had previously seen and noted the promise of his developing art style during his last year at art school back in 1952, and it was Steve Ditko's art idol and teacher, Jerry Robinson, who first introduced him to his future, historically relevant, collaborator.

Back in mid-1951, Martin Goodman had moved his publishing operations from the Empire State Building to 625 Madison Avenue (commonly known today as the Revlon Building) and rebranded the comic book division "Atlas Comics," reflecting the name of the distribution company he recently acquired to establish more control, and profits, over the conveyance of his product. It would be here, at the end of 1955, in an office on the fourth floor of the 16-story building, where Ditko would first receive assignments and deliver work to Stan Lee under his editorship.

Taking its name from Madison Square, itself named after fourth President James Madison, the north-south avenue became the hub of the American advertising industry from the early 1920s with its proliferation of agencies and their "mad men" developing and employing increasingly successful techniques to sell products to a public ready for mass consumerism. With television beaming into a steadily-rising number of country-wide households and a demand for varied products growing, Madison Avenue became a name synonymous with the professionally slick and highly-effective sell — to such a degree that Joseph Goebbels made a special journey from Nazi Germany to New York in the early 1930s in order to learn of Madison Avenue methodology that he would later apply in his propogandist image-making and subsequent selling of Hitler as a leader to the German people.

When Steve Ditko entered Atlas Comics' small, two-office workplace on Madison Avenue to receive his very first assignment from Stan Lee (a four-page story ironically titled "There'll Be Some Changes Made" published in *Journey into Mystery* #33, cover-dated April 1956) the Editor-in-Chief, now aged 33, was a seasoned veteran of some 15 years standing as an editor and writer of comic books. Over this time, he had witnessed and survived the halcyon days of the 1940s and the wild-west publishing playfield of the early 1950s but now found his beloved comic book industry in an apparent state of slow decay and, no closer to completing or even starting that great American novel, lately spent an inordinate amount of his time wondering whether the signal to switch career lanes had finally arrived. A brief attempt to revive superheroes with the re-introductions of Captain America (now promoted as a "Commie Smasher!"), Human Torch and Sub-Mariner from 1953-54 had proved fruitless. Launched partly in reaction to the success of the syndicated television series *Adventures of Superman*, which first aired on September 19, 1952 with George Reeves memorably in the starring role, the Atlas hero revival was short-lived, largely ignored and soon forgotten.

The particular re-emergence of Captain America, with scripts from Lee and early art from a heavily Caniff-influenced John Romita, Sr., prompted a mocking response from disgruntled ex-Timely employees Simon and Kirby, whose similarly-patriotic costumed hero Fighting American quickly appeared on the racks in direct competition and with

the intention, as Simon later said, "to show them how to do Captain America right." Unlike their prior arrangement with Goodman, *Fighting American* #1 (May 1954) — initially a straight-forward action book then developing into a knowing satire of the comic book industry over the course of its seven-issue run — was published by the Prize Comics Group as a creator-owned character, a notable achievement within the work-for-hire industry.

After leaving National for military duty, the duo reunited to work for Harvey Comics and by this time had set up their own company, Mainline Publications, to feed contracted work through Crestwood Publication for its comic book imprint Prize Comics — an arrangement that had reaped substantial rewards for both parties in the late 1940s with the astonishing success of romance genre comics. However, both Crestwood and Mainline were fated to never repeat this success with both companies experiencing some collateral damage in the wake of the havoc spread across the industry by Wertham's book. Crestwood limped on for a few more years until it sold its few remaining romance comic titles to DC in 1963, and, for a time, Simon and Kirby entered the field as publishers themselves with titles such as *Fox Hole*, *In Love* and *Police Trap*. But Mainline Comics collapsed by the end of 1956, and, with Simon wanting to pursue a different career in advertising, the partnership with Kirby had organically come to an end, and the two parted company as well-wishing friends.

They would work together briefly once more when Simon returned to comic books to edit Archie Comic's short-lived Red Circle line of superhero titles in 1959 on the *Adventures of The Fly*, but their successful double-act of 16 years was effectively over. Kirby was a freelancer once again, and he returned for work on assignments from National along with a grudgingly reluctant availability once more to Stan Lee's Atlas line, where he became a regular artist on stories in titles like *Battleground* and *The Black Rider* together with frequent contributions to the growing number of fantasy/science-fiction comic book titles. Before the decade was out, Kirby would balance his comic book assignments to concurrently produce his first real success in newspaper strips with *Sky Masters of the Space Force* — a pre-space race era astronaut saga that ran from 1958-1961, notable for its realistic spacecraft designs that appeared sharp and luminous when Kirby's pencils were combined with the sleek inking of Wally Wood — happy for regular work since the demise of such from EC Comics.

The hearings and negative attention of the previous years had had the greatest impact on Bill Gaines' line of pilloried comic books, and his reaction was to close them all down and focus on one best-selling product. Additionally, Gaines defiantly changed the format of the product from comic book to magazine, thereby falling out of the restrictions of the Code along with the necessity to follow them, and the more familiar version of *Mad* magazine was launched, proving to be the publishers' eventual financial salvation.

Over the first six months of 1956, Steve Ditko would draw nearly 20 five-page stories for Stan Lee's Atlas Comics that saw print across the company's line of fantasy titles including *Astonishing Tales*, *Spellbound*, *Strange Tales*, *Marvel Tales* and *Journey into Unknown Worlds*. The first published comic strip to be credited in print as a collaboration between the artist and Lee was also the only story that Ditko did for Atlas at the time not within the fantasy genre but rather a western tale "The Badmen" appearing in *Two-Gun Western* #4 (cover-dated October 1956). Although the fantasy stories, mostly scripted by Lee, some from initial verbally-given plots, were narratively formulaic — predictably ending on a quirky, revelatory twist — it enabled the young artist to further develop his skills, experiment with panel layouts, inking techniques and devise visual iconography that he would later make uniquely his own (a crowd depicted as a circular series of "floating heads" surrounding the central protagonist, as an example).

Working Lee's method during this period seemed to be a liberating approach that initially encouraged Ditko to sharpen his story-telling imagination and, in turn, inspire creative innovations within his art to express it. "I was getting the experience I needed that freelancers don't usually get," Ditko would write to me in a letter from 2014. The current feast of work from Atlas would soon disappear, however, after a disastrous business decision made by

Goodman and the catastrophic events that followed it. Distribution was key to the survival and prosperity of his publishing empire, but Goodman, facing a scared and unsettled industry after the senate hearings, had decided to close his own financially troubled distribution arm Atlas News to sign a deal in late 1956 with the largest player in the market, American News. But the distributor itself was not, of course, immune to the effects of a damaged market, shedding clients no longer interested in displaying comic books at such a rapid rate the company would abandon the product entirely by early 1957 and soon after collapse.

Goodman found a letter on his desk one morning which effectively informed him that his comic books were no longer required by the distributor. Left stranded, with comic books in production but no means of shifting them to retail outlets, Goodman signed a highly restrictive distribution deal with industry leader DC Comics' own distribution arm Independent News Company, which allowed only eight titles a month from the company to be produced. For now, the publisher's dream of market dominance was over, contractually limited by his main competitor, now also earning distribution cents on every comic book Goodman published.

By necessity, the effect on his line of comic books (almost 30 pulled from production and canceled in one month) and staff of freelancers was brutally immediate. Only Stan Lee was retained to run the office, feed material to the printers for the allowed number of comic book titles from stories he'd built up in inventory (reportedly a large quantity stored in a closet which, when discovered by Goodman, greatly infuriated him) and it would have been his task also as Editor-in-Chief to inform all the staff, one-by-one, they were out of work. With assignments halted from Atlas, Ditko now made regular trips to Connecticut to resume connections with Charlton, up-and-running once again and offering as much work as he could handle, albeit at vastly reduced page rates. He would need to be fast and very productive to generate enough income to live on and cover his travel expenses. Joe Gill, his primary script-writer at Charlton, would have to be even faster, paid as he was, only $2 per page but eventually writing over 100 pages a week for the company.

With no editorial interference, Ditko was able to refine his artistic skills even further, creating comic strips in a wide variety of genres under a punishing and relentless schedule that demanded the development of skills through constant application and endurance. For Charlton alone in 1957, Ditko would produce a back achingly large number of comic book art story pages, approaching 500 in total. Keeping Ditko busy with a regular supply of scripts, Gill would meet and dine with the artist at the only hotel in town, where he stayed during his visits.

"He was very withdrawn. He was devoted to his comic book art and used to say that everything he did, no matter who he was working for — if he was working for DC for two times the money or if he was working for Charlton, he still did the same quality work," Gill recalled of Ditko in a 2006 interview published in *Charlton Spotlight* #5 from Argos Press. "My early comic book work seen in Charlton Press comic books — (showed) a kind of developing story/panel continuity," Ditko wrote to me in September 2014, continuing, "Many comic book fans used to complain about Charlton's press printing, colouring, compared to Marvel, DC etc. — but the colouring never bothered me. Their old colouring presses kept the artists ink-line details, textures, effects. I didn't have any standard for the company or the colourist." Ditko concluded with a riposte to 21st Century comic books, "I've seen some computer colouring used now where the colours seem too dense and covers up, eliminates, kills, details. Progress always means losing and gaining and it can be hard to know what is actually best. There will always be advantages and disadvantages."

The "Atlas Implosion" saw many comic book creators abruptly thrown out of work once more, and artist Joe Maneely was among their number. Before the disruption of the Comics Code and the distribution debacle, Lee quickly learned how to identify a particular artist, flagged up by a combination of ability and speed, and depend on that individual as the prime conduit for his plentiful but sketchy ideas. In the 1960s, those individuals would be Jack Kirby and Steve Ditko, but prior to

Opposite page: Ditko, pencils and inks, original artwork for the splash page from ***Tales of Suspense*** #26 from the story "The Face," October, 1961, ©1961 Marvel Characters. Above: Ditko cover art from ***Space Adventures*** #37, December, 1960, ©1960 Charlton Comics.

this Lee had worked in a similar fashion during this earlier period. The absolute star artist working for Lee at the time was Maneely. Renowned for not only his speed but for beautifully-rendered ink work and exquisitely detailed pencils, Maneely co-created *The Black Knight*, *The Ringo Kid* and *The Yellow Claw* while at Atlas Comics, and many other artists around the offices at the time, Ditko included, looked upon his artwork with admiration and awe.

On June 6, 1958 he dined out with fellow laid-off Atlas colleagues, including artists John Severin and Stan Goldberg but past midnight, Joe Maneely was killed when he accidentally fell between the cars of a moving commuter train on his way home to New Jersey. He was just 32. Goldberg remembered in an interview for *Alter Ego* magazine that Maneely told him he had lost his glasses while in the city the week before and, visually impaired, had no idea how he'd managed to get home on that particular day, "So, this day came and he went out drinking and went out to get some air between the trains and he fell off the train. When they found him, he was still clutching his art portfolio. The family had a rough time after he died. The Maneelys had daughters and a lot of bills. They had just bought a big house and had no money put aside."

Recalling Maneely, Lee said in 2004, "Had Joe lived he would have been another Jack Kirby. He would have been the best you could imagine." Experiencing both personal and professional losses, the embattled Lee hunkered down throughout this tumultuous period, until business was improving, inventory was exhausted and more freelancers were once again needed to fill the pages of Goodman's only-eight-a-month comic books. Larry Lieber, Lee's younger brother, re-joined the staff at this time and in 2010 he recalled to the author, "In 1958 I started writing comics freelance for Stan, some of the comic book titles I wrote were: *Strange Tales*, *Tales of Suspense*, *Journey into Mystery* and *Tales to Astonish*. Of course, I wrote a great many of the 'monster' stories drawn by Steve Ditko and Jack Kirby, (Lieber's first published script work for these titles was the Kirby-drawn tale "I Led the Strange Search for Manoo" in *Amazing Adventures* #2, cover-dated July 1961) although I seldom met Jack. I wrote my stories and mailed them out to him. He was very fast and very good. I don't actually remember ever meeting Steve Ditko as I worked with him the same way. I wrote comics more than I drew them at this time because Stan needed a writer. I don't recall if he needed an artist at that particular time. Also, during that period, I didn't draw too fast and I'm not certain that I could have earned a regular living by pencilling comic books."

Having weathered yet another storm, Stan Lee called Ditko in the summer of 1958 — the same year the artist would set up a studio office on 43rd and Eighth Avenue with fellow artist Eric Stanton that they would share for the next ten years — to say that things had improved, and the editor was able to offer new, regular assignments once again. This was good news to Ditko who could produce work at better page rates and take a little longer on each story with the execution of the artwork. His first assignment, a story titled "I Captured the Abominable Snowman," appeared in the first issue of *Strange Worlds* cover-date December 1958. Despite its suffocating new distribution arrangement, sales were buoyant on comic books increasingly offering stories about colossal "monsters" as a device to snare readers — generally, giant-sized versions of aliens, robots or creatures that would be discovered/fly in/erupt from the sea or ground and proceed to terrorize urban populations, stealing the original template wholesale from movies such as *King Kong* and *Godzilla*.

Together with a bi-monthly rota of other genre titles — western, romance, detective — and with all titles produced being anthologies, each containing five or six different comic strips per issue, Lee was now scouting out more artists to join or re-join his freelancer roster to generate the amount of material required. These included John Buscema, reportedly bumped into on the street by Lee, who lured him back to comic books and away from his current advertising work (he would later depart once again before the end of the decade and not return until the mid-1960s); Don Heck; Dick Ayers; Paul Reinman and returning Timely veterans Joe Sinnott, Carl Burgos and Larry Lieber. Forefront in Stan Lee's estimation of fast, reliable and creative artists were Jack Kirby and Steve Ditko, and although it was still some years away, with the assembling of these two individuals in particular and the other talented, experienced comic book creators in general, the foundations had been laid for what Lee would later proudly exclaim to be the "House of Ideas" — in time, a veritable powerhouse of incredible creativity, fantastic influence and amazing corporate value.

As the 1960s began, there was zero value placed on back issue comic books, even by the publishers themselves, who held no supply of such as any returns from retail outlets were received as stripped-off covers, the interiors already trashed. A reader suggesting that fans should trade previous issues with each other in the letters page of *Superman* #35 (February 1960) was roundly rebuffed by the editor's response — "Sorry, but old issues of magazines are known disease-carriers, so we can't encourage such swapping."

At this time, Ditko was successfully juggling assignments from both Charlton and Lee's Atlas-that-was (the company had quickly dropped all branding from its covers after Goodman signed the repressive DC distribution deal) and together with Joe Gill, created one of the decade's first original superheroes with the debut of Captain Atom in Charlton's *Space Adventures* #33 (March 1960). Atomized but miraculously reformed in a space accident when inadvertently trapped in an experimental rocket that exploded in flight, Allen Adam gained super-human, nuclear-based abilities through the event, donning a special costume designed to shield people from the lethal radiation his body now contained in vast quantity.

This narrative device echoed a growing social concern in the early 1960s about the safety and moral standing of nuclear weapons, following the routine testing of them in the Pacific in the mid-1950s along with terrible memories of when the United States became the only country in the world to ever use such weapons with its atomic bombings of Hiroshima and Nagasaki in 1945 and the devastating and lasting results that followed. Recent studies have also suggested that when the first plutonium-based atomic bomb test took place at White Sands, New Mexico on July 16, 1945, thousands of local residents over a 15-mile radius from ground zero, not evacuated due to the secrecy of the test dubbed the Manhattan Project, were exposed to dangerously high radiation levels.

In 1960, there was a feeling of growing paranoia about the seen and unseen effects of these hyper destructive weapons, and, slowly, a disarmament movement collected itself together to protest against the stockpiling proliferation game the superpowers would subsequently play. Perfectly safe within the confines of his red-and-yellow "super-suit" and leaving a sparkling trail of photons behind him as he flew, Captain Atom becomes both crime-fighter and a protector of America's space-program interests, introduced as a recurring character and going against the industry's current trend for individual stories in its anthology titles. Marking the first time that Steve Ditko would draw and create within the superhero idiom, Captain Atom was a perfect vehicle for the artist to apply more detail to his visualization of the musculature of the human form in dramatic and unusual poses — twisting and turning in flight or shaped by throwing a punch — developing a distinct and increasingly identifiable style.

During the same period, Ditko kept his monster-visualization skills sharpened with his runs on Charlton's *Konga* and *Gorgo*, two books derived from low budget model city thrashing monster movies. But the low page rates and repetitively uninspiring nature of Charlton's prolific "stack 'em high" output would lead Ditko to accept more work, and soon, for a time, exclusively, from the newly branded Marvel Comics. A small, unobtrusive MC logo in a box near the title logo would first appear on the covers of *Journey into Mystery* #69 and *Patsy Walker* #95 in June 1961, quietly heralding that Marvel Comics as a comic book brand had surreptitiously entered the market. Something was in the air it seemed in March 1960, as also making a debut appearance in the same month as Ditko's *Captain Atom* was DC Comics' superhero team the Justice League of America, appearing in *The Brave and the Bold* #28. Although perennial-sellers *Superman* and *Batman* and their combined family-group of titles had kept the superhero genre visible over the previous decade, and while little development had been given to a concept regarded by other publishers as creatively and financially exhausted, DC had been making steady progress, under the leadership of Editor-in-Chief Julius Schwartz in reviving reader interest in the genre that was uniquely-born of the product.

Prefaced without fanfare by the introduction of a character called Martian Manhunter introduced as a backup feature in *Detective Comics* #225 (November 1955) by writer Joseph Camachson and artist Joe Certa, a period termed The Silver Age of comics is commonly held to begin when The Flash was successfully re-imagined and re-launched in the pages of *Showcase* #4 (October 1956) by writers Robert Kanigher and John Broome with artist Carmine Infantino. This was followed by other successful costumed-character revivals — Aquaman in *Adventure Comics* #260 (May 1959) by Jack Miller and Ramona Fradon; Green Lantern in *Showcase* #22 (September 1959) by writer Julius Schwartz with artist Gil Kane. With the addition of Superman, Batman and Wonder Woman, these refashioned characters would form the original seven founding members of a superhero team that was currently selling out the comic books it appeared in — a friendly, super mutual admiration society guarding the shores of America and the entire Earth from threatening menaces and offering readers a selection of different heroes for the same ten cents. It took a leisurely game of golf with DC executive Jack Liebowitz and his presiding bragging about the hot cake success of *Justice League of America* to convince Goodman that superheroes were sales worthy once again (this story is in all likelihood apocryphal).

The publisher reputedly returned to the office that same day, fresh from the field, to deliver Stan Lee his instructions to develop a similar hero team book with the sole purpose of competing with, and capitalizing on, the success of DC's current star attraction. With speed being of the essence — who knew how long the present superhero sales fad would last? Lee took the challenge to his primary and lightning-fast artist Jack Kirby. Following a story conference and the production of a rare, typed synopsis from Lee (not made public until the 1980s and one which Kirby would deny ever seeing), the artist returned with a comic strip eventually named by one or the other of the creative duo (both would later make such claims) as *The Fantastic Four.* "I tried to make them typical Americans," Lee would later recall of their origins in a 1975 filmed interview in which he failed to mention Kirby once, adding, "They were surly, insolent, petty, jealous, greedy — and the audience loved them!"

A comic book title telling the story of a team of four quarrelsome adventurers connected by friendship, dysfunctional relativity and a shared space accident experience that gave them superpowers, their appearance and subsequent succession of characters that followed in this and other titles under the fledgling Marvel Comics banner, would eventually have a similar revolutionary effect on comic books and superheroes as The Beatles would have on popular music and Alfred Hitchcock on film directing. But the disgruntled, suspicious and argumentative relationship that typified the nature of the Fantastic Four team, and one of the reasons for the book's impending success, would later be mirrored in the years to come by the deteriorating relationships between Stan Lee and two collaborating artists in particular over authorship credit for the comic books they produced that had passed through his scripting and editorial hands. And, in time, when both Ditko and Kirby eventually gave voice or acted on behalf of their own concerns or beliefs, they would eventually be joined by those with similar stories of uncredited writing under Lee's system.

Back in 1957, when Jack Kirby was perfecting the same juggling act of working for two publishers simultaneously that Ditko was also very familiar with, Kirby presented a comic strip to DC Comics called *Challengers of the Unknown*. While it's unconfirmed whether the concept was Kirby's alone or a collaboration with either Joe Simon or Dave Wood (one of the writers for *Sky Masters*), the first story that ran in *Showcase* #6, cover-dated February 1957 told of four friends who, after surviving a plane crash together, decide that since they are all "living on borrowed time" they should unite as a team and accept "unknown challenges" for the good of mankind and for the sheer thrill of it. The all-male group were devoid of any superpowers but wore unifying purple jumpsuits and later adopted an hourglass symbol to accentuate their motivation.

It foresaw much of the story of Reed Richards, Susan Storm, Johnny Storm and Benjamin Grimm, who would pilot an experimental rocket with the intentions of "beating the commies to the stars" and, exposed to gene-altering cosmic radiation, return to earth after surviving a rocket crash together, bizarrely transformed. Genius-level scientist/inventor Reed becomes Mr. Fantastic, with the ability to stretch any part of his body; Susan becomes The Invisible Girl and his eventual wife; teenager Johnny, brother to Susan, becomes the hot-headed Human Torch in a reworked version of Carl Burgos' original and Reed's war-veteran comrade Ben becomes the orange bricked, super strong, lumbering monstrosity uncharitably named The Thing.

At the end of their first story in *The Fantastic Four* #1 (cover-dated November 1961 but on sale in August that year) the four decide to band together and "use our powers to help mankind" and would soon adopt unifying blue jumpsuits with a 4 symbol on the chest to accentuate the name of the team. Over the following issues, they would establish headquarters in the center of Manhattan called the Baxter Building from where they would live and bicker with each other like regular people as they routinely saved the world from the unknown challenges that would monthly present themselves. It began as a rehashed idea but for the majority of the decade that followed, *Fantastic Four* would emerge as the newly-branded Marvel Comics' best-selling flagship title, establishing templates and company styles original enough to set its characters apart from the once more burgeoning field and operate as a central concept around which an entire fictional universe of interconnecting characters, localities and continuity would be built. As the series progressed, the uber fertile imagination of Jack Kirby expanded at an astonishing rate, expressing stunning art and creating thrillingly original concepts, month after month, that left readers in eager anticipation for the next issue.

Developing new techniques of foreshortening to enhance drama and applications to render depictions of cosmic explosions and alien vistas, Kirby's artwork became the de facto house style for a distinctive new group of comic books. Coupled with the melodrama of Lee's unashamedly cliché-ridden but witty and engaging dialogue, something innovatively fresh and visually new transpired. With its third issue and the introduction of costumes for the team, Lee quickly proclaimed the *Fantastic Four* to be "The World's Greatest Comic Magazine!" above the logo on every cover and, for once, this wasn't unwarranted hyperbole. Within its first year alone, the title had introduced the shape-shifting, world-evading alien race The Skrulls, super-villains The Mole Man, Doctor Doom and The Puppet Master and successfully revived Sub-Mariner (unused since his last series was canceled in 1955) as a nemesis to humanity and a peculiar love rival for the affections of Susan Storm.

In the following nine years, the comic book title would introduce a parade of imaginative new creations including: Galactus (a God-like alien devourer of planets who comes to earth to consume it); The Silver Surfer (herald to Galactus, who surfs the space-ways to find planets for his master to devour only to eventually rebel on the side of humans); The Inhumans (hidden society of alien descent, each member of which is transformed into a super powered being by exposure to the Terrigen Mists); The Black Panther (king of a technologically advanced African country called Wakanda, home to the wonder metal Vibrainium and the first black superhero in mainstream comics ever) and a plethora of alien races including the blue-skinned warrior race The Kree; the mysterious passive observers The Watchers and the inhabitants of the other-dimensional Negative Zone, ruled by insectoid Annihilus. Instrumental to the explosive and rapid development of Kirby's artwork over the course of the series and the formation of all these many characters, was the meticulous inking that Joe Sinnott brought to each issue. His fine brush lines smoothed out rough edges, added depth which gave weight and clarity to Kirby's pencils and when Joe Sinnott joined as regular inker from issue #44 until the end of Kirby's tenure with issue #102 in September 1970, the synergy created by the combined artists made *Fantastic Four* a truly original, visually cosmic, reading experience and a rare moment of genuine comic book genius.

"When I first saw *Fantastic Four* #5 from Jack's original pencils, I couldn't believe how great the characters were. It was the first time I even knew that the *FF* existed and just from that one book, I knew Marvel was onto something big and it would be a great success," Sinnott wrote to me in 2010. "It was not the first thing that I had ever inked over Jack's pencils, however," the artist continued, "The year before (1961), I had inked a story called 'Pildorr the Plunderer,' a monster story that appeared in *Strange Tales* #94. Jack had pencilled it and Stan couldn't find an inker so he asked me if I could squeeze it into my schedule. Stan then gave me another story pencilled by Jack — 'They Called Me a

Witch' (*Journey into Mystery* #58). Stan liked the combo so much he asked me if I would do more with Jack, including a story called 'Titano' for *Tales to Astonish* #10, and that led eventually to *Fantastic Four*. Stan wanted me to stay on the book as inker and sent me Jack's pencils for the sixth issue but I was already committed to work on *Treasure Chest* for Dell, so I think I inked maybe a few panels and then had to send it back to Stan, uncompleted."

It was when Sinnott began to ink Kirby regularly on *Fantastic Four* the seasoned artist discovered a bold and innovative new style that kept pace with the torrent of ideas flowing from the pencil forever in his hand. "I believe Kirby's changing styles on the *Fantastic Four* art was due, in large part, to when I came on the book," Sinnott wrote to me, continuing, "I enhanced a lot of his art — the 'krackle,' added blacks, refined his women, made Reed more handsome. The Thing was my favorite character to ink even though he took time if you wanted him to look great. You certainly could see the change with issue #44 onwards and after previous inking by Vince Colletta, Dick Ayers and Chic Stone. People have told me this is when Jack Kirby and the *Fantastic Four* attained new heights and some say it became the greatest comic book ever produced. I feel honored to have been a part of its success." Sinnott added, "I first met Kirby in 1972 for a short visit and spent a whole weekend with him during the 1975 Mighty Marvel Comic Convention in New York. He was very gracious, but he never commented on my work over his pencils — never! Of course, Stan did, many times, but that's a whole other story."

Jack Kirby would later comment on the creation of *Fantastic Four* in a 1970 interview for *Rocket's Blast Comicollector* #81 not long after he left Lee's Marvel Comics, "It was my idea. It was my idea to do it the way it was; my idea to develop it the way it was. I'm not saying that Stan had nothing to do with it, of course he did. We talked things out. As things went on, I began to work at home and no longer came up to the office. I developed all the stuff at home and just sent it in." Lee had seemed to confirm this in an early interview when he said, "Some artists, of course, need a more detailed plot than others. Some artists, such as Jack Kirby, need no plot at all. I mean, I'll just say to Jack, 'Let's let the next villain be Doctor Doom' or I may not even say that. He may tell me; he just about makes up the plots for these stories. All I do is a little editing."

But, of course, in an industry that "had no strict division of labor, not even for changing a lightbulb," as Ditko wrote to me in 2015, the story was not so clear-cut, and both Lee and Kirby would make inconsistent claims of authorship over the library of comic characters the pair worked on together in the ensuing years that followed. Over the course of 1961 into the early part of 1962, while steadily developing *Fantastic Four*, Kirby would also co-create with Lee The Incredible Hulk, making his debut in the eponymously titled comic book cover-dated May 1962 and along with scripter Larry Lieber, the Norse-mythology based character The Mighty Thor in *Journey into Mystery* #83 cover-dated August 1962 ("When I wrote *Thor*, I created the name Don Blake and named the mythical substance the hammer is made of as Uru. Later, Roy Thomas gave the hammer its correct mythological name of Mjolnir," Lieber wrote to me in 2013). Artist Joe Sinnott also remembered his work on the strip to me in 2010, "I inked Jack on many other books including the first appearance of Thor. Here again, I was certainly impressed with the character and the story was just perfect to introduce this new character Thor. I especially liked the splash page with the very young-looking Thor holding up the big boulder. I felt that Marvel had another sure-fire hit on their hands." Add the size-reducing Ant-man, debuting in *Tales to Astonish* #35, cover-dated September 1962, also scripted by Lieber who created the name Hank Pym, to the list and an increasingly substantial secondary cast would build outside of the multi-faceted world that Kirby and Lee would reveal to readers through *Fantastic Four*.

Meanwhile, Steve Ditko had also been working with Lee over the same period, creating five-page science-fiction/fantasy stories in *Adult Amazing Fantasy*, which exclusively featured the collaborations by its seventh issue, cover-dated December 1961, proclaiming on the cover to be "the magazine that respects your intelligence." By the end of 1961, he would have delivered close to 600 pages of completed art pages with an increased contribution to the plotting of the stories and a necessary refinement of skills to produce such a quantity of material. While the stories were little more than better polished renditions of the twist ending tales previously done for Atlas, Ditko's art displayed a new sophistication and growing confidence that gave these stories an eccentrically creepy air and a unique visual appearance. Referencing his work during this period, one that echoed the comic books he read as a youth with their variety of different stories contained and presented over the rhythm of a five-page format, Ditko wrote to me in 2015, "With superheroes, U.S. comic fans didn't want the five-pagers but ALL superhero. So, killing creative imagination and preventing the purpose, goal of comic books of exploring a range of fiction/fantasy ideas for a one-idea comic book. Exploration should be a big part of publishing stories and art," blisteringly adding, "(As a result) Marvel and DC became closed-in, stagnant-like tribal societies."

By the end of 1961, however, the still young artist was just a whisper away from allowing a complex web-work of cumulative experience, combined with a remarkably individualistic creative vision to originate and deliver one of comic books' and popular culture's most enduringly cherished fictional characters. As he wrote to me in 2014, "One can always enter his or other creative worlds to see what kind of surprises he can find and there will always be risk-takers."

11. AMAZING APRIL '62 6 1/4 x 9 1/4 - 1 SP. V-789
AMAZING 15-P.1

1.

Chapter Three
Spider-Man Swings Out to a Pop Art World 1962-1965

Steve Ditko was 34 years of age in the spring of 1962 when he handed Stan Lee 11 pencilled comic book art pages containing the first appearance and origin story of Spider-Man and his teenage alter-ego, Peter Parker. He'd been a professional comic book artist for just under a decade at this stage, with a wealth of experience under his belt and increasingly distinctive story-telling skills informing his art style. In those 11 pages, everything associated with the character of Spider-Man known today was instantly established. From the visual — the flawlessly-designed costume replete with full face mask and alien bug eyes; the crawling on walls and shooting webbing from the wrists; the skyscraper web-swinging; the appearance of Peter Parker as an average-looking, hard-luck joe.

To the narrative — the radio-active spider-bite that gave the powers; the high school student's doted on home life contrasted with the ridicule and rejection of his peers; his youthful arrogance leading to despair that creates a neurotic, guilt driven motive to only use his powers for the greater good and not for personal gain. It clearly told the story of Peter Parker, a kind hearted but messed up orphaned teenager who fell backwards into superpowers and whose narcissistic actions indirectly led to the death of the only father figure he had ever known. This was heady stuff for comic book readers of 1962, more familiar with a diet of nigh-perfect, code-sanitized role model heroes like Superman and Batman, portrayed in their adventures as kindly adults devoid of any of life's afflictions or real concerns. Teenagers were previously relegated to side-kick status in comic books and generally introduced as a companion to the adult hero for the kids to identify with and to stop the hero from constantly talking to themselves as they patrolled the rooftops of whichever fictional city they protected. The fact that Spider-Man lived and operated in the real-world city of New York was also a major departure from what had gone before.

The heroes of DC Comics resided in fictional American cities and towns, designed to vaguely resemble real life counterparts (Gotham: New York on a bad day; Metropolis: New York on a good day; Central City: Chicago; Smallville: Kansas, and so on). Spider-Man joined Marvel's Fantastic Four, Ant-Man and Thor's alter-ego Dr. Donald Blake in that regard, but whereas they all dwelled in the gleaming towers of Manhattan, Peter Parker's stomping grounds were the decidedly down-to-earth Forest Hills, Queens. Today, New York's third largest borough with a population of over two million and home to both JFK International and La Guardia airports, Queens was originally built by a workforce of Jewish, Italian, Irish and German immigrants in the early part of the 20th Century who developed a community based on the principles of hard work, assimilation and family centered civic participation.

By the 1930s, the borough attracted middle-class Jews fleeing Hitler's Europe and became an area so sought after celebrities like Charlie Chaplin and Will Rogers had homes in the Kew Gardens neighbourhood. But political decisions in the early 1960s successfully destroyed this middle-class society with high taxes, inattention to schools and short-sighted social policies, and the Queens that Peter Parker would have been familiar with was one of closing businesses, diminishing job opportunities and ever-increasing crime levels. The modest, two-story fictional house in Forest Hills, where Peter was raised by his Aunt May and Uncle Ben Parker, was later given the real-world address of 20 Ingram Street in the comic book series in the late 1980s. Writer David Michelinie, often attributed as the instigator of this as it happened during his run on *Amazing Spider-Man*, wrote to me in 2019, " I actually had nothing to do with that. The address appeared in a print paste-up that was added after I had turned in my script. I'm told that someone at Marvel looked up the name 'Parker' in a Queens phone book, and got the address from that."

At the time of the release of director Sam Raimi's original 2002 *Spider-Man* movie for Sony, when newspaper *The Queens Tribute* researched the character's local connections, they discovered an Andrew and Suzanne Parker at the exact same address, where the couple had been living with their daughters since 1974 and ran the story as a bizarre coincidence. Stranger still, the neighbor across the road at 19 Ingram Street was a Terri Osborne, a surname infamous in Spider-Man lore as the name of his best friend Harry and also of Norman Osborn, alter ego of archenemy The Green Goblin.

Opposite page: Ditko, pencils and inks, original artwork for the splash page from ***Amazing Fantasy*** #15, April, 1962 ©1962 Marvel Characters. The first story featuring The Amazing Spider-Man.

The area was not named as the Parker residence in the series until a pin-up page in the first 1964 *Amazing Spider-Man* annual confirmed it as such. The Steve Ditko Spider-Man origin story comic art pages that Stan Lee took delivery of, eventually to add dialogue and captions to, were not the first version of a character with that name the editor had solicited. Jack Kirby, already producing the bulk of the work of Marvel's current output, was initially given the assignment. Lee had offered Kirby the same scant verbal instructions on a new hero called Spider-Man (which, in itself, would later bring counter-claims of ownership from Joe Simon) that he would soon repeat to Ditko — that this was to be an orphaned teenager living with an aunt and uncle, who becomes a superhero called Spider-Man and very little else. He expected the rest to be fleshed out by whichever artist he assigned the task to and his initial concern was that the idea — vague as it was — received a green light from Martin Goodman.

According to Lee, the idea was initially emphatically rejected, as he remembered to the author during a meeting in October 2011, "When I took the idea of Spider-Man to my publisher Martin Goodman he said, 'You're crazy! First of all, a teenager can't be a hero; he can only be a side-kick. Secondly, he can't have personal problems. Don't you know what a superhero is? And finally, you can't call a superhero Spider-Man because people hate spiders!' So, he just thought it was the worst idea ever." This story supports Lee's subsequent claims that, despite Goodman's concerns, and emboldened by his wife Joan's urge to "write the stories you want to." Lee went ahead regardlessly and introduced Spider-Man — a name Lee claimed to create, inspired he said, by pulp character The Spider — to an appreciative world in the pages of a comic book title that was doomed for cancellation anyway. However, an editorial text page in the comic book itself disputes this memory. Under the headline, "Important Announcement from the Editor!" Lee writes that the comic is simply changing format and promises, "As you can see, we are introducing one of the most unusual fantasy characters of all time — THE SPIDERMAN who will appear every month in AMAZING." The editorial added, "Perhaps, if your letters request it, we will make his stories even longer, or have TWO Spiderman stories per issue."

Martin Goodman was the owner, financial risk-taker and absolute decision-maker at Marvel and the reality was if he didn't like an idea, for whatever reason, it would never see print. It also makes no logical sense for Lee to defy his long-standing, wage-paying boss over a character he had barely conceived of and had little invested in. After all, which version of the idea did Lee take to Goodman in order for the publisher to initially reject it? The Kirby pencilled pages? The completed Ditko version? Or the same gossamer-thin premise he would offer both artists on separate occasions? What Lee was deeply invested in was his mortgaged Hewlett Harbour home together with the comfortable lifestyle his Goodman salary provided him and his British-born wife Joan Lee, nee Boocock (the couple were married in Reno, Nevada on December 5, 1947) and daughter Joan Celia Lee, known as J.C., who was 12-years old at the time. The great American novel may still have been alluding him, but comic books had proved to be a dependable source of income for Lee and little was to be gained by risking it all for what was, at that precise time, just another character name to be imagined in detail by an artist.

At Lee's behest, with or without publisher approval, Kirby went off to plot and pencil the first five pages of his version of Spider-Man and, notoriously fast, returned after only two days from the initial talk with the finished results. In Kirby's version, the lead protagonist was an unnamed teenage orphan who finds a magic ring that transforms him into an adult hero, dressed in a costume similar to Captain America — with a half-face mask, gauntlets and boots — and armed with a hand gun that fires webs. It fulfilled the nebulous brief the artist was given and Lee, rather than reject it as he later claimed, (as in this example from 2002, "I hated the way he (Kirby) was doing it. Not that he did it badly — it just wasn't the character I wanted; it was too heroic") proceeded to assign an inker by giving the pencilled pages over to Ditko.

In an essay titled "Jack Kirby's Spider-Man" published in Robin Snyder's *History of Comics* #5, May 1990, Ditko recalled of the pages, "The Spider-Man pages Stan showed me were nothing like the (eventually) published character. In fact, the only drawings of Spider-Man were on the splash and at the end (where) Kirby had the guy leaping at you with a web gun. Anyway, the first five pages took place in the home, and the kid finds a ring and turns into Spider-Man. The other four pages showed a teenager living with his aunt and uncle. The aunt was a kindly old woman, the uncle was a retired police captain, hard, gruff, and he was down on the teenager. Next door or somewhere in the neighbourhood there was a whiskered scientist-type involved in some kind of experiment or project. The end of the five pages depicted the kid going toward the scientist's darkened house." This was the totality of Kirby's Spider-Man with Ditko adding that "almost all of the bits of this 'creation' (the scientist/magic ring, etc.) were discarded/never used." As editor and scripter, Lee had seemingly considered Kirby's version to be in line with what he had been expecting or else would not have moved the pencilled pages to the next stage of inking, thereby involving Ditko.

It's possible, but highly unlikely, that he would have given the pages to Ditko solely with the purpose to solicit an opinion — this would have been from a humble freelancer on work from another artist on a concept that remained, at this stage, largely undefined. Without a specific and precise description of the character and its story from Lee, how did he imagine Ditko could have judged Kirby's version in order to offer an opinion on the merits of it or lack of? Nonetheless, an opinion is what Lee received as Ditko immediately made him aware that he considered the pencilled story pages he had been asked to ink an exact repeat of The Fly, a character Kirby had previously co-created in 1959 for Archie Comics, and the kid-turning-adult concept also a swipe from Fawcett's Billy Batson and Captain Marvel. It was then, and only then, when Lee decided to give the assignment over to Ditko — for the artist to start anew, to create something different and distinct from Kirby's generic, square-jawed heroes, something amazing and something called Spider-Man.

With Kirby's version now firmly rejected by Lee, Ditko set to work to create his own vision of a spider-based superhero. "One of the first things I did was to work up a costume. A vital, visual part of the character," Ditko wrote in the same essay published May 1990, adding, "I had to know how he looked before I did any breakdowns. For example: A clinging power so he wouldn't have hard shoes or boots, a hidden wrist-shooter versus a web gun and holster, etc." The instantly recognizable, red-and-black (blue used only a high-light in his earliest appearances), web-patterned, formfitting costume with its haunting alien eyes set within a full face mask was a true design inspiration from Ditko, who employed a balance of creativity with realism to achieve a genre classic. "With Spider-Man I knew I couldn't show a teenagers' mouth, chin area, so a full-face mask was needed. Also, anyone could be behind the mask," he wrote to me in 2016, citing a facet of the character recently explored to great success in the 2018 animated movie *Spider-Man: Into the Spider-Verse* and adding, "All costumes take time to work out, to work effectively in all situations. I may have had a colour choice for the Spider-Man costume but all this is too far back in history. Stan Goldberg may have had something to do with the colouring, he did a lot of Marvel colouring at the time."

Opposite page: Photograph of Ditko in the early 1960s. Right: Ditko, pencils and inks, original artwork from the last page of the of Spider-Man origin story from ***Amazing Fantasy*** #15, April, 1962 ©1962 Marvel Characters.

Stan Lee liked the original costume design of Spider-Man that Ditko had offered and set him off to complete the assignment. He would next have seen Ditko's fully-rendered pencilled pages detailing the story and begin the task of scripting them — adding story titles, narrative captions, writing dialogue in speech balloons and thought-bubbles and naming supporting characters. Next, the letterer — in this case, Artie Simek who would have, coincidentally, lettered the pages from his own home in Queens — would calligraph the script onto the artboards before they were returned to Ditko to apply inks over the pencilled art for print reproduction. In many cases, the artist working this method of production would add written notes around the borders of the art or (as in Ditko's case on these early issues) on separate pieces of paper to clarify events taking place and often suggesting dialogue. Lee would later explain to readers of Marvel comics dated March 1966 on the "Bullpen Bulletins" page how the process worked, while notably neglecting to mention Ditko, "It isn't generally known, but many of our merry Marvel artists are also talented story men in their own right! For example, all Stan has to do with the pros like Jack 'King' Kirby, dazzling Don Heck and darlin' Dick Ayers is give them the germ of an idea and they make up all the details as they go along, drawing and plotting out the story. Then, our leader simply takes the finished drawings and adds all the dialogue and captions!"

In October 2011, Lee said to the author in reference to the now-famous closing dialogue line of Spider-Man's origin story, "I remember when I wrote that line 'With great power comes

great responsibility' I just thought – Well, I need something to end the story with, I've gotta get him (Peter Parker) to say something and it just hit me. And it's funny, it's been quoted so often and I read it in so many different places. In fact, I remember now, that the Attorney General of the State of Rhode Island called me up, oh, six or seven years ago and said, 'If you ever come to Rhode Island I'd like you to come to my office.' I just figured why? Am I under arrest? He said 'I'd like you to read a plaque on my door that reads, 'With great power comes great responsibility.'"

Stan Lee would have scripted those well-chosen words in the spring of 1962, to clarify the plot and to accentuate the drama of the story that was before him on those eleven art pages. He'd done this before on thousands of pages by many different artists over decades and was very adept at reading the artist's storytelling intentions — especially if the artist was not working from a detailed script, an increasingly normal working practice he had established to cope with workload. These particular pages revealed the story of the "Amazing Spider-Man" as plotted, pencilled and inked by Steve Ditko, and Peter Parker never actually said those oft-quoted words in a moment of epiphany, as Lee incorrectly remembered to me. They were rather delivered in a closing narrative caption, written by Lee but inspired by the wordless, yet fully-imagined and evocative art panel before him of a mournful Spider-Man walking away, head down into the night — his tragically unique story already skillfully told by the artist who had conceived of his dramatic genesis. Because of the two completely different takes originally produced on the character — initially by Kirby and successfully by Ditko — it can be safely assumed that a Stan Lee-written Spider-Man origin plot synopsis, typed or hand-written, never existed to be given to either artist.

Any additional instructions offered by Lee were strictly verbal, which left a great deal of the creative process to the assigned artist and a clarity of authorship clouded by procedures and the passing of time. Kirby's version was a teenager who finds a ring and turns into an adult superhero with a web-gun, and the central theme of power and responsibility are completely absent — no spider bite, no peer group pressure, no attempting to profit from power leading to the death of Uncle Ben.

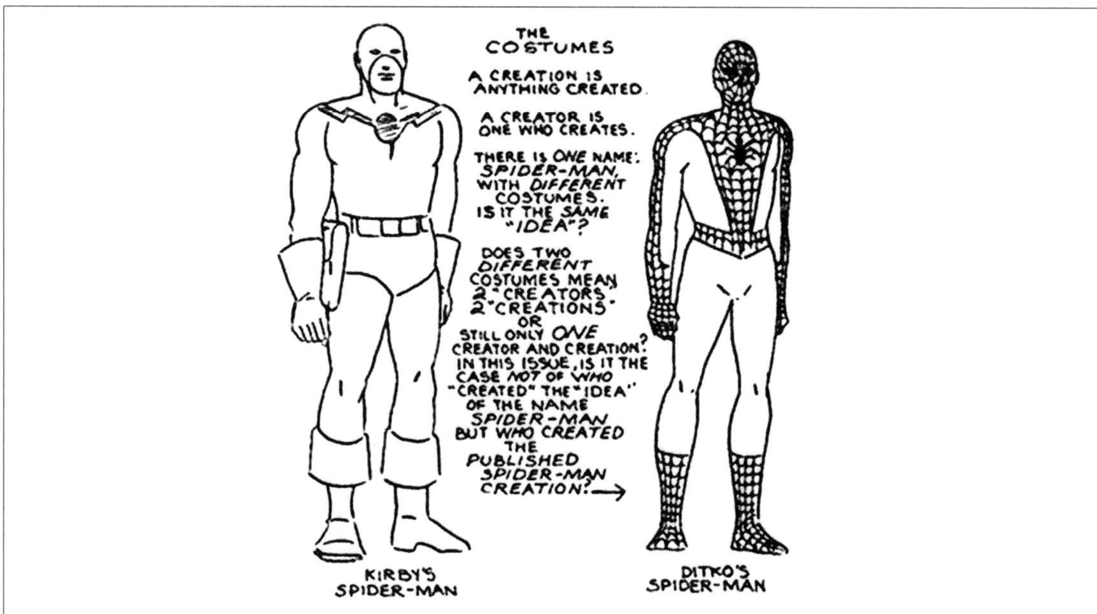

Kirby's un-inked pencil pages and the origin story they depicted have never been seen in any form and it's unknown to this day whether they still exist and, if so, who possesses them. Without examples of any of the five pages, it's impossible to say whether those pencilled pages contained any lettering that may indicate if Lee ever scripted any of them before handing them to Ditko. Outside of Lee, Kirby and Ditko, the only other person to ever claim to have seen any original Jack Kirby Spider-Man art pages is Jim Shooter, controversial Editor-in-Chief of Marvel Comics from 1978-1987, who says he saw a Kirby-drawn presentation page in 1969 and wrote in 2009 on his online blog, "I saw, and held in my hand, exactly one such page. It was a page of design drawings. I remember that his version of Spider-Man had a 'Web-Gun' and wore trunks. He was far bigger and bulkier than Ditko's version. There were no similarities to Ditko's Spider-Man costume. I think he had boots with flaps. There were notes in the margin that described the character, again, nothing like the Ditko version. I think there was something about him being related to, or having some connection with a police official, which was how he'd find out about trouble going on. It was a long time ago, I can't swear to that last item, but I can swear to the fact that it wasn't similar to the Ditko version. I remember thinking, 'This isn't at all like Ditko's.'" Shooter added, "Years later, in 1986, I had occasion to talk with Jack at the San Diego Comic Con. He insisted that he created Spider-Man. I told him that I'd spoken to Steve Ditko, Sol Brodsky, and other people who were there at the time, including Stan, obviously, and that they all agreed that Steve's version was the one that was used, though Jack did his version first. I reported everything I'd seen and heard. We talked about the costume — the bib and belt combo, the stripes down the arms, the mask, the symbols, a very Ditko-esque design. Jack was having some problems with his memory by then, but he thought about it for a minute, then said that maybe Steve should get the credit."

Despite this sentiment, in May 1990 Jack Kirby claimed he was the sole creator of the webslinger in an interview published in *The Comics Journal* #134 (February 1990) where he unreservedly states, "I created Spider-Man. We decided to give it to Steve Ditko. I drew the first Spider-Man cover. I created the character. I created the costume." While it's true that Kirby drew the cover to Spider-Man's first appearance, inked by Ditko, this was only after Ditko's original pencilled and inked cover was rejected by Lee on the grounds that the editor wanted a view looking up, not down, on the lead character. Ditko wrote to the author in a letter from November 2014, "Stan claims he rejected Kirby doing Spider-Man because Kirby made Spider-Man 'too heroic'. Yet, my original first *Spider-Man* cover, a subjective viewpoint, showed everyone up there in space with him and a kind of inexperienced Spider-Man action. Stan rejected it for a more heroic action scene and an objective viewpoint, the viewer is not up there with Spider-Man."

To illustrate the fundamental differences between what Kirby created and his own published version, and reacting to Kirby's claims, in *History of Comics* #5, May 1990, Ditko published the first drawing of Spider-Man he had done in over 24 years (opposite page), depicted standing near a version of Kirby's design for comparison, which Ditko drew either from memory or from material he had to hand. The drawing was accompanied by text written by Ditko where he simply asks "Is it the case not of who 'created' the 'idea' of the name Spider-Man but who created the published Spider-Man creation?" The subject of who created what would gather momentum over the coming decades with claims of authorship from both Kirby, Simon and Lee taking as many twists and turns as the plot of the average superhero saga. Ditko himself remained stoically silent on the subject for the most part throughout his life, offering the impression that he cared little but delivering rebuttals to what he saw as imbalances to the story when necessary. The truth was, whether he was creator or co-creator, whatever he originally intended to achieve with Spider-Man was, to his mind, ultimately subverted into something else entirely and the artist eventually felt that his collaborator was "working against" him.

At the time, it created an escalating disagreement between Ditko and Lee over the direction of the comic book series, with both creators feeling a paternal and propriety attachment to the character as its success grew. But the seeds of the conflict can be found in the origin story itself, with the first artistic clash concerning the very nature of Spider-Man emerging between Ditko and Lee over an issue that would later become an intrinsic part of the characters' visual canon. On the seventh page of the story, a large image shows Spider-Man being introduced to the world as a television personality — he's bathed in a spotlight while clinging to the wall upside down, face turned up, gazing out. It's a bizarrely contorted pose that, even in silhouette, would be instantly recognizable as the comic book web-spinner. A powerful and arresting ink line drawing, evoking the shock of the new in a single panel and an early example of Ditko's singular vision of the wall-crawling superhero. But Lee found the image too arresting and, fearing censorship from the Code, instructed Ditko to re-draw the page showing the hero standing upright on the floor instead, which the artist refused to do.

Ditko wrote to me in 2015 confirming this,"Yes, Stan wanted me to take Spider-Man off the wall because the Comics Code MIGHT object. Spider-Man (seen) as an unhuman creature, etc. I told him to wait until the Code actually objects. It didn't." In another example of how the

Above: Unused cover prepared by Ditko for ***Amazing Fantasy*** #15, ©2020 Marvel Characters; Stan Lee substituted one created by Jack Kirby in its place that depicts the same scene from a different angle. Ditko's cover was staged with the intention of including the viewer in the action, and the man in the bottom left corner could be a self-portrait of the artist. Below: A comparison prepared by Ditko contrasting his version of Spider-Man with Kirby's, ©2020 The Estate of Steve Ditko.

AMAZING 15 - P. 8
V-789
PART 2
NOW ANYBODY WITH THE INTELLIGENCE OF A SEVEN YEAR OLD KNOWS THAT IF A MAN APPEARED ON TV WHO SEEMED TO BE MORE SPIDER THAN HUMAN, HE'D BE AN OVERNIGHT SENSATION! ESPECIALLY WHEN HIS FEATS WERE PERFORMED WITHOUT THE HELP OF TRICK PHOTOGRAPHY! WELL, YOU CAN JUST IMAGINE HOW THE PUBLIC REACTED TO SPIDERMAN!
I'M SEEIN' IT WITH MY OWN EYES, AND I STILL DON'T BELIEVE IT!
V-789
SURE THEY LOOK AMAZED, INCREDIBLE, AWE-STRICKEN! WOULDN'T YOU???
AFTER ALL, WHEN WAS THE LAST TIME YOU SAW A MAN WITH HIS OWN FANTASTIC SPIDER WEB???
OKAY, SPIDERMAN-- CUT! THAT'S ENOUGH! DON'T SHOW 'EM TOO MUCH! LEAVE 'EM BEGGIN' FOR MORE!
7
8.

early Marvel characters were never conceived of whole cloth but rather developed over months through a creative process of trial and error: In Spider-Man's rites-of-passage origin story, when Spider-Man defeats and finally realizes that the killer of his Uncle Ben is the same thief he allowed through youthful arrogance to escape, two cartoon-like dots appear in the masked eyes to accentuate his surprise. These were never to appear again in any other Spider-Man story, and who added the incongruous dots was a minor mystery for decades. Was it Ditko at his own or Lee's behest? Another inker? The letterer, perhaps? But it was Ditko after all, as he confirmed to me in a letter from 2015, who considered then quickly decided against the visual effect for future issues. He wrote, "The eye through the usually blanked-out eye is just legitimate dramatic effect. We're not dealing with reality but with fiction and fantasy. The more that can be legitimately shown, explained, the more viewers will accept the exaggerated."

At the time Ditko drew the first Spider-Man story he was sharing office and working space with fellow artist Eric Stanton. The pair met originally at the Cartoonist and Illustrators School and had remained friends and collaborators since those days. Developing a career as a famed fetish artist, producing titillating bondage and domination "cheesecake" sexual imagery cartoon strips, Stanton had asked Ditko to assist with some inking of his pencils in the early 1960s, and the artist had obliged his colleague. In later years, however, Ditko would distance himself quite firmly from the work he assisted Stanton on, at one time denying he had done it and insisting that no proof existed that he actually ever had. His reticence to accept such work into his catalogue may have been caused by the conflict it could have created with his older self philosophy or, more likely, that he considered his real input into the Stanton-only credited artwork as negligible, without his creative influence and produced with the sole intention to help out a friend. Others may argue that the soft but present sexual aspect of the work is what Ditko, himself an individual that expressed very little of such in both his artwork and real life, was refuting.

At this point, no known long-term partners have ever been attached to him, and this side of Ditko's life will, like many aspects, likely remain forever private. In 2012, Stanton's daughter Amber wrote in an essay published in Craig Yoe's *The Creativity of Ditko* — a hardcover collection of reprint strips, "'You know, I co-created Spider-Man with a fella named Steve Ditko.' That's what my father told me when I was nine years old. Whenever my father mentioned Steve Ditko it was with a great deal of admiration and respect. From the late 1950s through the early 1960s, they shared a studio in Midtown Manhattan, not too far from Times Square.

"Steve was hired by a guy named Stan Lee to create a comic book super hero who was part-man, part-spider. My father contributed to the costume, the idea of the web-shooting out of Spider-Man's wrist and the movement which he made with his hands to release the web. I asked him why I had never met Steve Ditko and my father seemed sad. He said Steve had a very black-and-white view of the world, much like his pen-and-ink drawings. My mother later explained that when my father had told Steve he had fallen in love and was going to have a family, Steve reacted with anger and disapproval. Steve believed that people should not have children because the world was an awful place."

Opposite page: Ditko, pencils and inks, original artwork from the second chapter splash page of the of Spider-Man origin story from ***Amazing Fantasy*** #15, April, 1962 ©1962 Marvel Characters.

In interviews during his lifetime, Eric Stanton would recount some aspects of those details but summarize his involvement in the creation of Spider-Man as "practically nil." Ditko wrote to me in May 2015, "Someone is always bringing up someone other than the publicity claimed inventor, some prior assistant or stolen from some previous inventor etc. It happened with Thomas Edison and the light-bulb etc. I believe the creator of FM Radio who worked for a company was involved in a long court battle. He only wanted it known that he was the creator, not seeking any kind of cut, money etc. A company, for its own survival, has to claim ownership of whatever 'created ideas' a worker discovers."

Other potential influences can also occur by accident or be absorbed subconsciously, and such may have been the case of the New York-based Ben Cooper Inc. "Spiderman" Halloween costume of 1954, a widely-marketed children's costume that some have suggested may have influenced Ditko's Spider-Man costume design. There are similarities in the web-patterned structure, full-face mask and spider motif chest emblem but marked differences as well, and it can never be known if Ditko ever saw the costume or advertisements for it to derive any inspiration, subliminal or otherwise. In 2014, Ditko wrote brusquely to another correspondent after being sent a clipping of a 1954 Ben Cooper advertisement for the costume, "The burden of proof is on the person who makes the claim, assertion, charge. Some clipping etc, are not rational proof of anything but some clippings etc." His birth was convoluted with many midwives in attendance, but only one individual eventually delivered Spider-Man visually to the world, staying long enough to nurture early passages and guide the development of the comic book character to become the highly lucrative and well-loved one known around the world today.

Amazing Fantasy #15 — the comic book title containing Steve Ditko's first ever Spider-Man story — shipped to newsstands across America on Tuesday, June 5, 1962, despite its cover date of August. It was the final issue of the Marvel science-fiction/fantasy anthology series as the book would effectively rename itself *The Amazing Spider-Man* with its number one relaunch next issue after dropping the word "adult" from the title this issue. That same day in June saw the first Thrifty Acres Hypermarket open in Detroit, Michigan, combining groceries with a department store and introducing the world to the idea of a "superstore"; the Honda S360 was unveiled, and Richard Milhouse Nixon won the Republican Party nomination for Governor of California.

Just one day later on June 6, 1962, The Beatles held their first audition with producer George Martin at Abbey Road Studios, London. That same month saw President John F. Kennedy announce his plans for tax cuts while Lee Harvey Oswald returned to American shores after two years in Russia; Marilyn Monroe was fired from 20th Century Fox and began her swift descent; the first cosmic X-Ray source, Scorpius X-1, was discovered, and a second U.S. attempt to detonate a nuclear warhead in space, forty miles above Earth, failed once again. The missile was, coincidently, named Thor — very soon to debut as a Jack Kirby-drawn Marvel character. It would be another two years before Bob Dylan would declare that the "times are a changing," but Spider-Man was born into a world that presaged this, one dizzy with possibilities while simultaneously quietly fearful of their consequences — a perfectly accurate reflection of the comic book character itself. Today, *Amazing Fantasy* #15 is one of the collectors' market genuinely valuable and high investment comic books, with a 2011 sale of a near-mint example reaching over $1 million at auction, ushering Spider-Man into a very select company of just three superhero characters (the other two being, of course, Superman and Batman) whose first appearance, side-stapled, cheaply printed pamphlets have broken that eye-watering financial barrier. Collectively, the trio of comic books would have cost just 32 cents, when bought new from newsstands at the time of their respective issue.

With early sales figures promising and a steady trickle of positive fan mail encouraging, *The Amazing Spider-Man* solo title was launched with its first issue cover-dated March 1963 and guest-starring on the Kirby-pencilled, Ditko-inked cover, The Fantastic Four. From there, Ditko began to unveil his vision for the character with uncanny precision and astonishing speed. In just the first three issues alone, Spider-Man develops his "spider-sense," creates his hidden belt-buckle "spider-signal" and begins the practice of stringing up captured criminals in webbing (set to dissolve within an hour); as Parker he comes up with the notion of taking in-costume selfies in order to sell them to publisher J. Jonah Jameson's *Now* magazine (before being renamed *The Daily Bugle* in later issues) to help pay Aunt May's overdue rent, while Ditko also reveals a schematic cut-away design of how the wrist worn web shooters work and in quick succession introduces super villains Chameleon, The Vulture, The Terrible Tinkerer and Doctor Octopus.

In strips credited inconsistently as "Script by," "Story by" and "Written by," Lee not only erroneously refers to his lead protagonist as Peter Palmer (twice in the first issue) but also writes a confrontational speech for Doctor Octopus that begins, "And now, Super-man, I grow bored of this game!" Despite such inattentive mistakes, traces of Lee's later crowd-pleasing dialogue style could be found in Jameson's suggestion to Parker to take the money he'd just given him and "go out and buy some twist records." For the second issue of *Amazing Spider-Man*, the first with a fully pencilled and inked cover by Ditko, and displayed on the covers of all other Marvel comics dated May 1963, Ditko designed the corner box element — a combination of character image, company logo, issue number and price tag. The innovation successfully helped the line of comic book titles to stand out more on the racks and solidify the impression of a connected universe of characters produced by one publisher.

One inquiring reader noticed the cover addition and asked in the letters column of *Fantastic Four* #18 (September 1963) who was responsible, eliciting the following response from Lee, "Steve Ditko dreamed up the idea, and we're sure glad he did!" Ditko confirmed this in an essay written in 2008 for his *Avenging Mind* comic, "I suggested the corner box with a Marvel hero face and drew a face to show Lee and Sol Brodsky how it would look, and more important, how and why the Marvel title with a hero face would be quickly seen, recognized, no matter how comic books sold in stores were placed in racks." While introducing the classic super villain Doctor Octopus in the pages of *Amazing Spider-Man* #3, the same month also saw the debut of a brand new character from Ditko in the anthology title *Strange Tales* #110 (July 1963). Combining occult mysticism and Eastern philosophy with world-threatening supernatural challenges, Doctor Strange was the unlikeliest addition to Marvel's 1960's empire-building roster but became a vehicle for Ditko's art and story ideas to take full, mostly unfettered, form. The resulting comic strip, when it hit its stride within the hands of its creator, was breathtaking and startlingly fresh. As readers' desire to interact with the creators of Marvel comics increased, as evidenced by the rising tide of fan mail, Stan Lee kept abreast of all new fan-written publications, often feeding the fanzine editors items of news and interest.

It was in one such magazine that Lee confirmed that Ditko was the sole creator of Doctor Strange. In *The Comic Reader* #16 (February 1963), a publication founded by Jerry Bails, Lee wrote, "Well, we have a new character in the works for *Strange Tales* just a five-page filler named *Doctor Strange*. Steve Ditko is gonna draw him. It has sort of a black magic theme. The first story is nothing great, but perhaps we can make something of him. 'Twas Steve's idea. I figured we'd give it a chance, although again, we had to rush the first one too much. Little sidelight: Originally, we decided to call him Mr. Strange, but thought the 'Mr.' was a bit too similar to Mr. Fantastic. Now, however, I remember we had a villain called Doctor Strange just recently in one of our mags. I hope it won't be too confusing!"

Years later, in a 1975 television interview, Lee would contradict his own earlier published remarks that Doctor Strange "was Steve's idea" when he remarked on camera, "After we had all the other characters, at one point I said 'Gee, we don't have a magician and kids are interested in magic' and it seemed to me Doctor Strange was a good name for a magician." Lee did decide on the first name as "Stephen," according to Ditko, "It was Stan's little joke" alluding to a possible jibe at the artists' expense and adding, "I would never have used that name for Doctor Strange."

The artist would on occasion, however, work the names of people he knew into his stories. Stephen Strange, in the origin story, was originally a brilliant but selfishly arrogant surgeon, until an automobile accident robbed him of the dexterity of his hands and, seeking healing through unconventional means, travels to a Tibetan dwelling where The Ancient One offers a path to becoming "Master of the Mystic Arts" and protector of the material world. Recalling the character with pride, Ditko wrote to the author in a letter from September 2014, "Doctor Strange started out as a 5-page backup. Even some poor plots by Stan and others and incompetent inkers, didn't sink my basic ideas for Doctor Strange. One has to be willing to fail. Life offers no guarantees so why not explore the potentials? He never fit into Marvel's world of heroes but starting out as a 5-page filler was a great opportunity to try out all kinds of ideas. I don't know why Stan had others artists ink Doctor Strange. It could be he had inkers he wanted to keep and had to give them some work. Stan did not really understand the potentials of Doctor Strange. He was used to his usual 5-page ghost, haunted house type of stories."

That's how the series started, with uninspired plots and directionless drama, running contrary to the current superhero popularity wave — the future of the series seemed bleak in its early days. "Stan, at one point, wanted to drop Doctor Strange. I told him I should be writing the stories versus his usual type of stories," Ditko wrote to me in a letter from June 2016. The artist took over the plotting of the series along with both pencils and inks, and within a few issues, Doctor Strange emerged as a dramatically original series with a visual flair that seemed intent on transcending the medium. Lee remained as scripter on the series for a time, and his colourful language skills further enhanced the experience as he equipped the mystic sorcerer with memorable phrases when conjuring spells or opening dimensional portal doorways like "By the Crimson Bands of Cytorrak!" or "By the Eye of Agamotto" or "By the Hoary Hordes of Hoggath!"

Eventually, Lee passed the scripting duties on, exhausted of the best combinations. "Stan's phrasing writing dialogue could have taxed him; he tried to have another writer," Ditko wrote to me. He added in a letter from 2015 in summation of the characters' lasting appeal, "I'm surprised that *Doctor Strange*, who never fit into the Marvel Universe, continued to be published. It's like making a contradiction actually blend. But with the anti-hero comic book universe, anything goes."

A contingent of college student age Ditko fans saw *Doctor Strange* as an "anything goes" mind-expanding drug parable, with the hero remaining sitting at home in his Greenwich Village pad as his astral being engages in colossal battles with the forces of evil across alien landscapes in head-trips of kaleidoscopic proportions. The altered states of Doctor Strange were astonishingly rendered by Ditko, as the protagonist is thrown into bizarre, geometrically-shifting dimensional worlds, fighting heroically to save the material world from invisible and diabolical threats beyond our imaginations. For some of Marvel's student readers, increasing in number each month, reading *Doctor Strange* with a recreational drug of choice to the soundtrack of The Beatles' "Revolver," for example, was certainly a mutably compatible experience. Without intention, Ditko's surreal comic book strip connected to the counter-culture of the time to sit along comfortably with a new generation seeking new experiences.

In Tom Wolfe's novel *The Electric Kool-Aid Acid Test*, first published in 1968 and documenting the rise of the hippie movement in America, characters in the book look at Doctor Strange comics to gaze at Ditko's renderings of worlds beyond as a prelude to dropping acid. At the opposite end of

Above: Ditko original pencil artwork, unfortunately inked by George Roussos, who rendered the personality from the pencils, from ***Strange Tales*** #125, October, 1964 ©1964 Marvel Characters.

the spectrum and fundamentally opposed to such "irrational lifestyles," Ditko nonetheless continued to produce masterful work that found appeal with the perceptions and mindset of a much younger generation. When once asked by Marvel editor Ralph Macchio where he found the inspiration to create such peculiarly original vistas of dimensional worlds, Ditko replied simply, "Thought. I put a lot of thought into what another world looks like."

In one of the greatest oversights of this period of Marvel comics, none of the *Strange Tales* issues featuring Ditko's Doctor Strange strips were ever graced with an original cover of the character drawn by its creator. As he wrote to me in 2015, "I was never asked to do a Doctor Strange cover and Doctor Strange was not played up on the covers. It's a mystery to me as to why." Whether this was Lee's edict or Goodman's, who was known to generally dislike magicians and still regularly pulled rank over seemingly minor details on covers, often demanding the artist, through Lee, to redraw it from scratch, is unknown. Ditko, who says he never actually ever met Marvel's publisher, wrote to me in 2016, "How much the publisher — Goodman — had to say about covers, etc? He didn't like rats on the cover, for example. He certainly was aware of competition — DC and other comic companies. All publishers fought for space on news-stands, stores, outlets, with low profits on 10-25 cent magazines."

Generally, alterations to covers would be small enough to be performed by any artist who happened to be around the offices at the time — a task that often fell to staffer Marie Severin or later, John Romita. But a complete redraw would not only put added deadline pressure to the artist with regard to their other assignments, but also mean no payment for the rejected one. This would apply also to completed or partially completed interior panel pages. "You'd be shocked at the number of stories, actually editor-accepted, written, drawn — and NEVER published for one reason or another," Ditko wrote to me in February 2015, adding, "It's hard to understand or explain Stan's motives with his likes, dislikes and also his obsession with butt-shots! In one *Spider-Man* cover, I had Spider-Man leaping toward the Molten Man. Spider-Man was changed to leaping across the Molten Man and off the cover. What pleases an editor? They all have their likes and dislikes."

As the popularity of Fantastic Four, Spider-Man, Thor, Hulk, Ant-man (soon to metamorphize into Giant-Man) and ancillary cast increased, Lee began to have more regular assignments to hand out from his small office to his growing list of freelancers, including Don Heck and Dick Ayers, rearranging them on titles according to schedules and compatibility. Superman writer/creator Jerry Siegel briefly joined their ranks for a time, initially as a proofreader before Lee tried him out scripting Human Torch solo stories in *Strange Tales*. Siegel only scripted two Lee-plotted stories (one under the pseudonym Joe Carter) before leaving the company, with the editor considering his style not well-suited with what he had termed to be "the mighty Marvel style" of writing, in effect emulating Lee's own successful combination of melodrama, action and humour.

For artists on the top-tier books, it would be unthinkable to take Ditko off *Spider-Man*, or Kirby off *Fantastic Four* and *Thor*, but material required for Goodman's eight monthly titles, still including westerns and romance titles, provided additional work for all. One difference was that accepted work now had to fit the criteria of a rapidly-developing new house style, one that was exclusively derived visually from the dynamic, action-packed pencils of Jack Kirby and the powerful immediacy of his style that was on display in every Marvel comic he produced, together with the seemingly endless, yet all equally inspired, character creations the genius artist populated them with and the grand, Homerian-scale plots he wrote for them to play in. More than any other individual, it was Jack Kirby who built the Marvel Universe during an incredible period of unprecedented creativity in the industry, lasting throughout the 1960s, that not only provided a distinct, identifiable brand style and visual identity for Goodman's comic book division of the time but also a veritable treasure trove of valuable intellectual properties for future owners, merchandisers and film producers.

Very soon, Lee would be instructing all of his freelance artists to "draw like Kirby," using his artwork in style guides as examples of the artists' particular techniques of heightening the sense of drama in every panel by using posture, stance and foreshortening as methods to achieve this. Operating within his own, idiosyncratic but equally unique world, Ditko was exempt from such lessons, but with the two highly-gifted and individualistic artist/creators under his auspices, Stan Lee, directing the flow, no doubt felt a rising sense of triumph at the sudden success of their endeavors. "Marvel quickly became very popular, very fast during this period and I witnessed that Stan coped very well with the workload the popularity of the new titles created. If things were hectic in the office, it was a very pleasant kind of hectic," wrote Larry Lieber to me in February 2013.

In 1963, Lee gave his brother the assignment of scripting the first appearance of Iron Man in *Tales of Suspense* #39 (March 1963) — "When I scripted that book, I created the name Tony Stark" Lieber also wrote to me — from a plot credited to Lee and on art pages pencilled by Don Heck from Kirby's original designs and page layouts. With Ditko already well-settled into both *Spider-Man* and *Doctor Strange* but eager for more work, Lee assigned him to the pencilling of *Iron Man*, then appearing in an anthology title, not yet popular enough to warrant publication in a solo book. Today a flag-ship character for the company and a high number ticket-selling cinema attraction, due in no small part to the qualities brought to the role by New York-born actor Robert

Opposite page: Ditko recalls his early Marvel hero work in this letter from 2013.

2

As a kind of elitist news magazine, the growth of superhero movies, etc. called for some kind of time, coverage, judgment.

Stan claims he rejected Kirby doing S-M because Kirby made S-M "too heroic."

Yet, my original first S-M cover, a subjective viewpoint showed everyone up there in space with S-M and a kind of inexperienced S-M action.

Stan rejected it for a more heroic S-M action an objective viewpoint, the viewer not up there with S-M.

Stan may have had too many characters, titles to handle, write for so he needed some formula approach for everything.

It's seen with Dr. Strange's early Stan plots, Stories—about Ghosts, haunted houses, etc. and losing a consistent look having someone else ink Dr. Strange.

The ideas could be mine but I had no real right to them when published.

And it didnt matter. I was getting the experienc freelancers dont usually get.

I had a lot more freedom with Charlton press. It's too bad comic book fans didnt care to support them more. They have a weak excuse—poor coloring.

And comic companies not wanting to use me because of my Charlton Question and Witzends Mr. A. gave me more opportunities to get into self-publishing with Robin Snyder.

Downey, Jr., *Iron Man* remained a slow-burner throughout the 1960s, as Stan Lee said to me in 2011, "Now Iron Man, to me, is the most amazing character, but he had been the least popular character back then. When I say least popular, his book never sold quite as much as the other superhero books, although they all sold well. But *Iron Man* always got the most fan mail from our female readers!"

It's unclear whether it was under instruction from Lee or by his own edict, but Ditko redesigned the Iron Man armor costume — taking the original, striking but lumbering, robot-like design by Kirby and transforming into the sleek, red-and-gold, body-hugging metallic suit more familiar today. Ditko's memories on this to me in a letter from July 2016 were few, with respect for Kirby's original ("Kirby's Iron Man armor worked as a different, unique costume. Most superhero costumes can be changed in some ways. Different artists had different versions of Batman's headpiece and cape, etc.") and condemnation, without naming names, of how his original pencilled art was handled by the inker George Roussos — "The inker did a terrible job with very crude inking on my recreated Iron Man suit." The streamlined, new-look Iron Man debuted in *Tales of Suspense* #48 (December 1963), and although Ditko would only draw the series for three issues, the artist had left an indelible mark on the character's visual iconography.

Ditko was next offered by Lee a choice of three characters whose strips he could draw and freely re-imagine where required, The Hulk, Sub-Mariner and the jungle-based Tarzan re-tread Ka-Zar. Ditko decided on The Hulk, a character he had previously drawn for the sixth and final issue of its original, short-lived, sales-poor series, attracted also by the opportunity to draw the New Mexico environments the brutish emerald giant then inhabited. Ditko designed super villain The Leader and introduced the rage-induced cause of transformation to the series' lexicon (previously Bruce Banner's "Hulk-outs" were triggered by the setting of the sun) during his eight-issue run beginning in *Tales to Astonish* #60 October 1964.

In his last published interview for fanzine *Rapport* #2 in 1966, Ditko described his work-load at the time, "Just one 20-page story every four weeks means the writing and lettering have to be taken into account. I generally pencil five pages a day (I like four). The inking depends on how soon I get the story back after it's lettered. I can wait a week or as long as

three weeks. I have to pencil stories a lot differently than I naturally do when I do my own inking. For myself, I draw in line, or outline, sketchy in many areas, rarely putting in darks unless for a certain mood, and even then, it's just a slight indication. I like drawing with the brush — not just covering pencil lines with ink. Pencilling for others — all lines must be definite, dark areas positive. Like a complete ink job but in pencil. That's what it should be but I've never managed to do it."

With team books *The Avengers* and *The X-Men* debuting in their own series in the same month of September 1963 and both initially co-plotted and drawn by Kirby, Captain America revived once again and now reintroduced as a World War II "man out of time" finding a home within the ranks of *The Avengers* four issues later in March 1964 and the blind lawyer with heightened senses Daredevil following the month after (with art by returning Timely veteran Bill Everett), the Marvel stable of increasingly-popular characters was growing at an exponential rate, albeit still confined within the eight-titles-a-month-only distribution deal. In *Spider-Man*, the world of the teenage superhero was becoming progressively besieged with super villains Sandman, Lizard, Electro debuting in the comic book title's first year and adding to existing adversaries; a narrative template established of deep brooding and worrying about money, Aunt May's health and the spectre of Peter Parker's addictively-led other life as Spider-Man blocking his romantic intentions towards *Bugle* secretary Betty Brant. But along the way, the character is portrayed as slowly gaining in confidence also, standing up to class bully Flash Thompson, discovering that his spectacles were no longer needed to correct his eyesight and inventing the "spider-tracer" to aid his crime-fighting.

The second year of publication would further introduce Mysterio, Green Goblin and Kraven the Hunter with a selection from Spider-Man's rapidly swelling rogue's gallery grouping together as "The Sinister Six" (Dr. Octopus, Sandman, Vulture, Electro, Kraven and Mysterio) to threaten Spider-Man in his first King-Size 1964 annual that also had guest appearances from practically every other superhero in the Marvel Universe — presently defined as Manhattan Island where all but a handful of stories in the fictional publishing saga took place. Ditko provided six full-page splashes for the annual, depicting the finale of each individual battle, and the composition and rendering of these are masterful, displaying the artists' own confidence in his handling and execution of the character.

Along with the epic, lead story, Ditko also provided pages of other illustrated material for the annual indicating just how much attention the artist had given in sharply delineating characteristic aspects of the rising star superhero. In imaginatively constructed visuals, Ditko explained how Spider-Man's costume is designed to be worn unseen under street clothes (with shortened arms and legs and foldaway gloves and boots); described the two-way mirror lenses in the mask that allowed the hero to see out but disguised his eyes; noted variable ways Spider-Man could use his webbing as weapons, parachutes and even a sea-faring life raft; provided an explanation of how all his special powers worked and included a variety of pin-up illustrations of villains, supporting cast members and relevant locales to further illuminate the reader. With the hero depicted leaping and swinging in supple, kinetic, anatomically challenging poses, the drama of Ditko's Spider-Man played out against a gritty, shadow drenched backdrop among the steel and concrete skyscrapers of New York and its littered back-alleys and splintered wood waterfront locales, utilizing mundane features like water towers as part of the detailed landscape that Spider-Man would scamper over.

The artist would look out of his Eighth Avenue office window and sketch elements of the views he saw before him to enhance the reality of Spider-Man's surroundings. "All backgrounds have some kind of mood, emotional qualities, that one will react to. In art, certainly, settings, backgrounds, play an important role in attracting, supporting attention, interest etc. — some kind of reality, believability," wrote Ditko to me in April 2014 in response to my comment that, when reading *Spider-Man* as a child in the 1960s, his highly stylized but accurate version of New York was my introduction to the city, and I was fascinated by its proliferation of water towers. Adding, "A background may be the first thing the mind notices, 'sees,' and convinces." Ditko's Spider-Man and his urban environment convinced a lot of readers, engaged not only in his rooftop battles but also with the cast of the civilian characters and the conflicts of the everyday world practically intruding into the superhero antics and the slugfests the editor and reader demographic demanded. But having been in control of the plots of the comic book since its early days, the dedication and sheer hard work Ditko was putting into the writing of the series as well as the art, began to cultivate a gnawing and burgeoning feeling of unrewarded injustice for his efforts, and there was one currently within his professional circle who would have agreed.

Celebrated artist Wally Wood had joined Lee's list of freelancers early 1964, coming off a long and lauded run on *Mad* magazine to accept an assignment on the fledgling, audience-seeking title *Daredevil*, coming on for its fifth issue (December 1964) and becoming its main artist and story-plotter for the following seven issues. In *Daredevil* #7 (April 1965), a classic battle issue with Sub-Mariner, Wood took the wrestler-like, yellow-and-black costume designed by Bill Everett (with design input from Kirby) and refashioned its appearance to the familiar, all-in-one, completely red-hued design with the inter-locking "DD" chest symbol known

Opposite page left: Ditko original pencil artwork, Paul Reinman, inks, from ***Tales of Suspense*** #49, January, 1964 ©1964 Marvel Characters. Right: Ditko, pencils and inks, original artwork from ***The Incredible Hulk*** #6, March, 1963, 1963 Marvel Characters.

today. Wood also contributed Daredevil's adaptable billy club signature accessory, a weapon that transforms into a walking cane for Matt Murdock, the hero's sightless alter ego.

Despite Lee's delight in Wood's addition to Marvel's roster of creators, working from the editor's bare-boned plot suggestions resulting in uncredited and unpaid work and his aversion to Lee's personality, did not sit well with the artist, and despite a writing credit appearing in the final issue he would work on, Wood would leave what he saw as "Lee's regime" before it appeared in print. Prior to departing, Wood took Ditko into his confidence with his intentions, along with a suggestion that he do the same and join him to work on the artist's self-published line of comic books under his own Tower Comics imprint. With his own dissatisfaction mounting, Ditko listened carefully to his respected colleague but was not quite ready to cast aside a creation (or two) of such personal importance to his artistic integrity.

The narrative dichotomy of Parker's schizophrenic-like lifestyle reached its existential climax in the story titled "Spidey goes Mad!" (*Amazing Spider-Man* #24 May 1965) where a thinly disguised Mysterio and his "special-effects" find an easy route into persuading the over thinking superhero of his tenuous grasp on sanity — this was one four-colour hero who fought battles on many fronts with an introspective depth that could hardly be contained within the medium's thought bubble delivery system. Some tremendous influence was informing the complexity and struggles of the fictional hero, manifesting through the artwork and plot developments of the creative mind of Ditko, and that influence was named Ayn Rand.

Having first discovered her work in the early 1960s, ironically through Stan Lee who took particular note of the writer's definition of a hero, Ditko was now immersing himself and intellectually embracing the Objectivist philosophy postulated by Russian-born Rand, whose novel *Atlas Shrugged* had become a widely read best-seller in a 1963 paperback reissue edition. Advocating "reason, egoism and capitalism" and seeking to "reach the men of intellect, wherever such may be found," Rand, born Alisa Rosenbaum, grew up in St. Petersburg in the early years of the 20th century, witnessing the 1917 Bolshevik revolution and a communist takeover that stole her father's business, forcing her family into poverty as a result and created an era of combined collectivism and mysticism the writer came to loathe.

Looking to America as a successful role model of a free society, Rand studied philosophy, history and screen-writing in Soviet Russia before graduating in 1924, after which she promptly applied for a visa covering a "short visit" to the United States, never again to return to her land of birth. On February 19, 1926 she arrived in New York with her view from the ocean of Manhattan's skyline stirring her to shed what she later described as "tears of splendour." A dalliance with Hollywood informing her decision to pursue a fiction-writing career led Ayn Rand to her first major work and literary success when *The Fountainhead* was published by Bobbs-Merrill in 1943 after numerous previous rejections from other publishers. Steeped in romanticism and introducing the basic tenets of Rand's philosophy, *The Fountainhead*, written over a seven-year period, concerns the struggles of young architect Howard Roark defending his individualistic and modernist approach to building design against an innovation-scared establishment and its "second-handers," those who support conformity and the reflected glory of other people's triumphs. Filmed in 1949 starring Gary Cooper as Roark in a version that, despite providing the screenplay for, Rand "disliked from start to finish."

The Fountainhead received mixed reviews upon first publication but has now sold over 6 million copies worldwide and, at the time, made Ayn Rand a famous author and set the path clear for the writer to crystalize her opinions into the philosophy she would later term Objectivism. Rand's self-proclaimed "magnum opus" in this endeavour was her final novel *Atlas Shrugged*, first published by Random House in 1957, where the concept was personified in her fictional creation John Galt. In an America of the not-too-distant future, where businesses are highly restricted under governmental regulations, steel magnet Hank Rearden and railroad executive Dagny Taggart unite in their battles against the "looters" intent on stealing their profits and exploiting their productivity. Hearing the whispered phrase "Who is John Galt?" alluding to a mysterious individual persuading other "rational" business leaders to physically disappear from their companies in a collective "strike" of productive and creative labour withheld from the system, they eventually meet the saviour-like figure. All coming together under the leadership of Galt and intent on building a new capitalist society under the philosophy of individualism and reason he was preaching, the finale of the novel saw the gathered hopeful, confident of creating a lighter and more balanced world to carry the heavy burden that grew too much for Atlas to bear and which he finally shrugged off.

Ayn Rand had submitted her most concise (despite the novel running 1,168 pages) treatise on Objectivism and had raised a profitable banner she would carry for the rest of the life, although her final years would see her claiming welfare, an act her critics found inherently hypocritical, before her death from heart failure on March 6, 1982 in New York. Eschewing any religious, faith-based or supernaturalism beliefs with Rand writing the phrase "A is A" to describe the nature of reality and how minds should strive to correctly perceive it, Objectivism ran opposite to altruism in its elevation of individual self-interest, strident call for unfettered financial markets and the removal of any political or religious controls that may disrupt such pursuits. The essence of Objectivism was "the concept of man as a heroic being, with productive achievement as his noblest activity and reason as his only absolute." It supported civil rights, the right to choose and sexual freedom but seemed to contradict its own views with its rejection of welfare, religion and homosexuality. Rand elaborated further in a 1959 television interview, "I am primarily the creator of a new code of morality which has so far been believed impossible — namely, a morality not based on faith, not on emotion, not on arbitrary edicts, mystical or social, but on reason." Adding that "man's highest moral purpose is the achievement of his own happiness, and that he must not force other people, nor accept their right to force him, that each man must live as an end in himself and follow his own rational self-interest."

Short-handed to be a philosophy of "ruthless selfishness" by many modern commentators, it appeared with avaricious meaning in an episode of the dramatic series *Mad Men* when ad agency senior partner Bertram Cooper gave protégé Don Draper a fat bonus along with the advice to "Take $1.99 out of that $2,500 and buy yourself a copy of *Atlas Shrugged*," or with dismissive contempt as in an episode of *The Simpsons* when Marge seemed delighted to see a copy of *The Fountainhead* before being warned by daughter Lisa, "But Mom, isn't that book the bible of right-wing losers?" By 1962, the Objectivist movement had gained traction, with information centres opening up in New York, a monthly newsletter interested parties could subscribe to and regular talks and appearances from the Manhattan-based source of the material herself. Some reports suggest that Ditko regularly attended talks by Ayn Rand and met and spoke with her often, his fascination growing. Ace Comics publisher Ron Frantz wrote about his visit to Ditko's studio in 1987 in *Ditkomania* #90 (March 2013) where the artist "spoke with near-reverence about meeting Rand on several occasions and how he had often listened to her lectures at the Nathaniel Branden Institute."

Ditko rejected any confirmations in a letter to me from 2012, "Rand, etc. I can't prove anything about my past so whatever I say — or whatever others say or claim, all others will just believe what they want to believe." But he was happy to explain at length his own interpretation of Rand's thinking, "Rand offered a philosophy 'for living on earth' as she stated it. It's an individualistic philosophy not a collectivist one to impose on others like Communism, Nazism, Fascism, Socialism, Statism or some tribalism, with NO individual and property rights where all (except leaders) must sacrifice themselves to the cannibalistic feeding pot. Since man started writing, keeping records and publishing there has never been any real agreement on anything. The only agreement may be that there will always be disagreement. So, some authority, power, force regularly rules for a time until overthrown or replaced. As one gets older, one witnesses more but rarely the better." He continued, "Rand had this circular theory of knowledge. One is never through, knows everything about any subject. One deals with the subject, issue etc and goes on with other things. Living then at one point one circles back to re-examine the issue or topic with all the new understanding, knowledge for a better understanding and again at some point moves on — continuous circles for deeper and wider understanding. It cuts down on frustrations that one doesn't automatically have the answers, knowledge needed or wanted. Like with most things, one must earn them. 4BC Aristotle defined 'man is a rational animal.' History continues to show few believe in rationality so anything goes in the all grey world of NO judgments. The continuing global unrest just continues to prove that who has the power will determine what is right or wrong and facts are either emotional or by some authority."

The super villain adversaries to Rand's "rational" heroes were defined by the writer as "looters" and "moochers" with their self-entitlement demands for unearned benefits from the creativity, initiative, hard-work and successes of the "producers," a scenario that Ditko could presently identify with and see mirrored in events taking place around his current *Spider-Man* assignment and the work he was producing for it that remained unacknowledged. Putting the ideology of Objectivism into practice and armed with the principle of no compromise in both his personal and creative life, Ditko now approached Lee and demanded a printed credit for the plotting and writing work he was producing every month for the comic book or, like Rand's idealized protagonists, would withhold his creative labour in that arena. The credit the artist considered rightly due he would eventually receive but would also discover that there was a price to pay for stealing some luster from the king's crown with its attendant fall from favour.

In *Amazing Spider-Man* #25 (June 1965) Ditko received a "Plotted By" credit for the first time in the series, running alongside his usual credit as artist and remaining in place for the rest of his tenure on the book, but as he confirmed to me in a letter from July 2016, "I took over plotting, writing stories long before any writing credit. It took some pressure off Stan and the titles weren't ever late in publishing." Adding, "Since I was a freelancer, Stan Lee could have taken me off *Spider-Man* anytime he wanted — he did it once for a *Spider-Man* story pencilled by Jack Kirby, I inked it." (This appeared in *Strange Tales Annual* #2 1963.) Kirby would certainly have taken note of the development as this was the first time a Marvel artist had ever received any printed credit for story writing under Lee's method and the editor would begin by cheerily writing the credits as "Sturdy Steve Ditko dreamed up the plot of this tantalizing tale and it's full of unexpected surprises" but resort to referring to Ditko as "Scowlin' Steve" just two issues later. Lee's indignation in reluctantly granting the credit would seem to run deep, and the incident would herald a season of his ignoring and avoiding the artist with increasingly louder silence, refusing phone calls and never stepping out of, or inviting the freelancer into, his office when Ditko visited the Marvel offices. The original conflicts that helped create the rift between them were mostly involving Lee's scripting over Ditko's pencils that were, to the artist,

changing the style and tone of his original plots. Ditko's stance was, as he wrote to me in July 2015, that "Stan's writing style was completely wrong for Spider-Man. He treated teenage Peter Parker as a seasoned veteran with his nonsensical comic dialogue exchanges between a hero and villain. Creative ideas are no good if not used in a proper way."

Lee would make some acerbic comments on the duo's relationship in a pivotal interview published in the *New York Herald*, under the title "Super-Heroes with Super-Problems" on January 9, 1966 while also revealing an obvious disgruntlement over his demoted writing status on the title, "I don't plot *Spider-Man* any more. Steve Ditko, the artist, has been doing the stories. I guess I'll leave him alone until sales start to slip. Since Spidey got so popular, Ditko thinks he's the genius of the world. We were arguing so much over plot lines I told him to start making up his own stories. He won't let anyone else ink his drawings either. He just drops off the finished pages with notes in the margins and I fill in the dialogue."

Ditko would quit Marvel before the article saw print, and Lee's blithe comments would have played no part in his decision to leave but serve only to further validate it. For Jack Kirby, however, the manner in which the article, written by journalist Nat Freeland, not only substantially reduced his role in the creation of the majority of Marvel's superheroes but also painted an image of subservient creative dependence on Lee, along with the editors' down-playing of it, incensed the artist greatly. It proved to have a lingering impact on Kirby's feeling of satisfaction and security at a company where, although being named "King" by Lee in one of his name games, felt that not all was in accord within his royal court and the dividends of credit and reward the kingdoms he had constructed by imagination and pencil should have afforded him were not forthcoming.

As Marvel Comics' success and sales increased, editors at DC Comics held meetings to discuss their "garish, vulgar, badly-drawn" comic book covers and what made them so attractive to the readers who were buying them in ever-larger numbers, somehow connecting effectively to the new generational audience they were targeting. For titles cover-dated September 1965, the cover corner-box designed by Ditko suddenly changed and in place of the usual "Marvel Comics Group" line was the phrase "Marvel Pop-Art Productions," coined by Lee and explained to readers on an editorial page within, "So many of you frantic fans have objected to calling our Marvel mags 'comics' that we felt we just had to come up with a better name! And so, from now on, you are no longer reading comic books when you read our little masterpieces, instead you're reading a 'Pop-Art Book'!"

The faintly pretentious affectation would stand for the next three issues only before being discreetly and silently dropped, but Lee had touched on something that other creators would return to in later years — the selection of a new and less self-disparaging name for an entertainment medium now attracting an older and more sophisticated audience than in its previous history with a growing appreciation of the merits of a mostly disregarded artform. In the 1970s, Will Eisner would suggest the name "sequential art" as a more descriptive term but had more success with the phrase graphic novel when the writer/artist was credited with the invention of the format with his *A Contract with God* in 1978.

David Lloyd, the artist who created the celebrated *V for Vendetta* with influential writer Alan Moore in the 1980s and who cites Ditko as one of his greatest inspirations, said to me in 2013, "I think we should all try and ditch the term 'comics' and start using sequential art as much as possible — let's just slide it into the language. Of course, the phrase graphic novel, which really came about by accident, has been tremendously useful in helping to change people's perceptions and gaining recognition from the literary establishment. It's important that every medium should progress; otherwise they stay in the backwater of where they can be. We can produce anything,

SPIDERMAN 33-7
AND THEN--AS THE AGONIZING ACHE IN HIS LIMBS SEEMS UNENDURABLE--AS HIS SUPERBLY MUSCLED BODY SUFFERS THE TORMENT OF A VIRTUALLY INDESCRIBABLE ORDEAL--FROM OUT OF THE PAIN--FROM OUT OF THE AGONY--COMES TRIUMPH!
I DID IT! I'M FREE!
5

we can tell stories about anything you can imagine, but the creators are often hampered by the perception of the medium."

With Ditko now receiving full credit for the plots he was writing in the title, the second *Spider-Man* annual in 1965 featured a meeting between the arachnid hero and the artists' other character creation Doctor Strange, although Lee's tone for the credit he wrote in the issue had a condescending air and referred to the artist as "Stevey" and "Steverino," aware it would irritate the freelancer. Lee wrote, "This could be called our 'Be nice to Stevey Ditko' issue! We wanted to feature a really off-beat yarn for Spidey's annual and Steverino dreamed this one up!" With circumstance coagulating together in proper alignment, what Ditko would next dream up for the comic book series emerged as his three-issue masterpiece storyline that would bring of all of his intentions for the book successfully together and produce a story, and one particular scene, that would forever define the very character and nature of Spider-Man for all future iterations.

From *Amazing Spider-Man* #31 (where his plotting credit disappears for one issue) through to its iconic climax in issue 33, Ditko's "Master Planner" saga saw Peter Parker enroll into college, meeting Harry Osborn and Gwen Stacy for the first time; fight a variety of airborne and ground-level battles with packs of henchmen; suffer the worry of Aunt May's life-threatening illness and the desperate anguish in trying to locate the only serum that could save her, while thwarting those that also seemed to covet it. In the closing issue of the story-arc, titled "The Final Chapter!" with Spider-Man trapped under a mountain of collapsed machinery in a submerged enemy lair, with the serum in view but out of reach and the steadily increasing dripping of the outside ocean threatening to crash in at any moment, Ditko unfolds the sequence — the crushing odds, the physical and mental exertion — paced over five pages, with the number of panels decreasing but the size increasing on each subsequent page, building to a spectacular, single-page image of the hero caught in glorious, if transitory, triumph. Battered and exhausted, Spider-Man then snares the serum just before a flood flings him into a deliriously-fought battle with the remaining henchmen before facing his arch nemesis Doctor Octopus, the real schemer behind all it all.

Ultimately, having run this daunting gauntlet, Peter Parker is successful in staying alive himself and delivering the serum that saves his aunts fragile life while commended on his efforts only by the doctor, unaware of the true scope of them, who draws the blinds on his departing silhouette with the observation "Too bad there weren't more young men like him" to close the story. "There are continuing examples in history of men never quitting, never giving up," Ditko wrote to me in 2013, adding, "But the choice is always up to the individual."

In his scripting of the sequence, (which he would one day declare to be his own idea before a written rebuttal by Ditko corrected his errant memory) Lee built up the melodrama through inner monologue in repetitive but crowd-pleasing style, depicting the rising desperation of the predicament, although his captions lagged over its prolonged duration, lacking any real sense of literary drama ("Spider-Man fumes in helpless rage as the drops of water fall ever faster...ever larger...faster...larger...faster... larger!") and the final exclamation of "I did it! I'm free!" held none of the gravitas or memorable qualities of some of his previously scripted lines for the series. While Ditko had been quarreling with Lee over alterations to his stories and lack of writing credit, there were often mind games played out in the production of issues between the two collaborators, an example of one being when Lee provided script dialogue for Spider-Man in one lightly pencilled panel but was returned inked to the editor as the villain for that issue, the aptly name Looter. Perceived by Lee as a deliberate sabotage of the story, he made his angry reaction to the panel known around the office, along with his intention of "having it out" with Ditko, according to writer Steve Skeates, who was employed at Marvel at the time as an editorial assistant.

With Ditko's direction for the hero embodying aspects of the artists own convictions, such as Parker scoffing dismissively at student protesters on his campus and suddenly demanding fair recompense for the photographs he provided Jameson's Bugle, Lee also had issues with elements of the characterization and motivation that Ditko was providing for the character. For his part, Ditko intensely disliked Lee's dialogue style for the series, but in a correspondence to me from July 2016, his appraisal of the scriptwriting on *Spider-Man* softened a little, and he conceded, with reservations, that Lee's "corny captions" contributed to the rise of the titles popularity, "Stan's dialogue style of hero/villain wise-cracking, undercut the conflict of hero, villain — but it worked with readers who just wanted to be entertained. I believe Stan loved writing those corny captions. It added to reading appeal but undercut a more serious growth of a teenager in a heroic role."

Ditko added in 2014, "Stan may have had too many characters, titles to handle, write for, so he needed some formula approach for everything." Perhaps more finely honed than his character creation or plot hatching skills, Lee's formula yielded lively and verbose dialogue that became a key ingredient in the growing popularity of Marvel comics of the 1960s, hitting a zeitgeist of the time and contributing to an overall brand style. Under his editorship, the Marvel Universe of super-powered, problem-beset comic book characters was woven together as a cohesive whole, with frequent guest appearances by new heroes in well-established books. This not only aided the illusion of unity but also served as a canny promotional tool to sell new, up-and-coming comic book titles and cultivate a feeling that major developments could be missed if the reader didn't keep up with most or all of the books.

The exact same strategy was later employed in the 21st Century to create the Marvel Cinematic Universe in movie theaters worldwide with even greater effect and larger financial rewards. But while Lee had his editorial eye over the entire ever-expanding roster of characters and comic book titles, relying on Kirby for most of the creative heavy lifting, it was Ditko who had been planning the specific future of the web-slinger since inception. Ditko had won a major skirmish by becoming the first artist to wrest any writing credit from Lee with his "Plotted By" by-line but verbal instructions from the editor on new issues had become fainter each month and were routinely discarded by Ditko anyway, who confirmed this to me in a letter from May 2015, "Stan was willing to go along with my not using his usual monthly plots — like having Spider-Man battle Attuma or introduce a Spider-Girl, a purely monthly episode. He was, had to be, next issue orientated — Spider-Man fighting some villain, with no real continuity between monthly issues. Stan was also too concerned with fans, readers, to please their write-in complaints. And every fan has his particular complaint so even pleasing one means not pleasing others. (Example of) A fan complaint: I shouldn't show Spider-Man split-face, (with his) spider-senses, etc. If readers, viewers could see them so the people in the panel would also see them!" Adding, "The usual Marvel hero story was with some new villain every issue but very little personal life. Stan wanted to see the hero or villain on every page. It's why I first used the split-face device on Peter Parker which Stan thought would work," first seen as far back as *Amazing Spider-Man* #10 in March 1964.

Through creative differences, tensions caused by an overdue writing credit and an increasingly apparent personality clash, relations between Ditko and Lee had by this time deteriorated to a point where they no longer communicated at all and the first Lee would know of what was happening in the Spider-Man title was when he looked at the fully rendered pencilled art pages brought into the office by Ditko through Production Manager Sol Brodsky. In the last week of November 1965 — the same week that tens of thousands American citizens picketed the White House in protest of the Vietnam war and prevailing Pentagon advice to President Lyndon B. Johnson that US troops in the conflict needed to increase from 120,000 to 400,000 if operations were to succeed — Ditko delivered the art pages for his final issues of *Amazing Spider-Man* #38 and *Strange Tales* #146 (both cover dated July 1966 but appearing on stands in April of that year). When Lee first examined the pencilled *Spider-Man* pages he knew to be the last he would receive from Ditko, his attention must have been caught especially by the last four panels showing Ditko's final

renditions of Spider-Man in costume. After dispatching a crowd of rioters, Spider-Man turns to a store window display dummy bearing more than a passing resemblance to the editor and, for no discernible plot advancement reason, rages at the mannequin before delivering a solid punch to its strangely-smiling face.

The last image Ditko ever drew of Spider-Man for the comic book, showed the hero walking away, head down, with the permanently fixed smile of the familiar-looking dummy shown fallen in the foreground. "The shadow of Spider-Man isn't standing between you," Lee would script for that very last panel, alluding to a doomed relationship in the saga between Parker and love interest Betty Brant, but for Steve Ditko and Stan Lee it would remain exactly that for the rest of their lives, and the two collaborators would never work together again.

Back in 1964, Marvel's popularity, helped by Lee's clever marketing spiels, had grown enough to warrant the formation of its own fan club "The Merry Marvel Marching Society" (abbreviated to M.M.M.S) with early subscribers receiving a flexi-disc recording of the Bullpen's

Pages 72/73: Two sequential pages of Ditko artwork from ***Amazing Spider-Man*** #33, February, 1965. The first from the comic book, the second from the original pencil and ink art. This story and these images are now famous among comic artists and fans for their adept storytelling and are often referred to as "Spider-Man Shrugged," as the character prevails against literally crushing, overwhelming odds, ©1965 Marvel Characters. Above: Ditko's "split-face" technique seen here in a panel from **The Amazing Spider-Man** #17, October, 1964, a device the artist used to ensure a balance of the book's narrative between Peter Parker's personal life and its cast of characters and the superhero action Lee demanded, ©1964 Marvel Characters.

now familiar artists titled "The Voices of Marvel" as part of their $1 membership package. Quickly, the cramped Marvel offices were awash with $1 bills spilling out of hundreds of application envelopes daily as Lee's resourceful secretary, Flo Steinberg, kept apace of the deluge. The fan-club, running from 1965 to 1969, eventually became an effective platform for Goodman to market and sell associated merchandise featuring Marvel's brand of heroes. These included a six-foot "life-size" Spider-Man poster; a Spider-Man inflatable pillow and t-shirt designs featuring the web-spinner and Doctor Strange, all utilizing previously published Steve Ditko drawings and offering no royalty payments for their use. The flexi-disc record introduces all members of the Marvel Bullpen in its scratchy, audio recording with many staffers including Lee and Kirby taking part. Prophetically, Ditko is absent, having refused to participate on the day of production and referenced only in the following exchange of dialogue between Stan Lee and Sol Brodsky,

> Stan Lee, "Hey, what's all that commotion out there, Sol?"
>
> Sol Brodsky, "Why, it's shy Steve Ditko. He's heard you're making a record, and he's got mike-fright. Whoops! There he goes!"
>
> Stan Lee, "Out the window again? You know, I'm beginning to think he *is* Spider-Man!"
>
> Sol Brodsky, "You mean he isn't?"

As far as Lee's Marvel was concerned, Ditko was now most certainly "out the window," having made the jump of his own volition, in imminent danger perhaps of being pushed, and abandoning an environment deemed hostile and detrimental to his creative, personal and professional well-being. He wrote in an essay titled "Why I Quit *Spider-Man*" published in the ninth and final issue of his *Four-Page Series* in 2015, "So why did I actually decide to quit? One day I got a call from Sol. The next *Spider-Man* annual is coming up. Okay. Later, thinking about what I could do for the annual, I asked myself, 'Why should I do it?' Why should I continue to do all these monthly issues, original story ideas, material, for a man who is too scared, too angry over something, to even see, talk to me? At some point, I decided to quit Marvel, Spider-Man, Doctor Strange. My next visit to Marvel, I told Sol I was quitting Marvel and Sol told Stan. The only person who had the right to know why I was quitting refused to come out of his office or to call me in. Stan refused to know why."

Roy Thomas, a young writer from Missouri well-versed in comic book history, had joined the Marvel offices to work on staff only four months before Ditko's departure, and he recalled to me in 2012, "Steve Ditko would come in to the offices I shared with Sol Brodsky and Flo Steinberg and drop off or pick up work, but I didn't handle those pages; Sol did. I had few dealings with him, even though I dialogued two of his *Doctor Strange* pages. It was very exciting to do this even though *Doctor Strange* wasn't a particular favourite of mine, as I never cared a lot for magic strips. Stan had no idea why Ditko eventually left Marvel — and *Spider-Man* — so abruptly, but I was there on the day he quit — though I knew about it after the fact. At the time, Sol had a memo on his desk for a $5 a page rise for Steve, which was fairly substantial for 1965. I don't think he ever even got around to mentioning it to Steve, not that it would've made any difference."

A first-generation reader of, and subsequent contributor to, what would later be dubbed The Silver Age of Comics, Thomas was involved in comic book fandom from its early days, editing the fanzine *Alter Ego* in 1964, after succeeding its founder Jerry Bails. His work there came to the attention of professional creators, with some even contributing artwork to his publication. Thomas recalled to me, "The first professional artwork to appear in *Alter-Ego* (then hyphenated) was a Jack Kirby Thing pencil drawing. It depicted Thing holding up a sign that read '*Alter-Ego* or Bust!' Jerry Bails inked it apparently, and rather well, too. Steve Ditko sent Jerry a drawing for *The Comic Reader*, which was used in one of his issues in 1963." Learning his craft through *Alter Ego* and numerous letters of comment to titles (many published, including letters in *Fantastic Four* #5, 15 and 22), Thomas moved to New York and first found employment under the iron fist editorial rule of Mort Weisinger at DC Comics, then still more widely known as National. Weisinger notably edited the Superman titles throughout the 1950s and 1960s with great success and can be credited with introducing many new elements into the character's canon, including Supergirl, Krypto the Superdog, The Legion of Superheroes, The Bottle City of Kandor and The Phantom Zone. Despite his achievements, he was notorious within the industry for his heavy-handed approach to management, often accused of dominating writers' stories by quelling all creativity but his own.

Weisinger once said in response, "People have always accused me of being an egomaniac as an editor because I always gave the writers my own plots. I did that for a reason. If I asked a writer to bring in his own plots, and he spent a weekend on four of them, and I didn't like any of the four, then he's wasted a whole weekend." It was under this tyrannical leadership that Thomas experienced his first real work in the comic book industry. He wrote to the author in 2012, "Weisinger contacted me because of *Alter Ego* and we exchanged maybe one or two letters before he asked me to be his assistant editor on a several-week trial basis. The experience, though, was sheer hell. He was cruel — intentionally so, I think. He was almost sadistically (did I say 'almost'?) cruel — to subordinates, be they artists, writers, or editorial assistants. Very few of them ever had a good word to say about him. Except for not denying him a certain talent at guiding Superman during his tenure— and for that neither do I. He was a real browbeater, though. I didn't write anything during those two weeks, though I had written one *Jimmy Olsen* story before I moved to New York but only the general plotline of it was ever eventually used."

Swiftly, Thomas acted to escape the rigid corporate structure and entrenched ways at Weisinger's DC, seeking an improved working environment at Stan Lee's Marvel Comics. Thomas recalls, "Wanting badly to get out of DC, I contacted Stan directly, offering to buy him a drink, and he suggested over the phone that I take his writer's test. I did, and he hired me based on that, I presume. The writer's test was to dialogue four Jack Kirby pages from *Fantastic Four Annual* #2. The word-balloons had been taken out on the pages and they were black-and-white proofs." Thomas continued, "My first official title was Staff Writer and I worked 40 hours a week writing scripts at a small metal table with a typewriter on it in a small office. But my concentration was continually broken by being asked to do this or that and Stan would often come to me to check out some fact or other because I knew a lot about Marvel continuity. Very quickly I became Editorial Assistant and that worked out much better. The Marvel offices were pretty hectic back then with phones ringing all the time and many artists dropping in and out constantly. The only people regularly there when I went to work were Stan, Sol Brodsky, Flo Steinberg, Marie Severin and Steve Skeates. I did meet publisher Martin Goodman, but I don't recall when. Besides Stan, I had an especially good relationship with both Sol and Flo and with Marie it was mostly good, too. I very much enjoyed working with John Romita, Sr., on the rare occasions we did and I wish there had been more of them. Also, a very good friend of mine at the time, in fact we lived together off and on for a few years, was Bill Everett — the creator of Sub-Mariner back in 1939. I liked Bill a lot and found him irascible but interesting."

Herb Trimpe also joined Marvel Comics on staff in October 1966, the same month he was discharged from service in the USAF, through his friend John Verpoorten, who would become Production Manager of Goodman's comic book division after Sol Brodsky left Marvel for a time to set up his own comic book publishing company, Skywald. Despite his only previous reference point to Marvel being a single *Thor* comic he had read while serving in Vietnam, the 27-year-old artist joined to assist in the small, cut-and-paste assembly production department. Trimpe said to me in 2011, "I actually began at Marvel inking the Westerns — titles like *Kid-Colt* and *Two-Gun Kid*, but when I got on staff, it was because of an opening in the production department. Marvel had just bought a gigantic photo-copy machine which housed a camera, an adjustable table to shoot on, and the regular chemical baths you'd have for developing black-and-white photography.

"It was a full-time position with a reasonable $135 a week salary, copying art pages for the production department, but it also meant I could pick up freelance work as an artist on the side. Working for Marvel back then, fun is the main word that comes to mind. There was no great sense of self-importance by anyone or that comics themselves had any particular significance. It was just a pleasant working environment with nice people. Some of us went to lunch once in a while, and we had a team in the publishers' softball league. But there was basically none of the social aspect we see today, for instance at conventions when all the stars collect and spend long hours into the night getting hammered. This type of thing is hard to explain to people who are deeply into comics now. My first impression of people like Jack Kirby, Stan Lee, Steve Ditko and others were basically, 'Hi, how are you. Nice to meet you.' There was no 'buzz' no 'oh, joy!' Jack Kirby, of course, was a working comic book machine. He came into the office on rare occasions, and the number of times he did while I was there, I could probably count on one hand. Kirby had a special significance because his style was so strong and exciting, and he was fast. Speed doesn't mean much these days. But he was born to do what he did, no doubt about it. I had the pleasure of inking some of his pencilled pages, and Kirby could be inked while sleeping, drunk, taking a shower and many other things. It was all there, and he drew in a language that was immediate. It was easy, you had no choice. I didn't appreciate Stan, other than being a fun boss, until later. Stan was around a lot but once he moved to the west coast, the visits to the bullpen got less frequent. I'm not sure if I ever met Ditko, but I thought his *Spider-Man* had a special funky flair to it, and Peter Parker was the nerd he was supposed to be."

The entirety of Steve Ditko's work on *Spider-Man*, produced between 1962 and 1965, comprised the origin story, 38 issues of *Amazing Spider-Man* and two annuals — a total of 940 *Spider-Man* art pages, breaking down into 863 main story pages; 12 related strip pages; 28 pin-up pages and 37 covers. The gradual development and slow maturing of the character of Peter Parker was part of a carefully designed narrative thread that Ditko had given a great deal of thought to from the comic book's origin and was determined to enact, and this noting of the passing of time as a narrative device was one of many innovations the artist introduced that made the seminal comic strip a true original in the American genre of comic books.

While he considered that his editor Lee pandered too much to reader complaints, the amount of favourable fan mail and rising sales figures the book was attracting also convinced Ditko that his instinct for the character was correct and authentic. Ditko gave Spider-Man the most inventive collection of super villains in comic book history, surpassing even Batman's parade of adversaries. During his four-year-only run, Ditko created — or co-created but certainly solely designed — (in order of appearance) The Chameleon; The Vulture; The Terrible Tinkerer; Doctor Octopus; The Sandman; The Lizard; The Living Brain; Electro; The Enforcers; Mysterio; Kraven the Hunter; The Green Goblin; The Spider-Slayer; The Crime Master; The

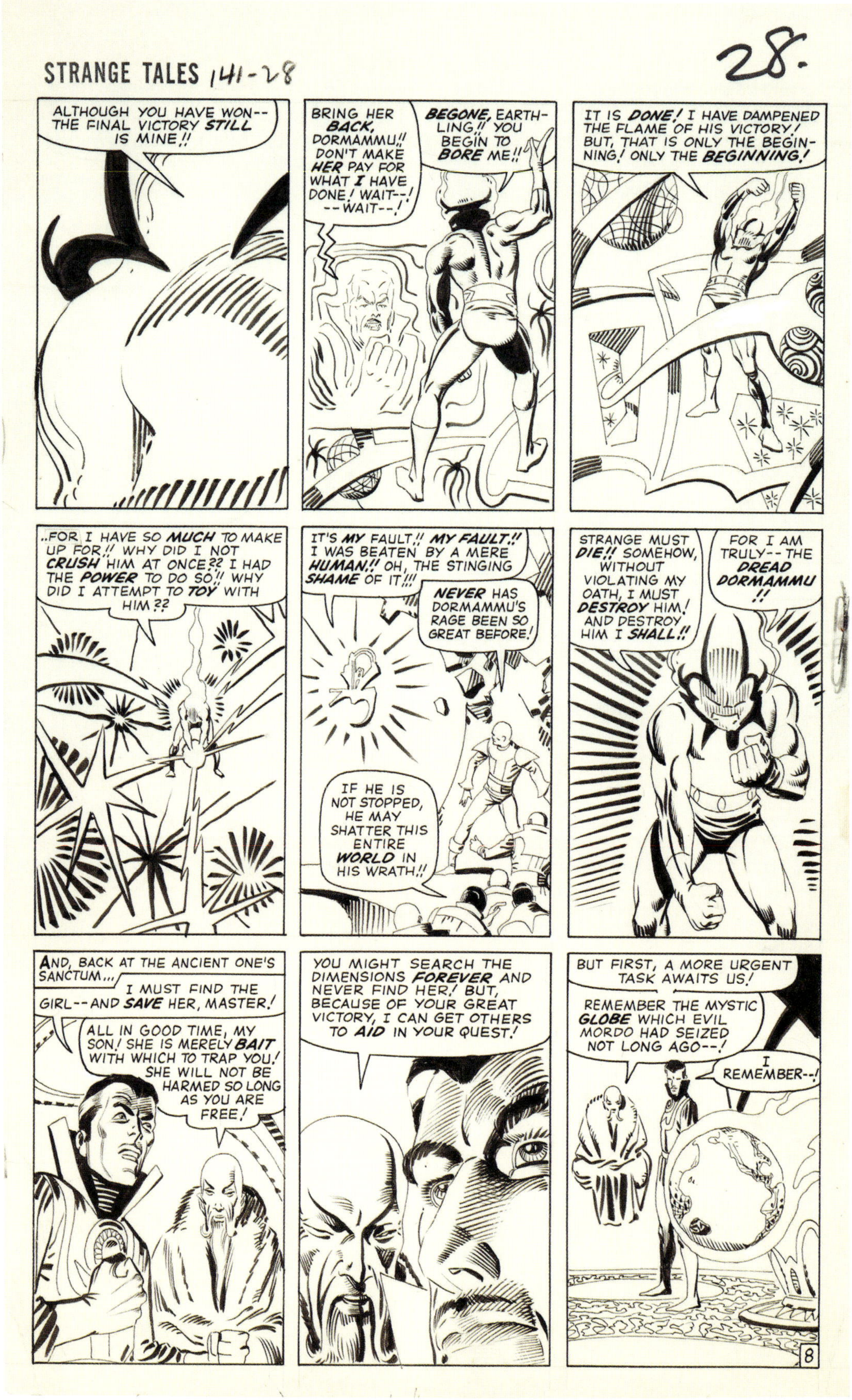
STRANGE TALES 141-28
28.
ALTHOUGH YOU HAVE WON-- THE FINAL VICTORY STILL IS MINE!!
BRING HER BACK, DORMAMMU!! DON'T MAKE HER PAY FOR WHAT I HAVE DONE! WAIT--! --WAIT--!
BEGONE, EARTHLING!! YOU BEGIN TO BORE ME!!
IT IS DONE! I HAVE DAMPENED THE FLAME OF HIS VICTORY! BUT, THAT IS ONLY THE BEGINNING! ONLY THE BEGINNING!
..FOR I HAVE SO MUCH TO MAKE UP FOR!! WHY DID I NOT CRUSH HIM AT ONCE?? I HAD THE POWER TO DO SO!! WHY DID I ATTEMPT TO TOY WITH HIM??
IT'S MY FAULT!! MY FAULT!! I WAS BEATEN BY A MERE HUMAN!! OH, THE STINGING SHAME OF IT!!!
NEVER HAS DORMAMMU'S RAGE BEEN SO GREAT BEFORE!
IF HE IS NOT STOPPED, HE MAY SHATTER THIS ENTIRE WORLD IN HIS WRATH!!
STRANGE MUST DIE!! SOMEHOW, WITHOUT VIOLATING MY OATH, I MUST DESTROY HIM! AND DESTROY HIM I SHALL!!
FOR I AM TRULY-- THE DREAD DORMAMMU!!
AND, BACK AT THE ANCIENT ONE'S SANCTUM...
I MUST FIND THE GIRL--AND SAVE HER, MASTER!
ALL IN GOOD TIME, MY SON! SHE IS MERELY BAIT WITH WHICH TO TRAP YOU! SHE WILL NOT BE HARMED SO LONG AS YOU ARE FREE!
YOU MIGHT SEARCH THE DIMENSIONS FOREVER AND NEVER FIND HER! BUT, BECAUSE OF YOUR GREAT VICTORY, I CAN GET OTHERS TO AID IN YOUR QUEST!
BUT FIRST, A MORE URGENT TASK AWAITS US!
REMEMBER THE MYSTIC GLOBE WHICH EVIL MORDO HAD SEIZED NOT LONG AGO--!
I REMEMBER--!
8

Scorpion; The Molten Man and The Looter. In all of the seven *Spider-Man* movies made and released at the time of writing this book, only one (minor) super villain, The Shocker, and one major character, Venom, used in the films, were not creations of Steve Ditko.

From the supporting cast members, Ditko notably delivered Aunt May and Uncle Ben; J. Jonah Jameson; Flash Thompson; Betty Brant; Harry and Norman Osborn; Professor Warren; Gwen Stacy and the teased but never revealed during his tenure Mary Jane Watson. Despite Lee's assertion that a teenager with personal problems was an element of the idea he originally took to Martin Goodman, in the development of the concept, it was Ditko who pushed for an even balance between super heroics and the real-life dramas of Peter Parker's complicated, working-class life in the yarn of the plots for the monthly series. When introducing The Green Goblin in *Amazing Spider-Man* #14 (July 1964), the artist refused to base the character's origins on Lee's proposed mythologically-based idea, saying that it would undermine the foundation of Spider-Man's real-world narrative to do so.

Theories suggesting that Ditko left Marvel over an issue with Lee concerning the civilian identity of the Green Goblin were groundless. *In The Comics!*, March 2009 in an essay titled "The Ever Unwilling" Ditko wrote, "I knew from Day One, from the first Green Goblin story, who the Green Goblin would be. I absolutely knew because I planted him in J. Jonah Jameson's businessman's club, I planted the GG's son (same distinct hair-style) in the college issues for more dramatic involvement and storyline consequences. So how could there be any doubt, dispute, about who the Green Goblin had to turn out to be when unmasked?" It would be John Romita, Sr., who at Lee's insistence took over pencilling duties on the book, who would eventually draw the dramatic reveal, in line with Ditko's seeded plots, in the very first issue produced after his departure. Interconnecting with supporting cast characters and past and future villains, Ditko had the next six months of *Spider-Man* stories planned out in detail at the time he left Marvel, and the series, so abruptly.

"I knew in advance the Spider-Man storyline. I had an issue/monthly sheet on the wall, like the best (worst) time for Aunt May to have a heart attack would be Parker's first day in college, etc.," Ditko wrote to me in 2016. This would have included more college years and more coming-of-age sagas for Peter Parker, along with new cast members and new super villains as the linear saga progressed and the leading role matured. The "can't catch a break," goof-up, forever-neophyte role the hero seems today perennially cast in, would not have been quite so clay-footed in Ditko's planned development.

Opposite page: Ditko, pencils and inks, original artwork from ***Strange Tales*** #141, February, 1966 ©1966 Marvel Characters.

I mentioned this characteristic aspect of Spider-Man to the artist once, and he replied in a letter from November 2014, "That's not usually understood. Peter Parker, a teenager becoming a hero, had to learn how to be a hero. He wasn't even like a rookie policeman or soldier with some experienced Sgt to train him, set him straight. Parker (Spider-Man) could make mistakes a hero like Captain America or Superman could never make. From grade school to college etc. Parker has to learn and grow up to be a hero." John Romita, Sr., said to Jonathan Ross in his 2007 BBC television documentary, "Steve's version of Spider-Man was true, but it didn't fit in with Stan's commercial sense. Any artist who fought him on it is making a terrible mistake. Ditko could have made a fortune." If riches were measured by the amount of positive influence on future creators, then Ditko would have been an extraordinarily rich man, such was the wide impact his art had on individuals that would later contribute their own talents to the comic book industry. Award-winning writer/editor and President of DC Comics between 2002-2009 Paul Levitz wrote to me in 2018, recalling his early first impressions of Ditko's *Spider-Man* and its special appeal, "I first encountered comics in cardboard boxes full of them owned by a couple of older kids on my block. Including an early *Spider-Man* (his first encounter with the Scorpion), leading me to identify the artist in my mind as 'the guy who did the ugly faces.' I read most of Steve's Marvel work as back issues, not off newsstands but I think his work on each had a very distinct voice: the animal-derived villains in Spidey, the surreal dimensions and entities in Doctor Strange — all very different from anyone else's art at the time. Both DC and Marvel had house styles dominating, but Steve was genuinely unique."

Artist P. Craig Russell was another young reader fascinated with Ditko's art and wrote to me 2018, "I read everything in the 1960s, you could do that then. Though the racks were full, it was nothing like today's seemingly-endless selection of comic books. I think I first saw Steve Ditko art through some pre-Spider-Man magazines like *Strange Tales* and *Journey into Mystery*. An easy style to recognize and maybe the first artist to influence me to pick up a pencil. Ditko was an absolutely unique, one-of-a-kind artist. So unique, that unlike Kirby or Neal Adams he never spawned a school of followers, as far as I know. He was a constant source of interest, in that his art was constantly evolving and an inspiration in that he never ever stopped drawing."

Writer/editor Marv Wolfman also wrote to me in 2019, "I absolutely loved Ditko's art from his early days on *Captain Atom* for Charlton and later his *Blue Beetle* books. His *Spider-Man* comics were revolutionary. Nobody but Ditko, no artist working then or now, could have ever designed Spider-Man to move the way he did or the mind-blowing world of Doctor Strange as Steve had. Others, even Jack Kirby who was always amazing, would have made Peter and Spidey more heroic. Ditko made him slender and creepy and not at all heroic, posing Spidey all twisted, grotesque and odd. All of which made him even more of a hero! I was a major Ditko fan."

In the beginning, when Lee's expertly-wrought suggested image of a creative, zany, friendly team Bullpen that was monthly pulling out comic book legends from their inspired minds under the benign direction of a "fearless leader" was structurally sound, Jack Kirby would visit the Madison Avenue Marvel offices regularly for next-issue story conferences with Lee on a number of different books but always with an emphasis on *Fantastic Four*, the company's premiere title throughout the 1960s. But as time went by, those visits from Kirby became fewer. "I didn't especially see much of Lee and Kirby working together since Jack came in less and less during the time I was there but they did confer when Jack came in once every week or so at the beginning," wrote Roy Thomas to me in 2013, adding, "I wasn't in on many of those talks. Jack appeared outgoing but he was really very guarded."

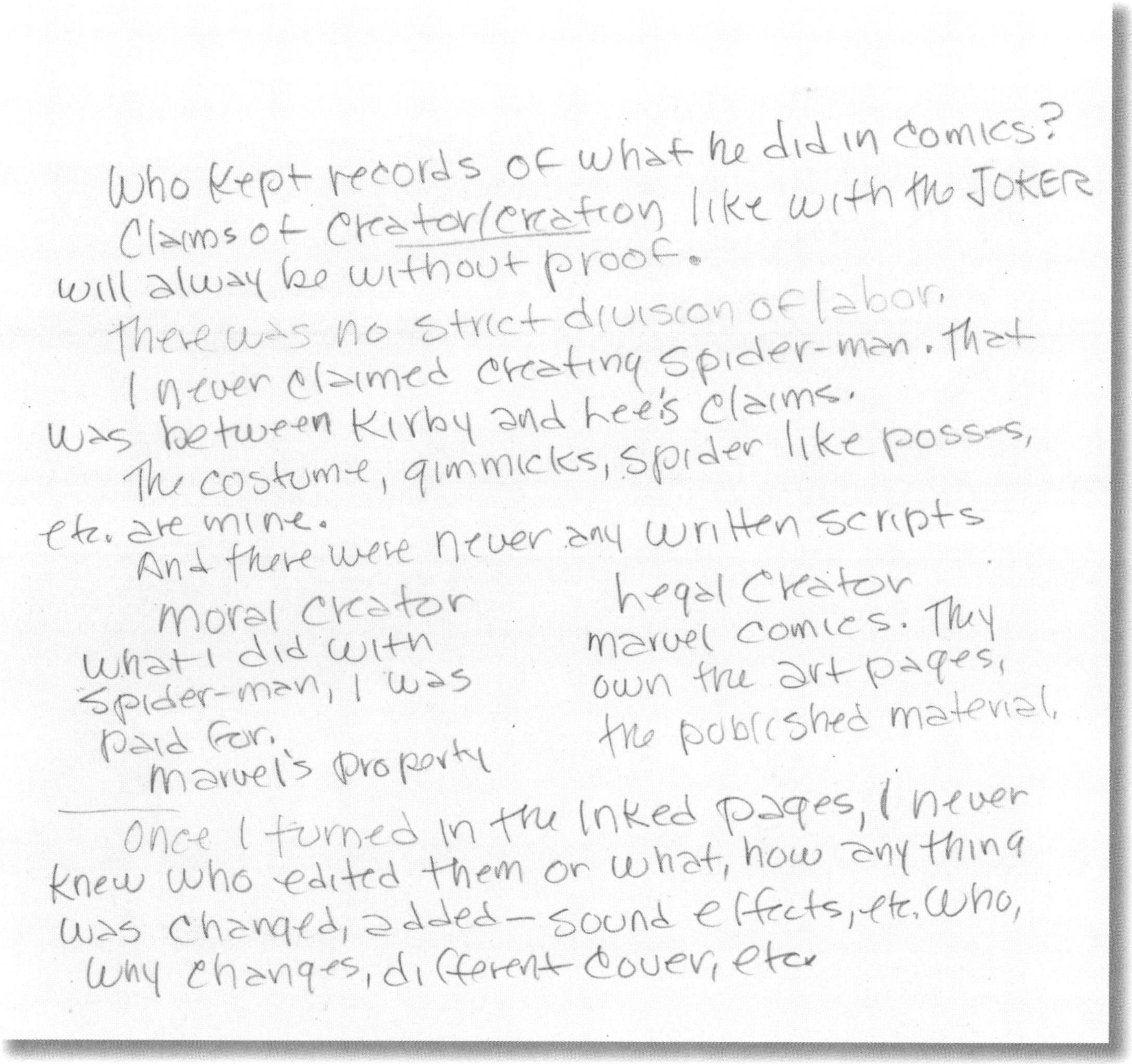

Who kept records of what he did in comics?
Claims of creator/creation like with the JOKER
will alway be without proof.
There was no strict division of labor.
I never claimed creating Spider-man. that
was between Kirby and Lee's claims.
The costume, gimmicks, spider like posses,
etc. are mine.
And there were never any written scripts

Moral creator
What I did with
Spider-man, I was
paid for.
Marvel's property

Legal creator
Marvel comics. They
own the art pages,
the published material.

Once I turned in the inked pages, I never
knew who edited them or what, how any thing
was changed, added — sound effects, etc. who,
why changes, different cover, etc.

Above: Portion of Ditko correspondence with the author from March, 2015, defining a "creator" in the context of comics.

With Ditko and Wood departed and Kirby keeping his own counsel away from the Marvel offices while still delivering his required assignments, the now-weathered House of Ideas seemed to be on shifting sands as other artists felt similarly motivated to challenge the unfair-funfair and inequitable division of labour that Lee's method seemed to generate. "The artists were doing the plotting, Stan was just coordinating the books," Kirby said in an interview published in *Comics Interview* #41, continuing, "The artists were the ones handling both story and art. We had to, there was no time not to!" And Gil Kane recalled in an interview for UK fanzine *Fantasy Advertiser* in 1986, "I made up a story, and Stan put in the copy. Stan made so many requirements of me as a writer, and a couple of times I said 'Look, if you don't like what I'm doing, do it yourself.' But he didn't want that, he just wanted to take the artwork home at night and there, from after dinner until two or three in the morning, he'd write a book." In the second volume of *The Dick Ayers Story: An Illustrated Autobiography*, 2005, the artist relates a confrontation with Lee, depicted in comic strip form.

After working as an artist for Marvel for some time with a gradual feeling he was doing unpaid writing work under Lee's system of production, one panel sees Ayers bursting into Lee's office declaring, "Stan, I think I should be paid for co-writing your stories! You don't even give me credit; you just sign your name as writer." Lee replies, "My-Oh-My, you do have an ego! OK, I'll add a couple of bucks to your page rate, but not your name as writer." This response echoed a previous one to letter writer Gary Rafferty, who asked in the letters page of *Amazing Spider-Man* #20, "Why does Stan always get top billing?"— and received the half-jokingly written answer, "Because Stan is so talented, lovable, clever and witty! And mainly because he's the bullpen boss!"

Not all artists working under Lee's method felt the same, however, with some sharing the editor's own positive views of the apparent creative freedom it offered collaborators. Herb Trimpe said to me in 2011, "Stan had a particular genius for allowing the artist to tell the story. He saw the artist as the one who visualized the story and the one to pace it. The writer was basically an ideas person and a scripter. The artist was the director of the movie — a very strong and influential position to be in." Some directors prefer to take the storytelling driving seat in their most personal of creations, knowing that the best art in its purest form comes always from within. The socially awkward, introvert character of Peter Parker, all the while hiding a heroic heart, strong moral fiber and iron will, is reflected well in the nature of its equally constructed artist/creator and while Stan Lee made Spider-Man's speech patterns the entertaining sum of his own brash, colourful and humour-filled personality, it was Steve Ditko who was the soul, spirit and true architect behind it all. But like all creative partnerships between talented individuals yielding ground-breaking, personality-informed works — Lennon and McCartney being an apt example — a little artistic friction and a handful of personal differences makes for a very special blend of creative magic indeed, despite how brief its effect may last.

In March 2015, Ditko wrote to the author laying out his clear view on his involvement in Spider-Man's creation, how he regarded his contributions today, along with a columned section where he defined all his work on the character until the title of Moral Creator. It was a term he had used in a previous letter to similarly define the role of Siegel and Shuster on Superman. Ditko wrote, "Who created Spider-Man started with fans wanting to interview people who did comics, they were more concerned with interviewing than with content, answers. Who kept records of what he did in comics? Claims of creator/creation like with The Joker will always be without proof. There was no strict division of labour. I never claimed creating Spider-Man. That was between Kirby and Lee's claims.

> The costume, gimmicks, spider-like poses etc. are mine. And there were never any written scripts.

Moral Creator	Legal Creator
What I did with Spider-Man, I was paid for. Marvel's property	Marvel Comics. They own the art pages, The Published Material.

Once I turned in the inked pages, I never knew who edited them or what, how, anything was changed, added — sound effects, etc. Who by and why changes were made, different covers etc. Once I did the job, turned it in, got paid, my involvement ended. It was all ancient history."

History that would be remembered as a major contribution to popular culture but for now deemed irrelevant by its creator, because Steve Ditko was moving on and leaving behind without a second glance, a successful, but now personally conflicted, character that perhaps he had invested with a little more of his self than he would care to admit. His aim now was to pursue new ways of working — to create but also to own his creations, in defiance of the corporate establishment industry and also, it would transpire, of a number of comic book fans that would read, and loudly condemn, his later subsequent conceptualizations of his now heavily Randian-influenced definition of what a true hero should be. "I prefer conflicts that are based on reality rather than based on fantasy," said Ditko in his last interview for *Rapport*. "When you get wound up with super villains, super fantastic gadgets and super incredible action, everything has to be made so deliberately that it all becomes senseless. It boils down to what you want a story to stand for. Every person, whether he wants to be or not, is in a continuous struggle. It is a struggle to keep his mind from being corrupted."

CHARLTON COMICS
700-1068
MYSTERIOUS SUSPENSE
APPROVED BY THE COMICS CODE AUTHORITY
12¢
CDC
NO. 1 OCT.
RETURN OF THE QUESTION
DITKO

Chapter Four
Rebel, Rebel 1966-1971

When Steve Ditko left Spider-Man dangling in 1965, leaving Marvel staffers and readers scratching their heads as to the reason why, he returned to his beloved Charlton Comics for increased regular work, taking a lower page rate than he had received at Marvel but encountering far less editorial interference. He'd been quietly accepting assignments from Charlton during his final months working for Stan Lee, with the first issue of his return to *Captain Atom* appearing on newsstands around the same time as his last *Amazing Spider-Man* comic. With a potential history of sniffing out moonlighting creators, Lee may have learned of this and considered it further justification for freezing the artist out of his inner circle in the year leading up to Ditko's departure. Of all the major comic book publishing companies that he worked for over his long career, Charlton is the only one that Ditko ever spoke fondly of in his correspondence to me — the artist produced thousands of comic art pages and many original character creations for the publisher during his thirty years working there.

In January 2015 Ditko wrote to the author, "Oh yes, I enjoyed working for Charlton Press. The editor Al Fago was willing to accept my art styles. I really enjoyed working on Joe Gill's stories, they remain a high point. Little enjoyment with most DC script writers. I've done some DC writers' stories that were boring to do. There was a lot of comic fan complaints about Charlton's 'poor colouring,' not buying Charlton, self-blinded to the stories, art. Many used to complain about Charlton's press printing, colouring, compared to Marvel, DC etc. — it was a poor excuse for not supporting them more."

At Charlton, directly after leaving Marvel, he developed over time what was named the "Action Hero" line, comprising revived and redressed new versions of Captain Atom and Blue Beetle together with a brand new creation, and one that would prove to be a controversial turning point in his career, The Question, in comic strips both drawn and written by Ditko. In the introduction to *Action Heroes Volume 2* hardcover edition 2006 published by DC Comics, who acquired the rights to the characters in 1983, Charlton and DC editor/artist, New York-born Dick Giordano wrote, "None of the 'Action Heroes' line would have happened if it weren't for Steve Ditko's discontent with the situation on *Spider-Man*. I was visiting his New York studio while he angrily insisted (as did Jack Kirby later) that he, not Stan Lee, was writing the scripts for *Spider-Man*. To make his point, he indicated a chart on the wall that clearly outlined the *Spider-Man* storyline for the next three or four issues. Stan, of course, did write the dialogue but Steve, whether rightly or wrongly, still insisted that he should get scripting credit."

Giordano would attend Charlton's New York office every Wednesday to meet freelancers picking up assignments and delivering finished work and continued, "During one of his Wednesday visits, Steve made a presentation of his ideas for the new Blue Beetle. He substituted Ted Kord for Dan Garret, the original Beetle, and kept the new character in the original continuity (I really loved the Bug — I thought at the time that it was a stroke of genius). Originally a Fox Comics character debuting in *Mystery Men Comics* #1 (August 1939), Blue Beetle developed as beat cop Dan Garret, empowered through a magical Vitamin 2X and an armored costume, then reimagined at Charlton Comics as archaeologist Dan Garrett, deriving super-powers from an ancient Egyptian scarab. In Ditko's version, debuting as a back-up feature in *Captain Atom* #83 (November 1966), millionaire industrialist Ted Kord inherits the Blue Beetle identity but without its powers and relies on his own ingenuity and considerable scientific and engineering skills to create a variety of gadgets to fight crime, including his land-air-sea all-purpose vehicle "The Bug," replete with insectoid legs. Giordano wrote further in his introduction, "Later came Steve's creation of The Question, a harder-edged hero whose actions in an early story allowed a bad guy to drown in a sewer — something that unleashed a flood of mail to Charlton. That just wasn't done in those days! I didn't see it as a big deal, but I was obviously in the minority. By today's standards, no one would even blink!"

By the standards of some observers in 1967, who blinked rapidly, the character itself would form a question in their minds regarding the validity of the artist's current work. Similarly devoid of any superpowers and dressed in a snappy suit and fedora, underneath which he wore a mask that rendered his appearance featureless and affixed by a special bonding gas provided by benefactor Aristotle Rodar that also changed the colour of hair and clothing, Vic Sage was a

Opposite page: Ditko cover artwork for ***Mysterious Suspense*** #1, October, 1968 ©1968 Charlton Comics.

crusading investigative journalist in regular life, operating in fictional Hub City and appearing as The Question in a swirl of green mist when required to fight crime and injustice armed only with his "rational" intelligence and a good right hook.

Having debuted as a back-up feature in *Blue Beetle* #1 June 1967, *The Question* cover-featured on *Mysterious Suspense* #1 October 1968, a one-shot title with a collection of strips intended for *Blue Beetle* before its lengthy publication hiatus and an effective curtain call on the character and on Ditko's "Action Heroes" line altogether. With the journalist alter-ego of the The Question expressing the political views of its creator, with another character in a strip saying of him, in dialogue written by Ditko, "That stupid Sage. A rumour spread about him speaking out against the U.N. Instead of denying it, he asks if decent people should deal with cut-throats and if not, why should free governments deal with dictatorships that enslave their own citizens and should we recognize the right of a dictator to make slaves of people?" The alter-ego was similarly free to employ his own "logically deduced" methods of crime fighting with a propensity for harsh realism and leaving a calling card marked with an image of a question mark.

The incident that Giordano mentions, where during a sewer-set battle The Question allows a criminal to potentially drown in the fast-flowing waters that he'd just punched him into, refusing to stage a rescue attempt. During this he commented that he'd "notify the police to retrieve them" if they survived the experience, displaying a ruthless streak in the character that echoed earlier Golden Age *Batman* scenarios but was completely out of step with the "love is all" sensibilities of the generation reading the comic books and the direction the decade would further pursue, in creative theory at least.

In retrospect, it seems a minor detail but an equally fast flowing stream of negative mail and condemnation of the actions of a fictional character would cause a lasting detrimental effect on Ditko's non-fictional career opportunities and the industry's perception of him and his produce. Ditko wrote in a letter to the author from April 2014, "When I did my first *Question* story for Charlton Press, the publisher of a leading fan publication attacked The Question and me. The publisher, publication, would decide what was proper fiction, fantasy, certainly not any writer or artist. The comic book industry, fandom made up of fantasies and fiction, came publicly down on me after the first *Question* story, it accelerated with Mr. A in *witzend,* and kept growing with comic book fan press publications as the anti-me grew. Some fictions are not to be tolerated it seems. Quite a confession." He was referring to an editorial written in 1968 by respected fan press journalist and long-time editor of Comics Buyer's Guide Don Thompson who wrote in *Comic Art* #7, "I have been increasingly disturbed of late by unpleasant developments in Steve Ditko's work. I am an admirer of his artwork, and, until recently, of his plots. But his work since leaving Marvel has been propaganda — and badly done propaganda at that — for a frightening philosophy."

In attempting to restrain the creator's infusing of his characters with his own personal convictions, the vehement criticism served only to inflame Ditko's desire to do so and further serve to create and consolidate a suspicious relationship between the artist and the collective fandom of comic books thereafter. He wrote to me his views in August 2013, "Comic book fandom deteriorated as it grew, expanded. Early fans, with their fanzines, were more interested in learning about what goes with creating comics, even creating their own characters, comic books. Later fans wanted to dictate with their opinions what should be done and editors foolishly pandered to them. Comic book fandom has become authoritarian. I don't give interviews; attend conventions so fandom remains childish, spiteful because they can't have their own way."

Ditko, once a supporter and occasional contributor to the early comic fanzines, had experienced previous disagreements with some editors over drawings of his that were reproduced without permission and eventually stopped sending out any such materials to the publications. In an unannounced visit by Ditko to the 1964 inaugural New York Comicon, a frantic mob-scene was created around him with some attendees who were close enough to exchange words with the artist recalling coming away severely deflated by meeting a comic book idol who had flatly advised against them seeking a career in the industry they loved, declaring that the work was hard, the pay was low and the rewards were few. For the artist himself, the experience of meeting his fans and admirers proved to be equally as traumatic and uncomfortable, ensuring that a convention appearance by Ditko was never again to be repeated. The event also formed an aversion in Ditko that made him wary or disinterested in meeting any fans at all, either individually or in a group setting, from this point on and for the rest of his life.

The aficionados and followers of the products that emerged from the industry Ditko was labouring in were steadily growing in number, and by 1966 comic book characters had begun to break out of their printed confines to find new audiences through the direct medium of television. With a growing number of viewers enjoying the wonders of colour programming the bright, primary hues of superheroes seemed a natural fit for a decade keen to distance itself from post-War conformity and its slate-grey memory. The first television series based on Marvel characters was *The Marvel Super Heroes*, a syndicated show produced by Grantray-Lawrence that featured Captain America, Iron Man, Hulk, Thor and Sub-Mariner in seven-minute segments of very limited animation that relied on previously-published artwork panels by Kirby, Ditko and Heck along with camera-manipulation to achieve its minimal effects.

Airing from September 1 to December 1, 1966, a total of 65, half-hour colour episodes were produced and widely syndicated across American networks, introducing the Marvel brand to countless households previously in ignorance of them. "See us on colour TV in the fall!" a promotional sheet proclaimed along with the boast that Marvel was the "fastest-growing line of comic books in the world with projected sales of 40 million for the year 1966."

Having first appeared in movie serials of the 1940s, Batman's ABC network television series, which ran for three seasons from January 12, 1966 through March 14, 1968, combined campy humour with colourful costumes, inventive sets and sixties-sleek props such as the turbo-powered Batmobile along with an energetically-charged cast of heroes and villains. With its memorably catchy theme-tune, on-screen comic book style lettered sound effects like "Ka-Pow!" or "Smash!" and dependably ludicrous cliffhanger endings, the show became a ratings smash, popular with children and adults alike. Actor Adam West who played the caped crusader with poker faced wit and a knowing self-deprecation defined the character of Batman for a whole generation so completely he could never quite escape the association for the rest of his career. (I met the actor once when he visited London in 2013 and during our conversation mentioned in passing that we shared the same birthdate, though separated by over 40 years. His reply, instantaneous and accompanied with a wry smile and raised eyebrow, was a perfect example of his acerbic charm when he said, without missing a beat, "How perfectly wonderful for you!").

The live-action *Batman* series produced a spin-off movie in its first year, with both versions reaching a far larger audience than Marvel's own primitive first attempt at a media translation of its characters. Some live-action sequences were filmed for the sparsely animated *Marvel Super Heroes* series with actors dressed as Captain America, Bucky, Hulk and Doctor Doom introducing the animated segments and the scripts for these were provided by Jerry Seigel. The previous year Seigel, together with Joe Shuster, had launched a fresh attempt to regain the rights to Superman with a legal request to renew the copyright on the character.

After the request was eventually denied, in 1969 the duo entered a new lawsuit against National Periodical Publications in a case that lasted five years through several appeals with an outcome that proved disastrous for Seigel and Shuster with considerable financial and creative loss for each of them. Concluding that the pair had transferred all rights to the character in settlement of the 1947 lawsuit, the judge ruled they had no rights to renew any copyright and found the case in favour of National. It would mark a decided turn of fortunes for both creators that would worsen over the coming decade.

Ditko's departure from *Spider-Man* may have shaken some of his most ardent admirers, but by successfully using and subtly adapting the artists' original template for the series, Lee and Romita had steered it to even greater popularity and increased readership. By now, Lee was devoting equal narrative time to the social life of the supporting characters, especially as Romita drew beautiful women exceedingly well and with Parker, once the outcast nerd, now an accepted, welcomed and noticeably more handsome member of a swinging late-sixties teenage in-crowd. With stories involving regular return visits by super villains from Ditko's back pages (with some Romita-designed additions including The Rhino, The Shocker and notably the mafia style crime boss The Kingpin, in more recent iterations on permanent loan as an arch-nemesis to Daredevil), Romita's Spider-Man was more muscular, his costume design more symmetrical, and the precise, bold lines of the artist presented an altogether more heroic looking character with a good looking supporting cast that played well against Lee's cliché ridden but entertaining dialogue. Within the narrative the comic book was, for the most part, caught in a repetitious recycling of previously used plots and situations, but Romita's direct and clean style appealed to many with his work emerging as a house-brand favourite at Marvel in the following decade.

Witnessing now from afar the growing success of the character he'd poured so much creativity into, fanned the flames of desire in Ditko to be able to produce future creations, free from editorial interference, that he owned not only the moral rights to but also the intellectual and legal rights. He found a kindred spirit in this endeavour with fellow artist, Wally Wood. Similar to Charlton, Ditko had been working for Wood on his range of titles produced for Harry Shorten's Tower Comics in tandem with his final Marvel work. A pivotal story Ditko drew in *Thunder Agents* #7 depicting the death of Menthor, one of the team members, would also have been on sale alongside his return to *Captain Atom* and his final work on *Spider-Man* and *Doctor Strange*. Ditko and Wood worked well together, sharing a mutual admiration for each other's artwork and an acceptance of each other's individualistic, quirky personalities.

New York-born artist Ralph Reese was Wood's assistant during this period and wrote to the author in February 2015, "In spite of their very different political views Woody and Ditko always got along well, perhaps because they were both unassuming in nature and shared a mutual hatred of Stan Lee. While I do have some respect for Stan Lee's contribution to the world of comics, it is well known that he did have a predilection for putting his name on other people's work. And as a person, he is a total phony. That is not necessarily always a bad thing in the world of business, and I do think he has a certain genius for self-promotion and therefore promotion of the Marvel brand. But both Wood and Ditko despised him. Not too surprising considering that they were both just the opposite in terms of personality. So, they felt like any very talented but shy and retiring artist type when confronted by such an overbearing and relentless self-aggrandizer — especially one who was basically ripping them off."

Wood, also an accomplished folk guitar player in a style reminiscent of Woody Gutherie, was a uniquely gifted artist who learnt his craft from past experiences working at Will Eisner's studio and similar places. He also knew how to put a great team together and many artists and writers, including Ditko, were called in for the *Thunder Agents* project — the

name being an acronym for The Higher United Nations Defence Enforcement Reserves. Among them was Reed Crandall, who drew the first *NoMan* stories for Wood and was a previous contributor to EC Comics, where the artist's delicate ink lines added layers to his accomplished pencils, projecting a fluid realism that added gravitas to EC's horror yarns. Years later, the artist now struggled with meeting deadlines, and Ditko took over drawing the character as a result in order for the book to fulfill its print schedule. Crandall continued to work sporadically in comic books until 1974, but his battles with alcoholism and deteriorating health, combined with few work opportunities from the industry, saw his final days working as a night watchman for a Pizza Hut warehouse in Wichita, Kansas before his death from a heart attack in 1982 at the age of 65.

Crandall had experienced what many comic book artists would, as their advancing years effectively rendered them obsolete in what appeared to be an increasingly ageist industry. Ditko wrote to the author in 2014, "A DC editor once said that DC won't hire any artist over 30. When it was pointed out to him that he was over 30, he said he's the 'exception' and in time, the over-30s disappeared."

Now 39, and after finding it difficult to work within Lee's edicts at Marvel, Wood occupied himself producing material for Tower and found inspiration through one of his fellow artists, Dan Adkins, who was working with him in his studio. Located in what was then a neglected Upper West Side area of Manhattan (today the Lincoln Centre area), in reality Wood worked out of his apartment at 76th Street and Columbus Avenue. Reese wrote to me in 2015, "It was a typical family-sized apartment which Wood shared with his then-wife Tatjana and most of it was their private space. The studio was a medium-sized room with space for three desks where Wood and whatever artists he had helping out, would work. There was also a small, windowless room off the hallway which served as the artograph room and was completely filled up with Wood's extensive photo-reference files and the artograph machine itself."

Renowned cartoonist and author Jules Feiffer remembered it in 2010, somewhat unkindly, as "A cartoonist and science-fiction writers' ghetto. It was just a huge room where the walls were knocked down. Dark, smelly and with all these cartoonists and writers bent over their tables." But Reese recalled to the author, "While Wood's old apartment on 76th street was not in a slum; it was not in an especially prestigious area or anything. At that time before gentrification there were still large areas of Manhattan where average folks could afford to live. Unlike, say, Gil Kane, who lived in a doorman building on the East Side and was known to be a snappy dresser and something of a womanizer, Wood never seemed to care much about the trappings of success. While most of his contemporaries went and bought houses in the suburbs, the childless Woods preferred the convenience of staying in the city. Also, I don't think Wood had much interest in taking on the hassles of maintaining a house. A great deal of artwork was generated there in the 76th street studio. In addition to myself, many other assistants came and went and performed various tasks according to their ability."

Reese became Wood's assistant and protégé at the studio in 1966 when he was a 16-year-old runaway from a New York juvenile detention facility. He recalled to me in 2015, "The pay was fifty bucks a week and the duties were pretty menial at first. The first thing that he told me was 'Don't call me Wally'. He always hated the nickname and preferred for his friends to call him 'Woody.' What possessed him to take a troubled young man under his wing at that time I can't be sure, but perhaps it had something to do with the fact that he was becoming middle-aged with no children. Maybe he sensed another rebellious spirit in me." It was at this apartment/studio where Dan Adkins told Wood about his dream to work on a self-published comic book with complete creative freedom and control along with a financial renumeration that reflected the creators' work and intellectual investment.

Adkins produced fine, smoothly rendered artwork but often grappled with deadlines and his own inner demons, familiar enemies of many a creators' working life. Artist P. Craig Russell wrote to me in 2018, "Dan Adkins was a very singular man who gave me my career. I met him when he was on a downswing. Though he was establishing a studio in Ohio at the time, he was finding it increasingly difficult to finish assignments, whether of his own art or of inking other artists. One night after he explained all his problems to me, I told

Above: Ditko, circa 1970s sitting in front of Mr. A artwork. Opposite page: Ditko, pencils and inks, artwork for a Mr. A splash from ***Comic Crusader*** #4, 1968, ©1968 The Estate of Steve Ditko.

him I thought he was depressed. He said 'Nahhh, that's not it.' Twenty years later in a phone call he said to me 'you know what my problem was, Russell? I was depressed.' He eventually returned to New York where he was assistant art director at Marvel and within the structure of a nine-to-five job produced a lot of inking work again."

Adkins' blithe comment solidified Wood's own desires to publish self-copyrighted material, he had a fair number of unused concepts and artwork built up for this purpose seeking the proper venue, and decided the time was now present to take the plunge into self-publishing. The magazine would eventually be named *witzend* (all lower case) and would soon become the platform for Ditko to create and present a character that embodied unconditionally the artist's Randian-informed beliefs — Mr. A. Reese recalls of the conception of *witzend*, "Wood figured he knew enough other artists with stuff just laying around, or who had original ideas that they wanted to copyright themselves before letting anyone else publish them, to make a kick-ass little magazine. Bear in mind that at this time, almost all comics and other illustration were still being done on a work-for-hire basis, so that the creators had no more right to their material than a bricklayer has to the building he constructs."

Wood started calling people, and after a couple of months the premiere issue of *witzend* began to take shape with an impressive selection of material, including an unpublished EC story by Frank Frazetta; Wood's own *Animan* strip; Gray Morrow's *Orion* as well as single-page illustrations from many others artists. The first issue of *witzend* appeared in the summer of 1966, and the Wood-written editorial declared that the magazine had a "no-policy" for creators — in other words, everything was permitted, within current state laws, with no editorial restrictions. While existing deadline obligations meant that Ditko was unable to contribute anything to the first issue, a further editorial page announcing future contributors said, "When it dawned on our friendly neighbourhood Steve Ditko that this means freedom, he immediately began to lose money at a fantastic rate by working on a secret project for us."

For Ditko, the opportunity that *witzend* offered felt like a path to creative freedom was beginning to open up before him, and he threw his support in with the project wholeheartedly, crafting his unpaid contributions to Wood's publication alongside his regular assignments for Charlton and DC, while also helping out in the office with general administration duties. This flag of rebellious creative independence now held aloft by Wood and supported by Ditko, was accompanied by a few others but notable for its lack of big names, working within the constraints of the major publishers, who all declined the invitation to participate — especially the guaranteed crowd puller, Jack Kirby. Kirby's workload at Marvel throughout the whole of 1966 was gargantuan, but his speed at drawing kept pace with the torrent of ideas that poured from him relentlessly, and his reluctance to see an opportunity with Wood's publication especially confounded Ditko.

In 2015 he wrote to the author, "It's a mystery to me why Kirby didn't contribute to *witzend*. I thought Kirby would be eager to create, copyright some ideas. I can't see Kirby with any 'workload' that could have prevented him from working up some five or three or ONE page showing his ideas, type of storyline, characters etc, and leisurely work up a full story. His creative ideas would have been secure." Adding that, "Too many comic book artists weren't interested in Wally Wood's invitation to create and copyright their ideas. They may have believed their steady company assignments would continue forever."

Despite the lack of supporters rallying to its cause, *witzend* continued publication and for its third issue in 1967 Ditko delivered his promised "secret project" — the equally-controversial comic book character, Mr. A. In his last published interview in 1968 for fanzine *Marvel Main* Ditko said, "Mr. A's 'power' is deliberately knowing what is right and acting accordingly. But it is one of choice. Of choosing to know what is right and choosing to act on that knowledge in all his thoughts and actions with everyone he deals with. No conflict or contradiction in his behaviour in either identity. He isn't afraid to know or refuse to act on what is right no matter in what situation he finds himself. Where other heroes choose to be self-made neurotics, the Question and Mr. A choose to be psychologically and intellectually healthy. It's a choice everyone has to make."

The character of Mr. A was forming in Ditko's mind at the same time he was preparing a distilled version of the same concept for Charlton, explaining the similar template found in *The Question*. In the same 1968 interview Ditko commented, "When Blue Beetle got his own magazine, they needed a companion feature for it. I didn't want to use Mr. A, because I didn't think the Code would let me do the type of stories I wanted to do, so I worked up The Question, using the basic idea of a man who was motivated by black and white principles."

Newspaper reporter Rex Graine wore an indistinguishable suit and fedora combo and a mask with a sculptured, expressionless human visage to fight crime in the guise of Mr. A, by name and nature the most overtly Randian of all of Ditko's comic book creations, visually personified by a calling card with one side white and the other black, a literal representation of Ayn Rand's "A is A" axiom. While The Question's morality was decried by simply allowing the possibility of a criminal to drown, Mr. A's actions were far less ambiguous. In the rooftop climax of his debut story he allows a teenage murderer named Angel to fall to his death, electing to devote his attention instead to a recently injured woman in need of urgent medical treatment. In the final panels, when even the rescued victim of the crime exclaims, "You're cruel! You don't have any mercy or pity!" Mr. A responds through Ditko's script, "I don't abuse my emotions. I have no passion for aggressors only for their victims, for the innocent. To have any sympathy for a killer is an insult to their victims. Even if you weren't hurt, I wouldn't have saved Angel," as the grim avenger is shown walking away, carrying the injured woman off to hospital with the cries of Angel's death plunge resounding in the background.

Appearing in two consecutive issues of *witzend* originally, Ditko would return to his uncompromisingly niche character throughout his career with further strips, illustrations and Objectivist informed stories, the majority of which were self-published. One of the few creations the artist owned the complete rights to, the intensity and forcefulness of the assimilation and presentation of the philosophy that influenced it, rendered Mr. A an intellectual property of limited commerciality, as Ditko agreed when I asked him if any film-maker had ever expressed any interest in translating the character from print to screen. "I never had any approach about Mr. A, it would never go over as a movie," he wrote.

Without the platform of *witzend* the concept may never have seen print but the production of the magazine was increasingly becoming a financial burden for Wood. Reese recalled, "The magazine never really made any money and probably barely managed to meet its own expenses if that, but it was an artistic success and has become a treasured collector's item. Looking back at it, I am amazed that it got done at all between the demands of doing the 'Thunder Agents' books and the other odds and ends he was taking on. Wood was a workaholic and he was cranking seven days a week." What Wood was attempting to achieve with his publication — returning creative power and present and future financial incentive to artists and writers — was eventually recognized by the comic book industry and later championed by publishers such as Dark Horse, Image and Fantagraphics, who began to offer creators similar deals within the mainstream industry.

But *witzend* was too far ahead of its time to effect any substantial changes during its published lifetime but rather inhabited a netherworld between newsstand comics and the growing rise of "underground" titles celebrating the era's free-spirited youth culture of recreational drugs and music, a genre best illustrated by the influential work of Pennsylvania-born cartoonist Robert Crumb, whose *Fritz the Cat* strips, and self-published *Zap Comix,* offered iconic imagery embraced and incorporated as a visual accompaniment for a particular contingent of a whole new freewheelin' generation.

In a testimonial to Wood's legacy with *witzend*, Ditko wrote to the author in September 2014, "Wally Wood did an outstanding thing for writers and artists, an opportunity to create and copyright what one creates, protecting and able to cash in on it at any future time. Wood deserves much more recognition, and too few appreciate what he offered those working in comic book publishing. I think Wally was disappointed in that so few professionals were willing to take advantage of such a great opportunity. I believe that is why he turned *witzend* over to Pearson." According to legend, Wood sold the rights for a nominal dollar to writer/editor Bill Pearson after the fourth issue with the direction of the magazine shifting radically under the new regime. Pearson continued irregular publication of *witzend* until 1985, with the contents of the title increasingly reflecting the particular interests of the publisher, with some later issues devoted exclusively to themes such as "good girl" art and actor W.C. Fields.

Ditko wrote to me in 2014, "Pearson confessed his contradictory editorial policies when he bought *witzend* from Wally. He exposed his being scared, even hostile, to other's fictions, etc. Pearson once asked me to submit something for the magazine. I did a 4-pager 'In principle' and he rejected it, violating Wood's original policy. As usual, some people in authority, having power, will abuse it. Worse, he collaborated with another artist to do a negative attack on Mr. A which he published. But that's his problem, not mine."

In the two-volume collected hardcover edition of *witzend* (Fantagraphics, 2014) which Ditko gave his blessing to — "I gave Bill Pearson permission to reprint my Mr. A and other original material to fully honour Wally Wood's *witzend* that gave writers, artists the opportunity to copyright their original ideas, created material, when published. A publication by Pearson without my material would have undercut Wally's achievement of the range of writer/artists ideas in fiction/ fantasy that Wally first published," he wrote to me in June 2014 — Pearson commented in his introduction to the volume,

"Steve Ditko was the first to be told about *witzend*, and second only to Wood in enthusiasm for the concept and quantity of material he contributed to the early issues. Wood believed in total anarchy, or thought he did, but he hadn't thought it through. Ditko believed in rigid governmental order, and maybe he still does. All I know is that the two were genuine friends, and aside from occasional fierce debates, they enjoyed working together whenever possible. When Steve dropped by the office one day, he volunteered to help with one of the necessary drudge jobs — addressing and stuffing envelope with subscription copies. He spent hours at it, and that was the time in his life when he was facing constant deadlines producing two new titles for DC Comics, *Beware the Creeper* and *The Hawk and the Dove*."

The "attack" that Ditko referred to came in the form of a comic strip called *Mr. E*, an overt ridicule (or gentle parody, take your pick) of *Mr. A* that ran in the same issue as the second part of a series by Ditko called "The Avenging World"in *witzend* #7, published in 1970. Scripted by Pearson, with art by Tim Battersby, the four-page strip was attributed to the fictional creator "Steve Diktato," with the character described as a "crusading moralist and amateur economist of the quid pro quo." Despite its satirical nature, the strip infuriated and aggravated Ditko who saw it as a personal slight and would contribute little to future issues of Pearson's magazine. For his final offering of the *Avenging World*, Ditko had eschewed the use of plots and specific characters and instead used an image of a scowling, wounded and bandaged world to introduce a 10-page editorial cartoon style, with full-page, text-heavy pages that read less like a comic book story but more of a manifesto with the artist in full out preaching mode, speaking out against "The Neutralist," "The Belligerent Protestors," and urging that "It is here, at the source, that one begins to clean up the 'world's mess,' here with a single person, with oneself" and that there could be "no compromise on basic principles."

The views, personal opinions and attendant themes that Ditko was stridently articulating would dominate his artistic endeavours thereafter and were firmly held, lifelong convictions, reiterated in correspondence to me, as in this example on the human condition from September 2015, "With the global conflicts going on everywhere, it's faith and force against faith and force. The 'human' race has learned nothing during its long existence. It's rational in technology — building the latest gadgets like the internet — but irrational in human relationships, more like tribal societies. We're in the computer, internet age, etc, with a little understanding, interest, or care of how we all came to be. The rot is being found at the top. It's almost a daily occurrence of some politician, city official etc, arrested for corruption going on for years. Politicians are power-seekers, lusters. They want to set the terms for all others so there are all kinds of compromises, shady deals. The continuing global unrest just continues to prove that who has the power will determine what is right or wrong. There's an old saying about people, 'Dumbing down and Deviations up,' an inverted pyramid."

Or in this example from a letter written in March 2015 on his philosophical views, "Religion is a primitive, early attempt at a philosophy of life. Religions stagnate, demand obedience — by force as the early history of religious wars, Protestants vs Catholics, Inquisitions, etc. Aristotle's 'Man is a rational animal' is rejected by the overwhelming majority, totally by religions. Philosophy is a comprehensive view of man, life, in regard to the real world and rejected by today's intellectuals. It's too early to see the start of a better world, life. Today, it's more a rejection of philosophy as having any real validity, knowledges, truth. Men's minds, creative in some areas, destructive in other areas. It seems some lessons can never be learned."

Notwithstanding, Ditko would spend the rest of his career in an attempt to teach the readers of his work, lessons that he deemed to be of monumental importance. The cumulative effect would further alienate a greater portion of his audience with the artist's casting as an outsider zealot now assured. An outcome, not unexpected or lamented by the artist, who concluded in a letter to me from February 2014, "No one is going to change minds that are unwilling to be changed, minds already set in their ways, direction, as the history of the human race continues to show. In a world of instability there will always be choices to be made, with no guarantees. It's the old 'one always has to pay the price.'"

Wally Wood's *Thunder Agents* group of comic books remained successful until 1969, but the price he paid for such success caused machinations from both DC and Marvel that resulted in a lost distribution deal, which halted the titles dead in their tracks. Reese remembers, "That was what really killed the series, if I remember right. It was a bitter blow to Wood." Ditko also confirmed in a letter from 2016 that "Wally's comics had distribution problems. They actually sold well." The demise of his Tower Comics work coincided with the dissolution of Wood's first marriage and a prolonged period of infrequent industry assignments. Wood first moved to DC, working on *Captain Action*, *Superboy*, *Hercules Unbound*, *All-Star Comics* and *Power Girl*, where the artist contributed to the character's visual identity by noticeably enlarging the size of her breasts and designing a costume to accentuate them.

No stranger to sexually charged visuals, Wood was the unsigned and undeclared artist of an infamous and widely circulated poster known as the "Disneyland Memorial Orgy" depicting well-known and rigorously protected Disney properties indulging in uncharacteristic and graphically explicit behaviour, with dollar signs emanating from a familiar-looking castle above them. For obvious reasons, Wood never admitted to being the artist of the image, which originally saw print in the May 1967 edition of satirical magazine *The Realist*, remarking in 1981 on the subject, "I'd rather not say anything about that except it was the most

pirated drawing in history with everyone printing copies of it."

Also at DC, Wood collaborated once again with Ditko in 1975, inking his pencils on a character Ditko had created with Paul Levitz named Stalker. Levitz wrote to me in 2018 in reference to the work and the artistic reunion, "It was a staged collaboration; I wrote the script then Steve created the visuals without any real back and forth. Teaming Steve and Woody probably came from Joe Orlando. Joe had an elfin twinkle in his eye and a great sense of humour. I learned many things large and small from him, but most significant was how to get good work out of creative people, and that readers value sincere efforts more than insincere ones, no matter how polished. Steve was a perfect storyteller and I enjoyed and admired the work we did together. I stare at the original art to a *Stalker* cover he did every day in my office."

In one of his final assignments, Wood returned to the Marvel superhero he'd help define when he inked artist Frank Miller's pencils for the cover to *Daredevil* #164 (May 1980). It would be his swan song on the character for Wood's declining health and the consequences of his addictive personality led lifestyle echoed the lyrics of a later Bob Dylan song, "It's not dark yet but it's getting there." Ralph Reese recalled of Wood's final days, "I was still renting desk space at Neal Adams' Continuity Associates when we got word that Woody was in the VA hospital at downtown Manhattan. Larry Hama, Jack Abel and I got together and went down there to see how he was doing. At that time, he had already had a couple of strokes that left him blind in one eye and partially paralyzed on, I think it was, the left side. Besides that, his kidneys were failing, and he was told he needed a transplant. We went on down to the Veterans Administration Hospital (where Wood could always get free or low-cost treatment as a vet) and went to see him there. He looked terrible. Although he was still only in his mid-fifties, he looked ten years older and just beat to hell. We chatted about his health problems and prognosis. He mentioned he was probably going to have to go on dialysis. At one point he and I went into the smoking lounge to have a cigarette. I asked him what his plans were once he got out of the hospital, thinking that maybe we could find some way to help him out. He told me that the first thing he was going to do was to go and get a drink. What can you say to that? Here the guy is obviously dying on his feet and surely knowing it, but yet and still…. After some rather awkward moments of well-wishing we left him there, and I had a strong feeling that it might be the last time we would see him alive."

Wally Wood took a gun to his head on November 2, 1981 in Los Angeles at the age of 54, coincidently the same day as Ditko's own 54th birthday. Wood reportedly said towards the end of his life "If I had it all to do over again, I'd cut off my hands."

Publisher Jim Warren had learned the hard way about magazine production and distribution through his experiences in the early 1950s producing a Playboy-inspired men's magazine titled *After Hours*. It was a brief and bruising episode that left him deep in debt and facing obscenity charges in his native Pennsylvania, but through it he met his future collaborator editor, writer and Hollywood literary agent Forrest J. Ackerman, who offered the publisher the idea for his first real creative and financial success. *Famous Monsters of Filmland*, first appearing in February 1958, was a magazine presenting articles, interviews and plentiful black-and-white photographs in celebration and examination of monsters of the movies, with a special emphasis on the films produced by Universal Pictures beginning with *Dracula*, starring actor Bela Lugosi in the eponymous role and *Frankenstein*, with Boris Karloff as the stitched-together, reanimated creature, with both films released theatrically in 1931. Profitable and popular, the magazine enjoyed a 25-year publication history and enabled a move for Warren Publishing to produce comic strips in a similar magazine-sized, black-and-white format beginning with *Creepy* #1 in late 1964, accompanied in early 1966 by *Eerie* #1 and culminating with the debut of the sultry, scantily-clad blood-

Above: Ditko, pencils and inks, original artwork from ***Showcase*** #75, 1968, the first appearance of Hawk and Dove, ©1968 DC Comics. Opposite page: Ditko, pencils and inks, original art from ***Creepy*** #12, 1966, ©1966 Warren Publications.

sucker Vampirella, co-created by Ackerman with artist Trina Robbins in July 1969.

The EC-inspired horror story comic magazines employed the services of many gifted artists of the time who delighted in the colourless medium, allowing them to pour lavish attention on their ink rendered pages, presenting sophisticated stories, exempt from any Code restrictions. Looking at the fine but time-consuming detail artists such as Alex Toth, Russ Heath, Tom Sutton and Angelo Torres were applying to their work for the horror titles and war title *Blazing Combat*, and despite the higher than average page rates, Ditko initially regarded Warren assignments as a "money-losing contest" among creators working competitively to impress one another. But the respect and friendship that Ditko had for the writer/editor of the line, Archie Goodwin, eventually persuaded him to also contribute his talents and work for the company.

With a sympathetic, encouraging editor, free from any Comics Code restrictions, and aware that his work would be seen and judged alongside that of his artistic peers, Ditko created a series of comic strips, the majority from Goodwin scripts, that each displayed some of the most accomplished, dramatic and masterful art of his career.

Utilizing a variety of techniques, the artist had perfected, from the sinuous cross-hatching on *Room with a View* (*Eerie* #3 June 1966) to the brush-applied, ink-wash details and subtle layers on *The Fly* (*Eerie* #7 January 1967), Ditko revealed his craft in stunning detail. By the end of his work for Warren, the artist had added charcoal to his rendering tools and produced a total of 16 stories for *Creepy* and *Eerie* until late 1967, when Warren Publishing hit financial straits and no longer able to offer the attractive page rates that had lured so many fine artists. Goodwin resigned as editor, tired of delivering second-hand excuses for late payments and cut page rates to his rota of artists, and Ditko saw no further reason to work for the company. But the body of work Ditko had produced for Warren, remarkably alongside all his other obligations, remains an artistic triumph during one of the artists' most prolific and innovative periods. He recalled to me in January 2015, "With my experimental Warren work (I give) thanks to the editor Archie Goodwin for the stories he wrote that gave me the opportunities to really experiment with visuals. Archie really challenged me to stretch, allowing me to experiment. Instead of the usual 'NO, NO' I got with most editors, comic companies for some company 'house look.' So, Archie is one of the rare ones."

While leading the quiet revolution with Wood, Ditko's new character creations were causing a backlash against the artist with fans and professionals alike. For his work at Charlton, that didn't constitute a problem for him but when seeking additional work at DC Comics and other publishers, it most certainly did. Ditko wrote to the author in 2014, "My first work for DC Comics had editors split on my doing any work for them and I heard of editors who wanted me but were pressured by others not to use me. The anti-me grew further." Ditko expanded on his reflections on past relationships with publishers in a letter to me from 2016, "The superhero comic industry editors confessed such fear of a different fiction/fantasy story, idea, art — what a humiliating confession. Charlton Press editors wisely let the artist develop his own styles, even story ideas, etc. DC editors were more like kings. Marvel's Lee — personal, picky, not intrusive but still, his Marvel had a pile of rejected art pages, a couple of my covers, rejected stories in their 'vault' etc. Why should any comic book fiction/fantasy story/art become so anti, not fit to be published? Can it be because comic book editors, fans, fan publications can't stand the comparison with their own mind, beliefs etc? — being compared, questioned, even judged by implication." Despite the editorial intrigues surrounding him at the DC offices during this time, Ditko delivered two memorable new creations for the company, beginning with The Creeper. First appearing in DC's *Showcase* #73 (March 1968) in a story plotted and drawn by Ditko with dialogue assists from Don Segall, the character was launched in his own series *Beware the Creeper* (June 1968) in a series co-written by Denny O'Neil that only saw six issues in its original run. In the comic book, Jack Ryder was a talk show host based in Gotham City, but the on-air expressions of his uninhibited views caused his termination from the position with the opinionated character

CREEPER
SUPERMAN
DC
NATIONAL COMICS
HA HA HA HA HA HA HA
Beware THE CREEPER
APPROVED BY THE COMICS CODE AUTHORITY
HA HA HA HA HA HA HA HA HA HA
THE MANY FACES OF PROTEUS!

pursuing a career in personal security instead. A case involving a rescue attempt of scientist Doctor Yatz reveals a need for Ryder to infiltrate a mobster's masquerade party, and he dons a skin-tight yellow, red and blue costume with shoulder fur trimming along with a green wig and facial makeup for this purpose. Nonetheless discovered by the mobsters, Ryder is deeply wounded by a stabbing and Yatz attempts to save his life by implanting an electronic device of his own making directly into the wound itself along with an injection of a special healing serum. This results in Ryder gaining enhanced strength, speed and agility together with a maniacal laugh that's not only a constant accompaniment to every Creeper appearance but also able to be controlled in pitch and volume to cause psychical pain to criminals, in extreme application by freezing the blood. "I enjoyed doing the antics of The Creeper," Ditko wrote to me in June 2014, but his collaboration with O'Neil was not without friction with both individuals polar opposites in their own political beliefs. Irritated by The Creeper expressing sorrow at the fiery death of a criminal in one issue, Ditko wrote a stern response on a later O'Neil script asserting that "once a person had committed a crime, they were a criminal for life," and it was the final incident that severed the creative relationship. While The Creeper came across as a traditional, if bizarre, superhero saga — with echoes of Ditko's Spider-Man apparent in the scenes of the lithe, acrobatic character leaping over city rooftops in similar and very distinctive poses — the conflicted solider/pacifist relationship of brothers Hank and Don in *Hawk and Dove* trod more familiar current territory for the artist. With a third element in the guise of the brothers' father Judge Irwin Hall, known for imposing maximum penalties on the convicted, introduced as a voice of "logic" to the brothers' differing personalities embodying force and compromise, Ditko's triangular-designed drama was stage-set for examinations of his Objectivist beliefs translated through the superhero medium with both editor Giordano and scripter Steve Skeates questioning whether comic books were the correct forum in which to do so. Both of Ditko's new series for DC were abruptly cut short and not by any editorial influence, as the artist suffered a second illness in a reoccurrence of the tuberculosis that interrupted his career over a decade previously. While not as serious or prolonged an episode, Ditko was absent again from the industry for a period of some months and during recovery may have found time to catch the *Spider-Man* animated television series that first aired on the ABC network on September 9, 1967 and ran for three seasons until June 14, 1970, all the while noting its lack of credit for the artist and absence of any royalty renumeration dropping through his letter-box. With its enduring theme song assuring that Spider-Man "does whatever a spider can," written

by multi-Academy award-winning lyricist, the appropriately-named Paul Francis Webster and composer J. Robert Harris, the cartoon series improved slightly on the limited animation range of Marvel's previous outing, with the first season also produced by Grantray-Lawrence but taken over by Krantz Film through the direction of Ralph Bakshi for its second and third, by this time syndicated, season. Despite its overuse of stock footage of the web-swinging, wall-crawling superhero, it utilized characters and imagery from Ditko's seminal run, gaining popularity with subsequent reruns and introducing the franchise to thousands of viewers.

As the progressive, tumultuous and epoch-defining decade of the 1960s came to an end, the remaining foundation stone supporting the creative powerhouse that took Goodman's stale and floundering line of comic books, transforming them into a cultural phenomenon and a collection of properties that netted the publisher around 15 million dollars when he sold his Management Magazine Company, including the comic book division, to Perfect Film and Chemical Corporation in July 1968, shifted loose when Jack Kirby phoned through to Stan Lee with the blunt news that he was resigning from Marvel. In the summer of 1970, after previously announcing to management that he would be leaving unless his annual salary was increased (currently around $35,000, a princely sum by 1969 standards), Kirby didn't wait for the response

Opposite page: Ditko, pencils and inks, original cover artwork, ***Beware the Creeper*** #2, July/August, 1968, ©1968 DC Comics. Right: Ditko, pencils and inks, original interior page artwork for ***Showcase*** #73, the first appearance of the Creeper, March/April, 1968, ©1968 DC Comics.

before deciding to take his leave of Marvel Comics. A year before, joining the millions of worldwide viewers captivated by America's historic July 20, 1969 moon-landing — even working the event into the narrative of one of his final issues of *Fantastic Four* — Kirby was thrilled to witness Neil Armstrong's first footprints on an alien world and wondered then if he should take his own "giant leap" into the unknown and respond to an offer from DC's Editor-in-Chief, Carmine Infantino. In truth, Kirby's dissatisfaction with his present employer concerned an issue separate from finance and mirrored Ditko's own reason for leaving four years previously — the recognition and due credit for the comic books he was writing as well as drawing for the company under Lee's system of production. Kirby left *Fantastic Four* with issue 102, a book he handed in only half-completed and took up a generous offer from Infantino to create his new work exclusively for DC Comics. He said, "As things went on (at Marvel), I began to work at home and longer came up to the office. I developed all the stuff at home and just sent it in. I had to come up with new ideas to help the strip sell. I was faced with the frustration of having to come up with new ideas and then having them taken from me. So, I was kind of caught in a box and I had to get out of that box, and then DC came along and gave me the opportunity to do it." In an April 1975 interview for UK fanzine *Fantasy Advertiser* Lee commented, "I really don't know why he left, I think it was a personal thing and Jack never told me. I've heard that he was tired of doing things he never owned, to copyright his characters, a share of the profit and so on. I wish I'd had the same thing and I don't blame him. The thing about Jack is, though he's a good story-man and artist, I feel he needs some control, some editing. He tends to get too wrapped up in what he wants to do he forgets what the reader might want. The trouble with Jack is that he's too imaginative and tries to put every idea he can think of down on every page and make it a whole new original thought and action. That isn't a good story. You have to build up a mood — take one idea and stretch it over a few pages to milk the utmost drama from it. It's a matter of pacing and Jack goes too fast; you don't have a chance to catch your breath reading his stories." While at Marvel, Kirby had previously been offered an Art Director staff position, overseeing all art that passed through the offices and an increased salary but not the writing credit that he sought. Lee said, "Many times in the past I had asked Jack to take an executive staff job at Marvel. I felt if he were willing, I'd give him my art director duties; he could supervise the artwork and I'd concentrate on the editing and handle the scripts. We would be full partners with his salary equaling mine. However, Jack never accepted the offer. He told me he'd prefer to freelance. I was disappointed because I felt that the two of us, working as a team, would have been dynamite. But that's what irritates me about people telling Jack how unfair it was that I made more money than he did. He could have had exactly the same financial arrangement as I did, but he never accepted it." But Kirby felt that he had encountered "A lot of ingratitude. It hasn't left me bitter; it's just that it shouldn't work out that way. If there's anybody who knows Stan Lee, I'm the guy who knows him. Stan Lee as a person is no better or worse than anybody else. I wasn't competing with Stan. I got along very well with Stan. We were very good friends. And, my God, I came up with an army of characters! I felt that his (Lee's) plans, somehow, didn't mesh with mine. Stan was already a publisher at that time and could call the shots. If you can call the shots on somebody, you win." Industry scuttlebutt was now awash with stories of credit-grabbing being the prime reason for Kirby's departure from Lee's Marvel with Joe Simon, a previous collaborator, making his own observations on the subject in a satirical strip he scripted that was published in a 1966 edition of humour magazine *Sick*, where an artist is shown subserviently bringing artwork to an editor, saying, "I'll make the changes, Sam. I draw so many different characters, I get confused sometimes." The cravat-wearing, tea-sipping, grinning editor responds, "Alright, do the whole book over and have it on my desk in an hour — we've got 20 other books to get out today," and finally, the punchline, "And don't forget to sign my name to it!" A similar, thinly-disguised dig appeared in DC's *Angel and the Ape* #2 in February 1969 in a story titled "The Most Fantastic Robbery in History," with writer/artist Bob Oksner presenting a panel showing two characters, resembling Lee and Roy Thomas, with the editor "Stan Bragg" declaring to his assistant, "Why are you so ungrateful? When you write good stories with good artwork, don't I sign it?" The story was inked, ironically enough, by Wally Wood.

As with Ditko, Thomas was a witness to the day when news of Kirby's resignation broke, stunning the members of Marvel's offices with John Buscema asking how they could possibly continue publishing the comic books without Kirby. Thomas wrote to me in 2013, "I remember when Jack quit Marvel for the first time. Stan told Sol Brodsky first and then me about the phone call he'd just had with Jack. Stan seemed confused, a little hurt and quite unhappy, naturally. But he never bad-mouthed Jack, that day or any other." Marie Severin, often drawing humorous caricatures passed around for staffers amusement, crafted her own tribute commemorating Kirby's exit by mounting a cigar butt the artist had discarded on his final visit to the offices, on a plaque with a hand-drawn speech bubble pointed towards it that read "I quit!" along with the caption "Jack Kirby's Cigar Butt." Severin hung it on the office wall in her own working space next to a 1970 calendar with the date July 12 marked with a notation. Present at both events that signaled the end of a particular era in Marvel Comics history, Roy Thomas mastered his craft as Stan Lee's protégé, then developed his own considerable writing and editorial skills, understanding and knowledgeable of the existing portfolio of Marvel characters and their continuity, eventually adding tremendously to their number himself. Thomas learnt quickly from Lee, with a simple edict remembered in summation, "I guess the greatest single thing that Stan ever taught me was, To tell the story." Putting this into practice, Thomas would enjoy a long run as writer of *The Avengers* writing the memorable "The Kree-Skrull War" saga in the late 1960s and recently used as a narrative backdrop in the movie *Captain Marvel* (2019). Thomas recalled of the artists he worked with on the title to me in 2013, "Don Heck was good and dependable, though not too thrilling. John Buscema was the absolute best artist on the Avengers, with great work coming in from him month after month, yet there was something special about Neal Adams' work. The deadline problems came about with Neal because of his over-commitment with other stuff and this coloured my feelings about our run on the book. But it resulted in the "Kree-Skrull War" (running through *Avengers* #89 to #97 between 1971/72) becoming even more of a landmark than it would otherwise be." Thomas would briefly revitalize the *X-Men* with Adams in the same period, then successfully and faithfully introduce Texas-born writer Robert E. Howard's 1930s pulp character Conan the Barbarian to comic books with its debut in December 1970. This departure in using material from existing franchises would spear-head a gradual but ultimately wide-reaching move for the company to licence other media properties for adaptation to its "mighty Marvel style," increasingly so as the decade progressed, in what would prove to be a significantly shrewd marketing decision. Thomas recalled to me, "It wasn't hard at all to convince Stan of the concept. He and I agreed we should go after a sword-and-sorcery character, but not necessarily Conan. Barry Smith — now Barry Windsor-Smith — got the art assignment because he was relatively new to the industry and he accepted the lower page rate the title had, plus I felt his art had a special quality that might work on Conan. John Buscema had been lined up to be the original artist but had to withdraw because his page rate was too high and Martin Goodman wanted to get the licensing fee back. I don't recall much about when I first met Barry, except I thought him very enthusiastic and it was definitely energizing to my writing of the title to see his art develop in the way it did. His attention to detail caused deadline problems as we went along but we dealt with it as best we could. Barry always worked away but never tried to blow the deadlines off. Of course, John eventually came onto the title with #25, after Barry left, and stayed with the character for the rest of his career. In fact, I would go so far as to say that John was first and foremost my favourite artist of all that I ever collaborated with. Of the new Conan stories that I wrote during this time, I probably liked 'The Citadel at the Centre of Time' the best, in the black-and-white magazine *Savage Sword of Conan* #9. John Buscema actually hated Alfredo Alcala's inking on that story, and on his pencils in general, but the readers liked it and I felt his detail (and to some extent Ernie Chan's in *Conan the Barbarian* and also Tony DeZuniga's illustrative style) helped keep a continuity going from the super-detailed artwork of Barry Smith's original work. I met John many times, though we were not really friends or anything of that sort. We mostly talked business. The original Robert E. Howard Conan stories, written in the 1930s, are eternal because they are elemental and because they loot from various historical periods to create a viable ancient world."

In an entirely different form of looting, the historic original art that Ditko produced for Marvel Comics, supposedly stored secure within the company, was beginning to appear for sale at conventions by the end of the decade with one report claiming that the entire Doctor Strange story from *Strange Tales* #129 was offered for $5 a page at the St. Louis World Science Fiction Convention in 1969 along with more Ditko work and hundreds of other pages from such artists as Kirby, Adams and Joe Kubert. The report further indicated that the sellers of the artwork were current employees of both Marvel and DC Comics but attributed no names to the particular two individuals. "A lot of original art was stolen from the companies by people within the companies," Ditko confirmed in a May 2013 letter to me. While many were happy to acquire the original art of Ditko's classic Marvel work at nominal prices, many more were keen to join in the growing tide of complaining anger leveled at the artists' contemporary offerings. "Fools talking, fools believing," was how Ditko dismissively regarded his critics, adding in a letter to me from June 2014, "Too many fans are copycat thinkers and responders. It's the old 'One neighbourhood dog barks at something and the rest of the neighbourhood dogs bark with the bark.' Few fans make claims based on their actual first-hand experience, abilities, or are qualified to judge a writer's or artist's work. Too many vocal fans want to be seen as publicly important with their opinions, complaints and I know this also about some professionals. It's pragmatism, truth is what works now, in the short term."

For Steve Ditko, the short-term as the decade of the 1970s dawned, involved producing as many pages of comic art as he possibly could in order to build a livable wage, filling Charlton titles such as *The Many Ghosts of Doctor Grave*, *Ghostly Tales* and *Ghost Manor*, working in an editorial-interference free zone for a dependable employer but seemingly trapped within a repetitive diet of 5-page "haunted house" type stories that had previously restricted his creativity at Lee's Marvel. Ditko had failed in his attempts to gain an audience tolerant to his personal expressions of a "rational and logical" superhero, but the dream of the liberties of self-publishing was not yet dead, though its road ahead would prove to be rocky.

ALL NEW STORIES and ART
CHARLTON COMICS
00658-272
APPROVED BY THE COMICS CODE AUTHORITY
GHOSTLY
TALES FROM THE HAUNTED HOUSE
NO. 92
FEB.
CDC
20¢
GHOSTLY TALES
TAKE IT AWAY!
LEAVE US ALONE!
FREE US!
STOP!
HA! HA! HA-HA! HA!
THERE IS NO ESCAPE FROM THE POWER OF THE "GHOST CATCHER"
HE-HE! HA HA! HA!
00658
VANDERCOOK

Chapter Five
Rise of the "Anti-hero" 1972-1989

"The attacks just spread. There were editors at both Marvel and DC Comics who wouldn't use me now and even pressured other editors not to give me any assignments," Steve Ditko wrote to me in April 2014, recalling an aspect of his 1970s comic book career that saw him struggling to receive regular work from the industry he had helped to reinvigorate in the preceding decade. He added, "So, a comic book industry that started out doing fictional/fantasy characters became restrictive, not open to someone's fiction/fantasy or hero. The then-editors, all comic book fans, seemed afraid of the creatively different; they didn't know how to judge anything objectively, only emotionally. Too many editors just refused to let buyers decide; refused to let buyers have choices with the widest range of fiction and fantasy. One shouldn't be surprised at the degree of anti-heroes in comic books today."

Something was certainly changing in American comic books of the early-to-mid 1970s, especially at the renovated "House of Ideas," with a fresh generation of young writers and artists entering the field, bringing with them new ideas, new artistic sensibilities and new ways of working. As the decade progressed, veteran creators such as Ditko or Kirby were increasingly regarded as "yesterday men" with their art styles reminiscent of past glories in a medium fast exploring new expression in the art and notably in the writing of a new breed of character creations. "What made Marvel Comics in the 1970s so different from comics before or after was that you had sophisticated stories told in dumb ways, as opposed to comics in the 1980/90s which were the exact opposite. Writers like Steve Gerber and Don McGregor were the kings of this — they were writing their lives down on paper, using comic books as a vehicle but essentially doing akin to what The Beatles were doing with music in the 1960s, telling their lives through their stories," British artist Phil Winslade said to me in 2013 describing Marvel's 1970s output and the effect of their brash new comic book creators. "It's only natural, young people coming in and wanting to take over, get rid of all those above them. Everything keeps changing with every new generation," Ditko conceded in a letter to me from November 2014.

Opposite page: Ditko, pencils and inks, original cover art from ***Ghostly Tales*** #92, February, 1972, ©1972 Charlton Comics.

Roy Thomas became Editor-in-Chief at Marvel in 1972, the first to succeed Stan Lee in a role he'd held permanently since 1945, with Lee taking a back seat to concentrate on college lecture tours and exploring media licensing deals but still a presence at the company's offices. "Stan was very much still around in NYC until 1980/81 — he was there and in charge even if I was Editor-in-Chief," Thomas wrote to me in 2013, continuing, "With all the scripting I did as well, it meant I just worked hard as hell, but it got difficult. I was relieved to pass the Editor-in-Chief post on; though I was unhappy it hadn't worked out better. The bullpen changed greatly from the time I first got there to this point. I liked it better when there were fewer people around." Returning to work in the industry at this time after a child-rearing absence, artist Ramona Fradon wrote to me in 2013, "I was amazed at how things had changed in the years I'd been away, this was 1973 and the 60s had done their thing! Compared to the staid, conventional offices I remembered at DC, Marvel was chaotic. There were no offices, just cubicles inhabited with long-haired, scruffy people half-buried under papers, coffee cups and various other things that were spilling out into the aisles. But the biggest shock of all to me were the actual stories. There was this Amazon named Thundra in *Fantastic Four* who kept pummelling The Thing. I had retired before the women's movement changed the parameters of acceptable super-heroine behaviour, and I had to make a drastic attitude adjustment. Everybody seemed to be suffering from some kind of angst, unlike the straight-forward and simple adventures of Aquaman I had been used to." Under Thomas' editorship, the expedient "Marvel Method" process of production continued to be used with the young writer taking charge of Lee's seasoned juggling act as additional new titles were added to the workload regularly. Fradon continued, "Roy called me one day and asked me if I'd like to do an issue of *The Cat*. It was a female character that had been drawn and written by women, and I guess they were looking for another woman to carry it on. I was totally confused when he handed me a single paragraph and expected me to create a 17-page story out of it, and, of course, my lefty brain immediately realized that I would be drawing and writing a story without getting paid for both!"

From a staff of just Stan Lee and a secretary in the late 1950s, through the universe-building freelancers and growing production staff of the 1960s, the Marvel Comics offices were now an accurate reflection of the bustling New York streets outside — full of young-blooded idealists coming into the industry with their own particular visions and influences. Some wanted to continue the traditions set down by Lee, Kirby and Ditko, while others wished to express increasingly personal statements through their own comic book creations and the once-sedate office environment had changed accordingly in tempo with the new decade. "The Marvel offices were a bevy of activity with everyone busy moving paper from one place to another, proof-reading, art corrections with lots of original art everywhere. It was way pre-digital age, everyone was enthusiastic, and it was really something to see," artist Val Mayerik said to me in December 2018, adding, "The offices then were small — an elevator ride to the fifth floor of just about half-a-floor of an office building on Madison Avenue. Stan had a corner office and was very accessible, you could just walk right in and ask him a question. There was no security, nobody wore badges. It was a completely different time."

Creator of cyborg-soldier Deathlok the Demolisher in 1974, the late artist Rich Buckler remembered the period's frantic pace of production when he wrote to me in 2012, "The whole time I worked at Marvel I wasn't on staff or on an hourly wage like John Romita or Larry Lieber. So, I had to work fast and work a lot, or I wasn't earning. I was always working against the clock — we all were! I drew many covers in-house at the Marvel offices and they were all usually done as fast as possible. The way I remember it, while drawing all of those covers it seemed like there was barely any time even for erasing let alone re-drawing. Romita was the Art Director and seemed to be the one guy who knew most what Stan liked. He could be a bit heavy-handed at times, but I considered myself lucky to be there so I never complained."

Marv Wolfman also recalled the time as "Totally insane but lots of fun. Everyone was a huge comics fan and we were all trying to push comics further and further." Wolfman became editor of Marvel's black-and-white line of comic magazine titles in 1974 before ascending to Editor-in-Chief from 1975-76, succeeding Len Wein, who in turn, took over from Roy Thomas in the position. "We were the new guys with new ideas in town, and that's why the Marvel offices environment was buzzing," wrote artist Frank Brunner to me in 2012, continuing, "I knew many of my fellow young Turks: Bernie Wrightson, Mike Kaluta , Jim Starlin and Gerry Conway, but the big hangout was at Neal Adams' Continuity Studios a few blocks away. I have many memories from those days but I'll pick a *Doctor Strange* related one as I was already a big fan of Steve Ditko's original work on the series when I became its artist in 1974. I was in New York briefly (I'd moved to the Bay Area in northern California) and, because I was doing *Doctor Strange* at the time and knew the girl up at the Marvel office who opened all the fan mail. I grabbed some unopened letters to look over and see what the readers were saying about the book. The very first one I opened up was from Hawaii and inside was a huge joint of rolled marijuana (Maui Wowie)! We went into some empty room, passed the joint around and after a few minutes we all had the same thought.... LUNCH!!!! (Laughs) And when we finally decided where to eat, after a rather wild taxi ride across town, I thought I must be doing the right kind of stories in *Doctor Strange*! (Not just for kids.) The fans were great and often showed their appreciation in different ways. That whole period was crazy fun."

Paul Gulacy was another young artist receiving accolades for his highly-detailed artwork on *Shang-Chi, Master of Kung Fu* — the first of Marvel's mid-1970s titles to capitalize on the current popularity craze of Kung Fu and marital arts in general and the extraordinary screen presence of Bruce Lee, together with his mysterious death at a young age, in particular. Gulacy wrote to me in 2012, "Often, I visited the Marvel offices in New York, and the halls were crackling with energy and excitement. Regularly I would see Stan, John Romita, John Verpoorten and a whole bunch of production people. Once in a while, other 'new' artists would also visit including Walt Simonson and Howard Chaykin. We were the new kids on the block. Bear in mind that some of these guys were living in the city and some were like me freelancing across the country. For me it was this crazy gig, hanging out with my old friends, going to clubs and parties, chasing girls and getting high!"

Despite the amount of work consistently generated by the major publishers and the increasing number of new creators needed to fulfill it, freelancers outside of New York City were still rare and unlikely to garner frequent assignments as P. Craig Russell wrote to me saying, "I worked in Ohio for my first 20 months so that I could finish college but found that by the end I wasn't receiving work from Marvel and so moved to New York in January of 1974. By showing my face around the office I was able to re-establish myself."

Paul Levitz also recalled to the author in 2018, "I think American comics had perhaps 200 creatives working steadily circa 1972, and all but a handful of them were in the New York metro area. Only Western (Gold Key) had a second office in LA and a pack of freelancers out there." Part of the new wave artist immigrants from outside New York State, Val Mayerik said to me in 2018, "I was 22 when I first worked for Marvel. I met Dan Adkins, who lived not far from me in Ohio and took a bunch of drawings to him, knowing that he worked then as an inker for Marvel. He liked them and invited me to come and work with him, along with P. Craig Russell, who'd also approached him about a month earlier. So, we both camped out at Dan's place for six months and helped Dan ink some stuff. When Dan thought we were good enough, he called Roy Thomas, who first gave us work. So, in 1972, we took a greyhound bus, all three of us, and visited Marvel and met Stan, John Romita, Sr., and Marie Severin, who coloured a great deal of Marvel books at the time."

Russell wrote to me in 2018, "I recall sleeping in the reception room at Marvel for a couple of nights. I was working on pencilling my second issue of *War of the Worlds/ Killraven* which was also my first inking job, and first colouring job and it was behind schedule. Hence, not leaving the office for 48 hours, working all night, getting a few hours' sleep, and being awakened when the 'suits' came in the following morning. I remember one giving me the quizzical stink-eye as he passed by as I roused myself from the sofa in the front office. I had zero dealings with Stan. I got on an elevator with him once and he gave me a sideways glance, as if to say 'who is this kid?' and that was it."

If the Marvel offices appeared to be a disjointed portrait of barely-controlled chaos, this was in stark contrast to the "editors in suits and ties, clean and orderly desk tops and shelves, a quiet professional atmosphere" over at DC, as writer David Michelinie, who entered the industry around this time, remembered to me in 2019. "It was a publishing house, as opposed to the fan-oriented chaos of Marvel," he added. Paul Levitz also recalled, "In the DC offices in 1972, the older guys were counting down to retirement, hoping the field would last that long but being professional and serious to the end. The new kids were excited to be on the inside, full of enthusiasm but looking to what the next gig could be after comics." Before his promotion, Roy Thomas was the first scripter to succeed Stan Lee on *Amazing Spider-Man* (beginning for a short run with issue 101 October 1971) where he co-created Morbius, The Living Vampire in the pages of the title. Thomas wrote to me, "I loved Spider-Man but didn't care much to write him. Mainly I remember Gil Kane and I having fun devising Marvel's first vampire character Morbius in the title. The Comics Code had just changed, relaxing some rules and now allowing vampires, werewolves and zombies to appear in comics for the first time since the 1950s. This happened just as Stan had to leave the comic for a few months, so I wound up doing the story from scratch. Gil Kane and I were originally planning to use Dracula, but Stan said he wanted a more super villain kind of vampire and so Morbius was born." This relaxation of the Code in 1971 heralded a period of renewed popularity in monsters made traditional by Universal Pictures with Marvel publishing *Tomb of Dracula*, *Werewolf by Night*, and *The Frankenstein Monster* in quick succession along with many other iterations of horror-based characters, which, for a time, took prominence over Marvel's superhero line. Despite gorgeously rendered artwork by Eisner-trained artist Mike Ploog on other titles, the stand out and longest running book from the entire crop was *Tomb of Dracula* when the series was eventually in the hands of writer Marv Wolfman and artists Gene Colan and Tom Palmer, a few issues after its debut in April 1972. Colan, a veteran of the industry, who Wolfman remembered to me as a "wonderful man and a great artist, nobody drew like Gene. I only have fond thoughts of him and miss him greatly," had an atmospheric, cinematic art style with the ability to convincingly render a wide range of human facial expressions in shadow textured, realistic environments that lent itself well to the gothic adventures of the *Lord of the Vampires* and its supporting cast of characters. Wolfman had joined Marvel originally in 1972 after spending some years previously working for DC and remembered an incident to me in 2018 which inadvertently struck a blow for creator recognition rights along with highlighting how petty some alterations made by the Comics Code were before the loosening of some rules and how strong its influence could still be felt, "The DC horror comic books back then did not include creator credits. Each horror comic had a host character introduce the stories. Gerry Conway wrote the intro pages in *House of Secrets* and, knowing I wrote it, joked that the story was 'told to the host by a wandering Wolfman.' The Comics Code rejected this because back then werewolves, wolfmen, vampires, etc. were not permitted. DC informed them that Wolfman was my real name and they weren't trying to get around the rule. The Code insisted that DC credit my full name, so that's how I got my first credit on the horror books. After that, every writer received credit."

Prior to the selling of his company to the conglomerate now known as Cadence Industries, Martin Goodman had renegotiated a better distribution deal with DC publisher Jack Liebowitz before breaking with it entirely and signing a limitless contract in 1969 with Curtis Circulation Company. Retained within the comic book division as publisher, Goodman was now free to pursue a strategy of market dominance by aggressive product saturation and, together with its ever-increasing roster of colour comics, Marvel's line of black-and-white magazine-format titles that Wolfman headed up spawned a multitude of additions with an aim to grab that particular market-share from its prime originator, Warren Publishing. It begun tentatively with *Savage Tales* (May 1971), *Dracula Lives* (June 1973) and *Savage Sword of Conan* (August 1974) but soon grew to monster proportions with titles as diverse as *Planet of the Apes*, *Deadly Hands of Kung Fu*, *Monsters Unleashed*, *Marvel Preview* and *Tales of the Zombie*, to name just a few of the initially one-dollar range.

The magazine-sized comic book was a format that was favoured by Stan Lee and was something he'd previously tried once before some years back in April 1968 with the short-lived *Spectacular Spider-Man* title. The 35-cent title was twice the size (and price) of a regular comic book with a painted cover by Harry Rosenbaum, interior art enhanced with ink-wash details by John Romita and Jim Mooney and a script from Lee that contained the usual costumed slug-fests, coupled with a more "adult themed" storyline in which the ensemble of characters talked about politics a lot. A second issue appeared in this magazine format but now in full colour and returning to Marvel basics by proclaiming the return of the Green Goblin on its Romita-painted cover. The experiment was quickly wrapped up with the title being cancelled, having failed in its bid to find a whole new demographic of reader and instead finding itself lost and buried on magazine racks.

During Marvel's 1970s magazine explosion, however, its success saw the company with a sudden need to employ artists adept at intricate linework that would shine within the monochromatic format and appear sophisticated enough to appeal to a slightly older audience, justifying its one-dollar price tag (five times the price of a regular 20-cent book). Marvel needed quick, high quality artists willing to work at a lower page rate than their colour comic counterparts to fill the pages of their magazine line, and like Warren, the company looked beyond U.S. shores to recruit artists from the Philippines and South America. One such artist was Pablo Marcos, who left his native Peru in 1970 to migrate to New York with his family and work for Warren's *Eerie* and *Creepy* magazines before his muscular, visceral art found a perfect home in Marvel's black-and-white line — especially on Conan and Simon Garth, the zombie character he refined with writer Steve Gerber ("I worked on Steve's Zombie scripts from the third issue until the end of the series. Steve was a great writer and an extraordinary person.")

Marcos first met Sol Brodsky at Skywald Publishing, not long before the Marvel veteran returned to the company. "When Sol left Skywald and went back to Marvel he promised me he would help me find work there also. At the time, he was the assistant to Stan Lee. I constantly saw Stan at the offices, and he would often assign me different covers to draw. Stan was very active, sociable, guiding us, expressing his ideas across to the artists in a gentle but stern manner. I felt comfortable at the Marvel offices. I worked on over 100 covers for the Marvel UK line, under the direction of Larry Lieber. I was producing four covers a month at the time, in addition to some interior pages. I drew many for *Planet of the Apes* and *Captain Britain*, although I enjoyed working on the covers for *Dracula Lives* the most. One cover I especially remember showed the hero Captain Britain attacking the Queen of England! Back then, I was able to ink 45 pages in a week when working on them 12-14 hours daily! On a regular 32-page comic, where it involved both pencilling and inking, it used to take me about a day per page."

With Goodman and company shareholders intent on market domination by ambitious publishing schedules with a constant emphasis on variety through volume, the licensing deals that Marvel would sign as the decade continued were diverse and plentiful, adding a bizarre mix of characters and concepts published alongside its usual superhero fare, the majority of which existed outside the connectivity of the Marvel Universe. Some licenses mined further properties derived from pulp fiction such as *John Carter, Warlord of Mars*; *Tarzan* and *Doc Savage* while others used established and currently popular franchises like *Planet of the Apes*, recently airing as a syndicated television show with actor Roddy McDowall linking the show with the five movies that preceded it, beginning with the iconic Franklin J. Schaffner directed 1968 original with Charlton Heston in the starring role.

Others still championed currently-dormant movie franchises such as *Godzilla* and *2001: A Space Odyssey* together with adaptations of recently released movies including 1976's *Logan's Run* with Marvel's short lived comic book version of the movie notable for its early artwork by future superstar artist George Perez , whose detailed style developed on the series before becoming synonymous with character cluttered superhero team books. Co-author of the original 1965 novel that postulated a future society's brutal solution to surplus population, and owner of Perez's original art for the cover of *Logan's Run* #1 (January 1976), William F. Nolan recalled the MGM film to me in 2011 as "a fun, rather silly popcorn drama. Colourful but basically empty and with several lapses in logic. The changes the studio made took the depth out of the novel, and I did not like the old man with the cats. I thought that Michael York and Jenny Agutter were superb, however, and elevated their script roles. When they re-make it, it should be dark and savage, similar in tone to *Blade Runner* The original movie was far too bland with Logan vulnerable in his costume 'pajamas.'"

An altogether different Logan, code named Wolverine, was a feisty, claw-handed scrapper revealed in the final panel of *Incredible Hulk* #180, before appearing on the cover of the following issue, cover-dated November 1974. An ancillary character for the book, introduced as a third dramatic element in a battle scene, Wolverine became part of an ensemble of "outsider" characters in a revival of the "All-new, all-different *X-Men*" in May 1975, later developing as one of Marvel's most popular and bankable properties in his solo outings, both in comic books and movies. But, in an example of Ditko's comment in a letter to me that "there was never a strict division of labour in comics," the specific individual contributions of the small committee of creators involved in the introduction of Wolverine, each playing their own part to ensure a monthly publication hit its schedule, are clouded by time and memory.

Roy Thomas certainly coined the name *adamantium* for the unbreakable metal Wolverine's extendable claws and skeleton are made of ("I'm really pleased to have stumbled upon such a great name for this metal which Wolverine's body is laced with. I hope someday a real metal or element is named after it," wrote Thomas to me in 2013) and also had a role in the character's genesis. Thomas said, "As to the creation of Wolverine, 'created' is a word of infinite stretchability. Yes, Wolverine was my idea — I told Len Wein I wanted a character who was short, even shorter-tempered, nasty (like a real wolverine), and Canadian. That was a creative act, sure, just like Stan's few sentences to me about the origin (and name) 'Man-Thing' could be considered as 'creating' the character. But Len Wein was the guy who came up with the story (stories), and my understanding — based on things he's said — is that he conferred with Romita on the costume and look. Even so, since Herb Trimpe added to the story while drawing it, I feel Wolverine really has four creators. Len Wein might feel he has two. I don't know how John Romita feels."

Herb Trimpe, the artist who drew Wolverine's first appearance, remembered there being two prime creators of the character, but neither of them were the actual team assigned to that issue, himself included. The late artist wrote to me his views on the subject in 2011, "I'd like to set the record straight on Wolverine. It was Roy Thomas and John Romita, Sr., who co-created the character — and by that, I mean the concept and also the visual appearance. The two worked together. I know because I was there. I did have the privilege of bringing the character to life in the pages of *Hulk* with Len Wein, although none of us knew at the time what Wolverine was destined to become. I've been asked by art collectors to recreate the cover drawing for *Incredible Hulk* #181 at least fourteen times! And Wolverine is certainly the most requested-for sketch I get at conventions." Trimpe continued, recalling his signature run on the title, which visually defined the appearance of Hulk for the period, "In retrospect, I would consider my run on Hulk as the highlight of my comics' career. It was certainly during a time when working in comics was the most fun. As for the character itself, I really thought that Stan and Jack nailed the original concept of the Hulk as being very much in the Jekyll and Hyde vein and I preferred that to superheroes. I really don't like superheroes all that much! (laughs) I had help on the first few issues I drew from Marie Severin who'd been drawing the title previously. Marie is a very funny, but astutely critical lady. Nothing got by her, but she was more than willing to help with anything you might need. As I got into the run, I worked mostly work from home. We lived in Manhattan at the time, and it wasn't far from the Marvel offices. A couple of blocks once, then a short ride on the subway another time. I liked to ink my own work because I could go easier on the pencils."

Roy Thomas was involved in the creation of many of Marvel's 1970s period character additions within the fast-paced production procedures of the times, and along with Wolverine and Morbius, his extensive co-creator credits include: Iron Fist ("I came up with the name the night I saw my first Kung Fu movie, which had an iron fist ritual in it. I went straight to Gil Kane, and from there we made it up together. The costume design was all Gil, with my kibitzing as I wanted the design burned into his chest"); Ultron ("A great design by John Buscema, based on a robot in *Captain Video* #3 which I showed him"); Killraven ("I came up with the concept of doing a comic bringing the H.G. Wells Martians back to earth 100 years after the original *War of the Worlds* novel (first published in 1898). I further based some concepts on the Artilleryman's speech as to what the world would be like under Martian rule and then brought in Neal Adams. He started working on the hero who would eventually become Killraven, though at that time he was called The Junkman. I bowed out of the series after that inaugural issue, too busy with a hundred other things"); Union Jack ("This is one of the few characters, along with Squadron Sinister, that I ever designed by drawing out a sketch. Then, Frank Robbins defined and improved it. Kirby just used it to draw a beautiful first cover for Union Jack's premiere appearance in *Invaders* #8"); Valkyrie ("I was very happy about this idea"); Brother Voodoo ("Stan wanted to bring back the title *Strange Tales* and needed a character to launch it. As a young teen I'd made up a Dr. Voodoo character, so I suggested a character by name. Stan said no to that but instead said make it Brother Voodoo. I gave a few roughs suggestions to Len Wein and turned him loose on it"); and Carol Danvers, later to become Ms Marvel ("I'm regretful about that last name, since it's also Supergirl's surname"). The kid from Missouri had learnt well from Lee, bringing his own considerable skills and ingenuity to bear and emerging as one of Marvel's most prolific creators during this era of continual creative and managerial flux for the company.

Maintaining his high-volume output for Charlton Comics, Ditko was concurrently seeking new avenues for the publication of *Mr. A* and his other Objectivist-informed works but was wary of contributing to comic fanzines after previous adverse experiences of non-returned original artwork by one and printing an image of Mr. A on a cover with a pink coloured background by another, which "shocked" and "dismayed" the artist, considering it contrary to the character's literal black-and-white identity and leading him to exclaim in a letter to its editor Bill Schelly, "Why is it I get burned every time I do something for the fan press?"

Ditko's first attempt at self-publishing came in 1973, in association with comic fanzine publisher Joe Brancatelli who organised the production of an over sized, one-shot edition titled *Mr. A* containing reprints and one new story. The partnership was brief, with the edition selling under half of its 5,000-copy print run and Brancatelli selling the remaining issues on to fledging publisher Bruce Hershenson. Picking up the mantle, Hershenson would print the Ditko one-shot titles *The Avenging World* in late 1973 followed over a year later in 1975 by *Wha...!?* and a revised edition of *Mr. A*, but with their high cover prices of 60-75 cents, the titles would remain largely unsold in the handful of speciality stores dotted across America and languish in dusty boxes with the publisher.

A professional poker player throughout the 1970s and 1980s, Hershenson would go on to set-up the online movie memorabilia auction site "eMoviePoster" in 1999, creating a successful, multi-million dollar company in the process. Back in the early part of the 1970s, Jack Kirby's work for

DC Comics following his departure from Marvel was characteristically grandiose in scope, comprising separate books *Jimmy Olsen*; *The New Gods*; *Mister Miracle* and *The Forever People* with stories that connected to a wider narrative canvas under the umbrella title of *The Fourth World*, and as visually dynamic and eye-catching as any of his previous work.

On all of the books, Kirby was editor, writer and penciller with some input into the selection of inkers assigned to the titles, which is how artist Rich Bucker received encouragement from an industry legend during his early attempts to enter the industry. He wrote to the author "My friend Shel Dorf arranged for me to audition as an inker on one of Jack's new books for DC. Jack thought that my inking didn't quite cut it, but he was impressed with my drawing. Jack told me, 'Rich, if you're ever in New York, look up Stan Lee at Marvel Comics and tell him I said to give you a job!' That was how he put it—always unequivocal and direct—that was Jack. A couple of years ago, I saw Stan and reminded him of that story. He replied that he remembered giving me my first Marvel assignment but felt compelled to point out that he would never do something just because Jack had told him to do it. He seemed quite sensitive about that. I remember clearly his exact words as he corrected me, 'More probably, Rich, I gave you that assignment because I am such a wonderful guy.' Going back to Jack, I remember one time when I imposed upon him to explain how he worked. I was hoping for some valuable insight into his drawing techniques and his creative process. Well, Jack said he never analysed that and didn't know how to explain what he did, he just did it. I found that answer both curious and totally unexpected because I was absolutely certain that Kirby was some kind of genius and always knew what he was doing."

Above: Roy Thomas, 2013, ©2013 Dylan Almond. Opposite page: Jack Kirby at the San Diego Comic-Con circa 1970s.

But the complete creative freedom that enticed Kirby over to DC proved to be a primary reason why his *Fourth World* books fell below expectations of sales and consumer acceptance, with the artist now providing self-penned, dense and peculiarly phrased dialogue to accompany the stream of inspired but unrelentless concepts that emerged from him, editorially unchecked, with Kirby's writing skills revealed as a poor cousin to his artistic ones.

In an interview for Tomorrow Publishing's *Comic Book Artist* #1, published in 1998, Dick Giordano said, "Jack was being paid more money for a page rate than anybody else at the time. Carmine was trying to beat Marvel by getting Jack Kirby, their co-creator. Sales on the *Fourth World* books weren't bad by today's standards but they were bad then, based on what we were paying Jack. Carmine didn't want to admit defeat, and it cost him a lot in pride in honour to have gone out and gotten Kirby and then have to say, 'I'm sorry we can't go ahead with them.' I think that Carmine was looking for a magic bullet, but Kirby wasn't it."

Kirby followed up with two new titles unrelated to his confused, brilliant and floundering comic book epic, including *Kamandi* and *Omac,* but the glow of the novelty of his tenure at DC had substantially dimmed, and the artist would soon be returning to the company headed up by individuals he had recently lampooned in an issue of *Mister Miracle*. Roy Thomas wrote to me, "That character was Houseroy, and I wasn't amused, but it didn't bother me all that much, either. Houseroy was depicted as a side-kick to another Kirby character, 'Funky Flashman,' and it was Stan that Jack was mostly aiming at, not me. But, like Stan, who arranged it, I was delighted to see Jack eventually come back to Marvel in the mid-1970s."

Granted a similar deal to the one he enjoyed at DC, Kirby returned to Marvel late 1975 to write and pencil his earlier co-creations Captain America and Black Panther along with new characters Machine Man; Devil Dinosaur and his final great contribution to Marvel lore, The Eternals. While continuing to insist on scripting and editing his own books, Kirby worked with Lee on one last project in 1978, a Silver Surfer graphic novel titled *The Ultimate Cosmic Experience*, published by Fireside Books in association with Marvel and marking the first entry from the company in the newly-christened format. It was the final bow of a creative partnership of incredible achievement and the original art to the cover with a Kirby-designed image of the Silver Surfer rendered in paint by artist Earl Norem proudly hung on the wall of Stan Lee's bedroom during his final years as a visual reminder to the editor of treasured glories past. The character was one that Lee felt a great affinity towards, at one point insisting that no one else should write his stories and provide the brooding, contemplative scripting of the Surfer's plaintive observations of humanity. For Kirby, who created the character to be an amoral being of superior standing and felt that Lee's appropriation as a eulogising philosopher was the exact opposite, his own rejected original art for the graphic novel's cover would have served to stimulate an entirely different set of memories, and by the end of 1978, the artist would leave Marvel once again and very soon, the entire comic book industry altogether.

"It was Disney that first inspired me to draw," Val Mayerik said to the author in 2018, continuing, "There was a weekly television show I never missed, and my parents took me to all the Disney animated releases at the time. I devoured the comic book adaptations of these films and also loved Carl Barks' art in the 'Uncle Scrooge' title." Such influences would later surface when the artist co-created Marvel Comics' unlikeliest cultural success of the 1970s — the cigar-smoking, world-weary, highly opinionated Howard the Duck. For a time, the satire-stuffed series was one of Marvel's top-selling books of the mid-1970s, briefly out selling even *Spider-Man*, with the character receiving national press exposure by running a spoof presidential campaign in 1976, America's Bicentennial election year, and picking up thousands of real votes, perhaps from those disgruntled with the other non-fictional choices on offer during the highly fractious, après Watergate political period.

Howard appeared in a monthly comic book, a syndicated daily newspaper strip and eventually made such a quack that, in time, the lawyers at Disney took notice of its success and visibility, legally forcing Marvel to radically alter the appearance of Howard, including the wearing of pants, to disassociate the character from its own precious Donald Duck. The writer and soul of Howard the Duck, this improbable cultural rebel, was Steve Gerber, a prolific and highly original writer, who essentially used the cartoon-like character as his personal mouthpiece to espouse views and satirize many aspects of 1970s America.

In writing that veered from genius to insanity, with the alien Howard reacting to and sharing verbose and damning observations of the world of "hairless apes" he'd been thrown into, Gerber's highly personalised approach and idiosyncratic language skills created a unique and engaging reading experience and something far different from what the medium of comic books and the expectations of what the adventures of a cartoon duck should yield. Gerber himself summed it up quite succinctly when he said, "The book is existentialist, and its main joke is that there is no joke. Life's most serious and most incredibly dumb moments are often distinguishable only by a momentary point of view."

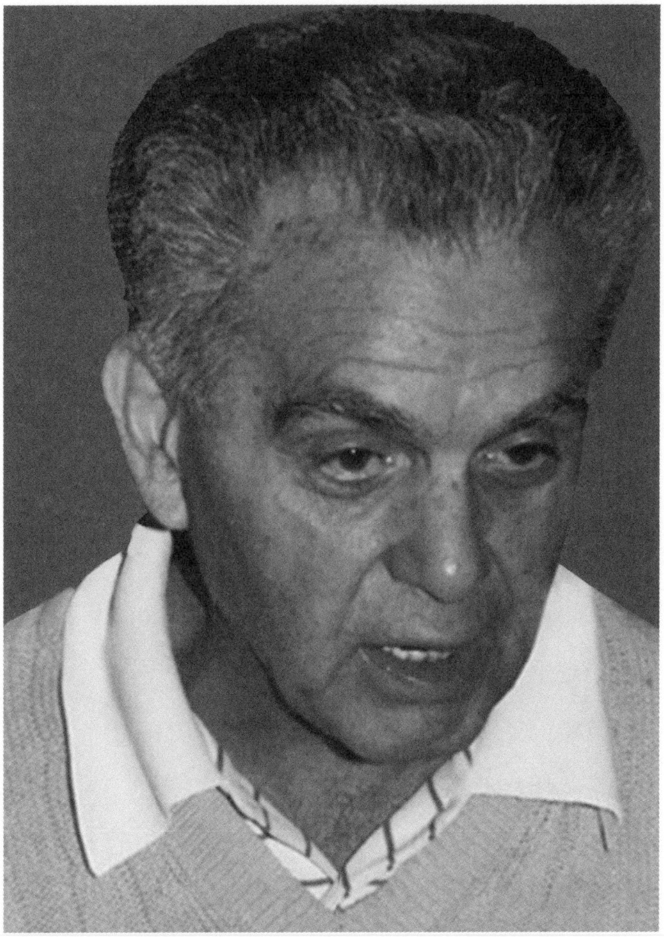

Contrast that with the view of screenwriter Gloria Katz who, in adapting the comic to the screen for George Lucas in a much-derided 1986 movie, declared, "It's a film about a duck from outer space. It's not supposed to be an existential experience." The movie would render the character undesirable for media translation until recent, brief cameo appearances in Marvel Studio's *Guardians of the Galaxy* movies revived awareness of Howard's acerbic charms.

Steve Gerber was a comic book writer best associated with Howard, but his time at Marvel in the early to middle-1970s was one of high productivity and fresh originality. Following a long run on *The Defenders*, during which he revived the *Guardians of the Galaxy*, he also dug up a Zombie character from Marvel's 1950s Atlas era, retooling it as Simon Garth in *Tales of the Zombie*. Gerber defined the emphatic nature of Man-Thing during his tenure on the title, which hit its peak in December 1974 with the disturbingly realist "Song-Cry of the Living Dead Man" story in *Man-Thing* #12 and also created new characters for Marvel including Starhawk and Omega the Unknown. Gerber had written the first comic book appearances of glam rockers Kiss, initially in an issue of *Howard the Duck* and then in a magazine that was not only authorized by the platinum-selling recording artists but also contained traces of their own blood in the printed ink, proven within by photographs of all members, in full stage makeup and costume, receiving extractions for that purpose.

This move by Marvel to license comic books contributed to or based on real-life stars from the music industry produced random one-shots, like a Beatles illustrated life story or *Marvel Premiere* #50 December 1979 featuring horror shock rocker Alice Cooper in a story written around his current "From the Inside" LP release. At the time, Marvel Comics were definitely cool-by-association, with *Paul McCartney Wings 1975* "Venus and Mars" LP including a track titled "Magneto and Titanium Man" along with images of the characters, lifted directly from comic books, projected onstage during his concerts and Marc Bolan remarking in a 1976 interview, just a year before his untimely death in an automobile crash, "I've been into Marvel since 1967. The Silver Surfer, in particular, was one I liked and Doctor Strange was another. At that time, they were very weird compared to the other comics on the market. I'd like to write some comics for Marvel. I've actually got a book of science-fiction stories coming out soon. There's a couple of superheroes in it. One's a God from another planet. These super heroes aren't really like Marvel's, but they could be. Stan was very much into the idea of my doing this. It was lovely to meet him, really, he's a hustler, a solid gold easy hustler!"

In the 1980s, the author wrote material on English rock legend David Bowie including a concert tour book *Glass Idol* (Omnibus Press 1987), where I accompanied the tour across Europe, taking photographs of the concerts and notes for the book. On his appropriately named "Glass Spider" Tour of 1987, I met and spoke with Bowie on numerous occasions and, knowing his fondness for comics, once asked him about Marvel Comics of the 1960s and what he remembered of them. He recalled Jack Kirby's work on *Fantastic Four* then cited Steve Ditko's *Doctor Strange* and *Spider-Man* as the thing which "really impacted" him. He described the art simply as "fucking genius." And this was at a time when the superstar's stage set was a gigantic, 60 foot spider! Arachnids were a familiar reference for Bowie ("Spiders from Mars") and during his own semi-reclusive years while recovering from or battling recurring health issues, the singer was spotted in a rare public sighting while attending a pre-run preview of *Spider-Man: Turn Off the Dark* theatre show in November 2010.

On his final album, "Blackstar," released just two days before his death, Bowie sings "I'm not a Marvel star" on the title song "Blackstar." When Bowie died on January 10, 2016, the iconic entertainer had created art from his death with his final work unflinchingly addressing the issue, and a global interest story became also very much a New York one, as the singer had found family, happiness and security in the city he loved in the last decades of his life. During correspondence, I mentioned to Ditko the remark that Bowie had made to me nearly 30 years previously as we discussed the passing of the star and the upcoming sale of his art collection. He wrote in 2016, "It's news to me that he was attracted to my *Spider-Man* material. David Bowie did get a lot of newspaper space over here. I did read that he wanted to be cremated, his ashes to be spread over the ocean, he didn't want any burial plot for people visiting, some kind of shrine. He certainly was an art collector — fine art — 'over 400 pieces' — a personal museum! It had to give him a lot of pleasure and a peace of mind." (With this letter, Ditko included a cutting on Bowie titled "David Bowie was a Time Traveler from our Hyper-personalized Future" taken from the April 2016 issue of Reason magazine, to illustrate his current reading around the subject.)

I informed Ditko that in 1975, Bowie, together with his then-wife Angie (herself cast in the role of Black Widow for a proposed *Daredevil* television series that never got off the ground) were in casual talks with Stan Lee about the possibility of a Bowie-written Marvel comic. In "Stan's Soapbox" printed in all November 1975 dated Marvel comics, Lee wrote, "Hi to Angelic Angela Bowie and her titanically talented hubby, Dashin' David Bowie. The three of us are planning a real far-out surprise for Marveldom Assembled, if we can ever get together long enough to nail it down!" When I asked if Ditko may have considered returning to Marvel back then for the project, should it have ever come to pass or if Bowie requested his involvement, he surprisingly replied, "I might have done with an actual script depending on the actual content," thereby raising the tantalising, if long-lost, possibility of a David Bowie-written, Steve Ditko-drawn Marvel comic book! "So, he had his fascination with Marvel Comics. What could have developed can't be known. It remains another 'could have,'" Ditko logically concluded.

Recalling the writer/creator of Howard the Duck, collaborator Val Mayerik said to me, "Steve was a very nice guy, very amiable with creative ideas and a great writer. He was a little on the cynical side, which is no surprise if you've ever read any of his work. The kind of guy you could sit down with in a bar, talk about general things and have a good time. I'm not telling tales out of school when I say that he was chronically, almost pathologically, late with his work. All the projects he worked on eventually got killed because of this and artists had to work doubly hard to catch up in order to meet deadlines. It happened with me and Steve a couple of times, on a series called *Void Indigo* in particular. But for the most part, I loved working with him." Gerber perhaps provided an accurate description of himself when he wrote in one issue of *Howard the Duck* that "a cynic is just a fallen idealist, right?"

Comic readers love origin tales and Howard the Duck's is fairly unusual. He originally waddled onto the pages of *Adventures into Fear* #19 (December 1973) in a disposable cameo role for a *Man-Thing* story where he eventually meets his demise by falling, mid-quest, into a dimensional void. "Howard was created quickly and easily," Mayerik recalled to me, continuing, "They weren't full scripts in those days at Marvel. Usually three or four pages of a plot and it was pretty much up to the artist to determine the numbers of panels per page and POV (point of view) of the action and such. Steve did write full scripts as well as use this method, but memory doesn't serve if Howard came out of a loose plot or tight script. Steve described the character in the copy, he was introduced as one of a group of characters from different dimensions in a *Man-Thing* story, including a Gandalf-like wizard and a Conan-like barbarian. I just drew it and that was that. I don't know if Steve expected anything to come of Howard at the time; I certainly didn't, but the Duck went on to become a star while the other characters introduced along with him faded into obscurity. Steve said to me, 'Think of Groucho Marx as a duck,' so I gave Howard a cigar, a little derby hat, tie, vest and jacket. Steve added, 'Don't make him look like Donald Duck, make it look what an animated duck as a 3-D real world creature, walking down the road, would look like.' I didn't overthink it; I just drew it. Steve liked it right away, no revisions, and went with it." Marv Wolfman wrote to me in 2018 that "Steve showed me the very first Howard story in *Man-Thing* and was so excited because Val designed the character so perfectly and not at all like he expected." To the total surprise of all, especially Gerber, the Marvel offices were subsequently flooded with protest letters against the duck's tragic fate. One in particular expressed their view in no uncertain terms, mailing an actual corpse of a dead duck to the office with a note attached that read, "Murderers!" During his many convention and college appearances, Stan Lee was frequently asked by readers, "When are you bringing the Duck back?" Eventually the requests became so insistent that Lee was compelled to ask the Marvel editors, "What the hell is this 'duck' people keep asking me about?" With passions running high, Marvel brought Howard back with two solo stories in *Giant-Size Man-Thing* (an unfortunate convergence resulting in one of the most snigger worthy comic book titles of all time) where his fall through the void lands him in Cleveland, USA and "trapped in a world he never made."

In these first two solo strips and for the first two issues of the character's own series, Howard was drawn by Frank Brunner, who wrote to me, "I had just wrapped up ten issues of *Doctor Strange* and was looking for something completely different to draw and along came *Howard the Duck*. I was available so I called Steve Gerber and he sent me the script for "Man-Frog," Howard's first solo story in *Giant-Size Man-Thing* #4. I may not have been responsible for what Howard looked like; but Beverly Switzler, Howard's human girlfriend and constant side-kick, was 100 percent mine. Beverly was based on one of my girlfriends at the time. The character's name was Steve's idea, but the visual and her every nuance was my creation. The first issue of Howard was co-plotted by Steve and me. It didn't surprise me that an intended throwaway character became such a big cult hit in the 1970s because I thought Howard was such a wild departure from everything Marvel had been doing at the time, and college kids across the USA agreed. They made *Howard the Duck* Marvel's biggest hit until the *Star Wars* comic came out. Steve was crazy! And I liked that. He thought outside the box. However, later — after I could not come to terms with Marvel over my page rate—I quit *Howard* after the second issue. I guess I was thinking Marvel would re-consider, but they did not! So, I created *Scarface Duck* and *The Duckaneer* for Quack Comics, published by Star-Reach. Gerber didn't like that, but I couldn't just drop the whole thing because Marvel was being stupid and a tightwad!"

With Brunner's departure, Gerber was joined on the title by Gene Colan, who would remain on the series until its demise, with his fluid, dramatically lit, angle-altering art-style a perfect match to visualize the incongruous placement of a talking duck in a real world setting and the artist enjoyed working from Gerber's scripts. Colan said in 2008, "Steve was a very funny guy, and I would have to stop working in the middle of drawing a Howard strip because I would be laughing my head off!"

Together, Gerber and Colan crafted a sharp, funny and often poignant saga of a misfit lead protagonist unable to catch a break regardless of whatever universe he found himself in. At the height of the title's popularity in 1978, when Howard was appearing not only in his monthly colour comic but also every day in a newspaper syndicated strip, Gerber was unceremoniously fired not only from writing *Howard the Duck* but from the employment of Marvel Comics completely. Citing lateness of work from Gerber, and therefore breaching his contractual obligations, Editor-in-Chief Jim Shooter brought the axe down firmly, and Gerber found himself cut suddenly adrift. Two years later, Gerber embarked on a protracted legal battle with Marvel Comics, suing the company for copyright infringement by claiming sole ownership rights to Howard the Duck with the case that as it was originally created as an ancillary character it was not covered by the work-for-hire agreement he had with Marvel at the time.

In Gerber's attempts to take back ownership of Howard, he was aided by many other comic writers and artists who banded together to form "F.O.O.G" ("Friends of Ol' Gerber" in a parody of Marvel's 1970s fan club incarnation "FOOM") to help raise funds for the legal case. These creators included Jack Kirby, who gave his work at no charge to co-create and pencil *Destroyer Duck* for Gerber, published through Eclipse Comics, and featuring the eponymous hero's attempts at crossing dimensions in order to "rescue the little guy." All profits from the sale of the comic book went to aid Gerber's legal costs fund, but eventually he would lose the case in late 1982, conceding that all rights, title and interest were the property of Cadence Industries. Steve Gerber found employment in animation and television script writing for a time (he co-wrote an episode of *Star Trek: The Next*

Generation titled "Contagion") then returned to comics to write sporadically for a number of publishers, including Marvel. But the success and accolades he enjoyed by writing the often indignant opinions of *Howard the Duck* were never to be repeated, and Gerber slid into a world of relative obscurity. In 2000, Gerber returned to Marvel to write his final *Howard the Duck* series under the more adult-oriented imprint Maxx Comics. Artist of the series, Phil Winslade said to me, "I'm proud to have done it, but it's tinged with regret. The *Howard Maxx* series we really talked Steve into doing despite his own reservations, and some great material came out of it, especially the final issue with Howard having a conversation with God that makes some clever comments on creatorship, ownership and work-for-hire. (As in this example, where God reveals to Howard that he created the universe as a work made for hire adding, "The universe was a contract job. I made it but legally speaking, I'm not its creator. It's considered a contribution to a collective work called 'Existence'") But I think that Steve hoped that Howard would return to the level of popularity enjoyed in the 1970s and when the Maxx series came out, it sold OK, but received little or no response and this disappointed Steve greatly. Howard is an extension of Steve Gerber, it really is. And when he was writing it in the 1970s it was an incredibly popular character but this meant it got under a lot of radar and attracted so much legal wrangling it really meant that Steve couldn't work in comics for a long time after." Val Mayerik recalled to me, "Steve was very generous. During the height of his litigious activity against Marvel, he was working in animation in LA making pretty good money and needed me to give a statement to his attorney. I could have given it over the phone, but he flew me out to LA, took me out to dinner and I got to know him then even better than before. I spoke to Steve a few years before he died when we were thinking of reviving 'Void Indigo'. He wasn't an old man but had a profound lung disease. I wish I'd spent more time with Steve and pursed more projects with him. It's that old story of making sure you spend time with people you care for before they're gone. I have more of a relationship with the Duck today than I ever did before. The reason for this is that Steve is gone now and when people want to know about the inception of the character, they turn to me for answers. I find that I'm warming to this character now like I never have before and do many commissions of Howard and hope to do many more. I've been creating a series of paintings of Howard and the Man-Thing travelling through time — little vignettes like in Howard talking to Ernest Hemingway in 1920s Paris, all kinds of crazy stuff. I did receive all my original art back from Marvel but that was in the mid 80's and at the time neither the Duck or I were hot items in comics, being overshadowed by Miller et al. Back then I couldn't give those pages away and having no collectors' instincts, did not foresee them increasing in value to the extent that they have. So, I sold them all very cheaply to a collector in the early 1990s."

Gerber's latter works include the DC/Vertigo series *Nevada* that featured a Las Vegas Showgirl and her pet Ostrich, characters that were revived from a brief visual appearance in a 1970s *Howard the Duck* comic book and the DC series *Countdown to Mystery* with Doctor Fate. While hospitalized in Las Vegas, Nevada, Gerber continued to work from his bed on this series until his death on February 10, 2008. The year previously, Gerber had been diagnosed with idiopathic pulmonary fibrosis and, while on the waiting list for a lung transplant, had passed due to complications arising from his condition. He was sixty years old.

The character's co-creator Val Mayerik summarises the essence of the oddball fowl with the understanding that "Howard the Duck is part of that ensemble of fictional characters and real people that embody the rebellious spirit of their times." Concluding, "Steve Gerber had the stones and the temerity to sue Marvel over the rights for the Duck. He didn't win but it was a landmark case that ultimately paved the way for writers and artists to receive royalties for the characters they did create at Marvel. When I attend conventions now, I don't know if the people who really like the Duck are aware of Gerber's efforts to try and regain control of the character, which really set a precedent for the way things are today."

Martin Goodman didn't immediately leave the company he'd founded when he sold his interests back in 1968 ("Goodman did finally sell Marvel. The price was probably good for him," Ditko wrote to the author in 2016, adding, "He had enough experience to know what was to his best advantage — sell or continue competing with DC and all other new comic companies that could enter what was becoming a profitable field.") but remained as publisher until 1972 having prepared the way, he thought, for his son, Charles "Chip" Goodman to inherit the role from his father. It didn't work out that way with behind closed doors board machinations resulting in Lee being offered the position and Chip effectively ousted. Angered, in June 1974 Goodman re-entered that "profitable field" with an audacious attempt at market share grab by launching a total of 23 new comic book titles and five comic magazines, in quick succession, through a brand-new company he'd established and appointed Chip as Publisher, Seaboard Periodicals Inc. Under the imprint Atlas Comics, cheekily revived from the pre-Marvel name of the 1950s, the new endeavour poached many Marvel staffers with the lure of higher page rates and enhanced benefits including the return of original art, not a standard industry procedure at this time.

From his Fifth Avenue offices, Goodman also hired as editor, Larry Lieber who dismissed any inference of a sibling rivalry scenario when he wrote to me in 2013, "Goodman hired me to edit magazines. I was not aware of any other motive on his part. I went there to earn a living. Stan understood this and was sympathetic to my move."

Lieber had worked at Marvel, enjoying a long run both writing and drawing the western title *Rawhide Kid* from 1964, but found assignments scarce by the end of the 1960s.

"It wasn't an easy period because I had difficulty getting work from Marvel, and DC wouldn't give me any work (I tried unsuccessfully to get work from them) because I was Stan's brother, and I believe DC was suspicious of my attempting to work for them." But the ambitions of Goodman's instant mix character universe publishing venture, with titles such as *Tiger-Man*; *Ironjaw*; *The Brute* and *Planet of Vampires,* proved to be unsuccessful and the entire line folded within one year with not one of its titles lasting more than four issues.

"Publishing comic book titles is a risky, competitive business and with monthly titles and with no guarantees," Ditko wrote to me in March 2015 in reference to Atlas Comics Mk II, adding, "Many new comic companies' attempts to enter the business were short-lived like with Wally Wood. I don't know the problems with Marvel/Goodman's son Chip company. It's where Archie Goodwin, Wood and I did *The Destructor.*" After Atlas bombed, quite spectacularly, Lieber returned to the New York Marvel offices to edit the burgeoning line of reprint comics produced exclusively for the United Kingdom market. When Lieber came on as editor, the line comprised of no less than seven weekly series — all reprint, but requiring art generated for new covers and splash pages, many created by some of Marvel's top artists at the time such as Jim Starlin, Rich Buckler and Ross Andru. "I enjoyed being editor of Marvel's British reprint department. I think it might've been the only time in my comic career that I was on staff. I even got a week's vacation and flew over to the UK. I visited the Marvel office — met the people I had been speaking to on the phone and saw a great play in London. The time I spent there was a happy experience for me."

Writer/editor Danny Fingeroth had joined Marvel's staff in 1977 and recalled the UK division to me in 2018, "We were competing with weekly black-and-white comics like *2000 AD* and *Beano* that were the standard in Britain, so had to modify Marvel stories to compete in that marketplace generating some new material including new covers and splash pages, since we would split most stories into multiple chapters that required that extra material. We had two people in editorial and two people in production in the New York British department, which took up two windowless rooms in Marvel's offices. There were numerous freelancers who would stop by to deliver or finish work, and there were a couple who were there pretty much all the time, even though they weren't technically staffers. There was also a British Marvel office in London, and I spoke with editor Neil Tennant all the time. It was, of course, before he was a famous member of *The Pet Shop Boys.* I recall him being a pleasant guy to chat and work with. Marvel was a fun place to work. Most of the people were talented and very nice, with a few psychos sprinkled in. We all thought comics as a mainstream entertainment medium would be gone within a few years, and we should enjoy ourselves while it was still around, then go on to whatever we were really going to do with our lives. In late 1978, the operation moved over to the UK entirely, under the direction of editor Dez Skinn. I went into the mainstream editorial department and Larry went on to draw (and write) the *Hulk* newspaper strip, and then became the artist on the *Spider-Man* newspaper strip for more than 30 years, only recently leaving it."

Lieber said to me "I believe I'm the longest-running artist on the *Spidey* syndicated strip. Those dallies, and the syndicated Hulk strips which I wrote and pencilled are what I consider the highlights of my career." Lieber's work on *The Hulk* newspaper strip, in particular, garnered a rare, if back-handed, compliment from brother Stan when he remarked, "It's very good and also more dramatic than your work on the *Spider-Man* strip."

While American comic book imports with their superhero exploits were widely distributed to UK newsagents at the same time they were issued in the US, most home grown British comics were humour-based (*Beano*; *Dandy*; and *Buster*) and the comics that attempted a more varied and sophisticated attempt at story-telling such as *The Eagle* were few in number. Odhams Press was the first UK Company to reprint the 1960s Marvel material in sequential order under their Power Comics imprint, but prior to that, Alan Class Comics had been reprinting Atlas-era material as far back as 1959 and were the first to reprint any 1960s Marvel superhero material, including Spider-Man with the Ditko-drawn origin story first reprinted in Britain in *Out of This World* #17 in late 1964.

The stories in the Class Comics were not presented in any order and printed on pulp paper so coarse the chips were visible and with ink that stained your hands. Beginning in 1966, *Spider-Man* was first reprinted sequentially in black-and-white in the weekly Odhams title *Pow!* The comic also reprinted Kirby's *Nick Fury: Agent of Shield* strip along with UK-originated, humour-based strips like Mike Higgs' *The Cloak* and in companion titles *Wham!* and *Fantastic*, legendary British artist Leo Baxendale's *Grimly Feendish* — subtitled *The Rottenest Crook in the World* and a notable visual precursor to supervillain Gru in the 2010 animated movie *Despicable Me.*

By 1972, Marvel itself took over the reprinting of its comics for UK shores and began mining again from the beginning of its 1960s material. Commencing with *The Mighty World of Marvel* in October, reprinting *Spider-Man*, *Fantastic Four* and *Hulk*, with the first edition *Spider-Man Comics Weekly* following in February 1973 and eventually producing an extensive line reprinting, and swiftly exhausting, practically all of Marvel US back and current catalogue.

Soon there was a need for newly-originated material and *Captain Britain* became the first Marvel superhero character produced in New York but intended exclusively for a particular overseas market. Herb Trimpe was assigned artist on the series, due in no small part to his returning from vacation in the country with multiple photographic views and said to me in 2012, "I was working from plots from writer Chris Claremont. They were more elaborate than Stan would do, but definitely not full scripts. One thing I can tell you, I wasn't very enthusiastic about Captain Britain. I thought it was silly, and the fans in the UK would never go for it. It was like putting a square peg in a round hole. I thought, though I never mentioned it to anyone, that to use an American metaphor to express British heroism and steadfastness was ludicrous. I couldn't see the character in any other way than as an American in masquerade. I can't remember if I started to draw the strip while still in the UK, but I certainly used photos taken on the trip as reference. I can remember getting together with Chris — he came down to Cornwall and first mentioned the possibility of me drawing the book then. We were together talking on a deserted, wind-swept Cornish beach, and I think he first came up with the name then, although I can't be certain. *Captain Britain* was very much a committee book. I don't know for sure who designed the original costume, but to me, it looks a lot like John Romita's work. He was the guy in the NY office all the art went through and who did corrections and everything else. If John did it, there was never any need to add or change whatever he did. Stan Lee would have undoubtedly approved the final character design, however."

Ditko was aware of all the foreign edition reprints of his *Spider-Man* and *Doctor Strange* work and how soon they followed publication of the US originals. He wrote to me in May 2015, "Marvel material was reprinted; I don't know how early or where. I've seen some comic books from different countries — originals and Marvel reprints. It's interesting to compare the look with Marvel/DC, even Charlton's press look. With Marvel's growing success, reprints potential had to increase."

He reviewed the production values of one such British comic from 1972 that I mailed to him as an example, "The UK comic you sent — I don't know who did the cover — not Kirby." (The comic was *Mighty World of Marvel* #4, October 1972, and its cover was by Jim Starlin) "I inked that *Hulk* story. Real odd-green colouring. In a way, more visual clarity than usual with comic book colouring of Kirby's crowded panels. The grey on the Hulk diminishes his menace. A green Hulk works best. A no Hulk colouring — No impact, he fades into the background. I don't know who inked *The Fantastic Four Fight Back*. Spider-Man/Chameleon — mixed colour effect. Back cover — Vulture — grey tones fit him. Spotty coloured backgrounds, odd choices made by colourist. No colour on Spider-Man works best."

1977 was a year that saw the deaths of Elvis Presley; Groucho Marx and Howard Hawks; the first flight of the NASA Space Shuttle "Enterprise" Jimmy Carter sworn in as the 39th President of the United States; punk rockers the Sex Pistols banned from UK radio airplay with their number one single "God Save the Queen" during Queen Elizabeth II's Silver Jubilee anniversary celebrations and *Star Wars* was released to round-the-block queues across America.

In November of that year, Steve Ditko had reached his milestone 50th birthday but was finding little to celebrate in his career opportunities and had returned to the offices of DC Comics in search of work. His previously dependable employer Charlton Comics had experienced financial issues that resulted in all of its titles going on an assignment hiatus with material for its comic books gleaned from inventory or reprinted. This was a bitter blow to Ditko, who had become reliant on the company for regular work since he first began in the industry in the 1950s, and circumstances would not improve at Charlton but rapidly deteriorate over the coming years with the company ceasing trading altogether by 1985.

With the certainty of regular assignments from the publisher gone, Ditko found work from the major comic book companies difficult to come by and opportunities few in number, despite his previous accomplishments. As a result of Stan Lee's move from comic book editor to Hollywood mogul, *Spider-Man* made his live-action debut on American television on September 19, 1977 in a CBS series that starred actor Nicholas Hammond as the superhero in a limited effects production that attempted to remain faithful to its source material but possessed neither the finance nor creative direction to achieve it. A one-off television movie featuring Doctor Strange would air the following year, a production that called in a recent artist on the series for assistance as Frank Brunner recalled to me, "I had some involvement with the Doctor Strange ABC television movie that appeared in the 70s. I was contacted by a Universal TV producer, Phil Degere, who wanted me to design a toned-down Doctor Strange wearing trousers rather than tights along with several other characters for the TV movie. I didn't think his ideas were particularly good, but I worked with him, hoping for the best, and it was very useful to gain some Hollywood experience."

The original artist on the character was not contacted in a similar fashion, nor did Ditko receive any royalty payment for either television production starring his comic book creations. His only memory of the first media translation of his *Master of the Mystic Arts* was of its singular star name when he wrote to me "Yes, years ago, a one-shot movie of Doctor Strange. I may have seen a DVD, I have faint memory of John Mills in it. The Hulk can't seem to be made into a successful movie, but he had his TV success."

The third and final entry into this round of attempts by Marvel to find an audience for licensed live-action adaptations of its characters came with *The Incredible Hulk* which first aired on the CBS network on November 4, 1977, running for five seasons until 1982. Mixing "Fugitive" — style drama with slow-motion, tattered shirt, set-busting Hulk appearances and a haunting piano melody, the series, starring Bill Bixby and Lou Ferrigno made the green goliath a household name and popularized the phrase "You wouldn't like me when I'm angry."

Opposite page: Steve Ditko, pencils and inks, cover from ***Shade the Changing Man*** #1, July, 1977, ©1977 DC Comics.

Rising paper and distribution costs had seen a sharp rise in the price of comic books, and the anger that this generated produced a rapidly declining readership. With a standard comic book beginning the decade with a 15-cent price tag and ending at 40 cents, a 110 percent increase, all publishers were struggling to turn profits, and in Marvel's particular case, only the advent of a movie from a "galaxy far, far away" and its subsequent comic book adaptation saved the company from financial ruin during this period, as Roy Thomas, who championed the Marvel version long before *Star Wars* appeared in cinemas, remembered to the author in 2013, "In 1975 I met George Lucas when *The Star Wars* was just something in the works, not even a script quite yet, I think. Jim Shooter and Jim Galton said the comic adaptation saved Marvel financially during a difficult period and they would know. I just knew it sold very well, especially after the movie came out, but I never got that much out of it. And nothing at all from Lucas, which, I must admit, still grates even today. I felt him ungrateful, considering how badly he'd wanted a comic book done and how hard I'd had to convince Marvel to do it after they'd already turned it down. Still, I liked the movie, but we didn't turn out as good a comic as I'd have liked, especially after Howard Chaykin couldn't do full art beginning with issue two. But it was a very interesting period in many ways."

While Hollywood was reinventing science fiction by returning to its *Flash Gordon* serial roots, Steve Ditko delivered to DC Comics a brand-new character, Shade, the Changing Man and the artist's final work-for-hire creation produced for the company. Launched directly into his own title with the first issue appearing in June 1977, Rac Shade was a fugitive on Earth from the planet Meta and its military-based society, fleeing a false conviction of treason and its death sentence. Using a stolen "M-Vest" incorporating Meta-Zone technology that allows him to project force fields and visually transform into a monstrous version of himself, Shade attempts to clear his name while steering clear of the interdimensional "Area of Madness" and the Meta-Authorities' attempts to recapture him.

Despite the editorial frictions that Ditko remembered, there were some in the DC offices in simpatico with the artist and one in particular with whom Ditko enjoyed a lasting and productive relationship. Jack C. Harris was an editor and writer at DC at the time who handled Ditko's *Shade, the Changing Man* and remembers the artist as "a quiet gentleman with an iron-clad ethics code." Harris wrote to the author in 2018, "I first met Steve in the hallway of DC Comics. He was waiting to see Joe Orlando. I invited Steve to wait in my office. We had our first conversation there. Over the next few months, he did a few stories for the mystery titles I edited. Later, when Joe Orlando saw how well Steve and I worked together, he assigned me the editor slot on Steve's *Shade, the Changing Man* title." Before the title was given to Harris, however, Ditko had experienced some initial editorial resistance to the concept when he first mooted the idea. He wrote to me in June 2014, "*Shade, the Changing Man* certainly didn't fit into DC Comics' Universe. A DC editor at the time I brought the Shade idea, story in, told me 'Comic book fans won't accept an alien hero.' That very week, in the DC editorial offices, they were going over a movie script about Superman, an 'alien hero.' There's an editorial fear of ideas that they are not familiar with, instead of seeking, wanting creative ideas to explore, etc. They want safety — 'Don't rock the boat.' But fiction and fantasy need to be continually rocked."

Under the editorship of Harris, Ditko was able to fully realize his bold new creation, as Harris recalls, "He did extensive and detailed notes and sketches for many, single page ball point pen sketches for others. It usually depended on how far along the concept was in his mind. (He worked on) mostly full scripts for any strip that I wrote. Shade came in as completed pencils first, with notes which we discussed with dialogue writer Mike Fleisher. One time, Steve brought in some Shade pages and the story had called for a close-up panel of a left hand. As I went over it, I noticed Steve had

drawn a right hand instead. When I pointed out the error, Steve looked at the page, furrowed his brow, then looked at his own hand (held in his famous raised pinky-and-forefinger gesture — like Spider-Man was spinning a web or Doctor Strange casting a spell), smiled and said, 'Well, that's what editors are for!' Then he rushed off to redraw the panel. It's my favourite story of working with Steve."

Harris remembers visiting Ditko in his studio, with an invitation into his inner sanctum indicative of the professional respect he held for the editor, "The studio I visited was not the one he ended up in. The one I saw was a small one with one large window, a drawing board, a black-and-white portable television and many, many shelves crammed with books and movie stills, which he used for reference. Although he had a drafting table, he often drew on a drawing board on his lap, with the top edge resting on the bottom ledge of the drafting table." Although Harris remembers the DC offices as having "a very casual atmosphere" with staff socializing outside of the office, Ditko was never among their number. "The only time I recall Steve joining in was a few times he, Mike Gold and I, went to lunch together," Harris recalls. Not unsurprisingly, Ditko never talked about his early Marvel days, "Steve never spoke to me about his work at Marvel. Never. However, there was one time when Marvel published a little paperback edition of the first ten or so issues of *Amazing Spider-Man,* and I bought an extra copy to give to Steve. However, when I offered it to him, he quietly refused to take it. That was the only time I got any indication of his feelings about those years."

Some things still hadn't changed in the comic book industry of 1977, and Ditko gave all his new creations for DC Comics under the same conditions he had for Goodman's Marvel, as Harris confirmed, saying "I recall logging checks to be written for him, so that would have been work-for-hire. I have two personal favourites of all the work I did with Ditko: the pages he did for my *Wonder Woman Spectacular* (1978) and a little story called "A Demon and His Boy," which appeared in *House of Mystery* #258, edited by Paul Levitz. Working with all the idols of my youth, Ditko, Kubert, Infantino, Anderson etc. really was a dream come true!" Ditko's assertion that "Shade didn't fit into DC's universe" was borne out by the brief lifespan of the title, lasting only nine issues, despite being planned in advance by the artist up until issue seventeen.

When the announcement that filming had begun on Warner Brothers *Superman: The Movie*, a multi-million dollar production with a stellar cast including Hollywood royalty in Marlon Brando and Gene Hackman and promising newcomers with Canadian actress Margot Kidder as Lois Lane and Christopher Reeve in the starring role, Jerry Siegel took up his pen and, in exasperation of his defeats in previous legal battles, wrote a highly vitriolic open letter to the press, cursing the impending movie, "I hope it super-bombs," Seigel wrote. "I hope loyal Superman fans stay away from it in droves. I hope the whole world, becoming aware of the stench that surrounds Superman, will avoid the movie like the plague. The publishers of Superman comic books, National Periodical Publications Inc, killed my days, murdered my nights, choked my happiness, strangled my career. I consider National's executives economic murderers, money-mad monsters."

At the time of anticipation of the movie's release, both creators were now in their sixties, with Siegel working as a minimum wage mail clerk and Joe Shuster afflicted with rapidly deteriorating eyesight and living in relative poverty. With director Richard Donner preparing to launch Siegel and Shuster's creation as a profitable movie franchise, creator rights advocates Neal Adams and Jerry Robinson initiated a three-month PR campaign to raise awareness of the inequality of two creators struggling while Warner Brothers, parent company of DC Comics, stood poised to make millions in cinema ticket sales. In exchange for the commitment to never again contest ownership of Superman, DC Comics awarded Seigel and Shuster an annual payment substituting a pension, the medical insurance they badly

Above: Ditko, pencils and inks, original artwork for ***Ghostly Haunts*** #46, 1975, ©1975 Charlton Comics.

Focus
Ditko Draws Batman

These rare layouts of Ditko's take on the comic book character he loved as a child were commissioned by and saved for posterity by writer/editor Jack C. Harris who recalled to me in 2019, "These are from 1977; at the time, I was editing *World's Finest Comics* in its Dollar Comics format. The lead was Superman/Batman team ups, and the rest of the book contained various backup features, including short Creeper stories by Steve. Occasionally, we would need a fill-in artist for the lead. There was really never a regular artist on the lead at the time. Everyone from Kurt Schaffenberer to Garcia Lopez to George Tuska, and others had tackled it. It occurred to me that it might be fun if Steve tried his hand. So, he was going to work up some sketches of his take on Superman and Batman. He handed in these pages of Batman, but the 'powers-that-be' at the time didn't like them, so Steve didn't bother doing any Superman sketches (I would have loved to have seen those!). They had deemed the Batman take 'too violent,' which is ironic when considering the directions Batman eventually took. At least I had the foresight to keep these drawings!"

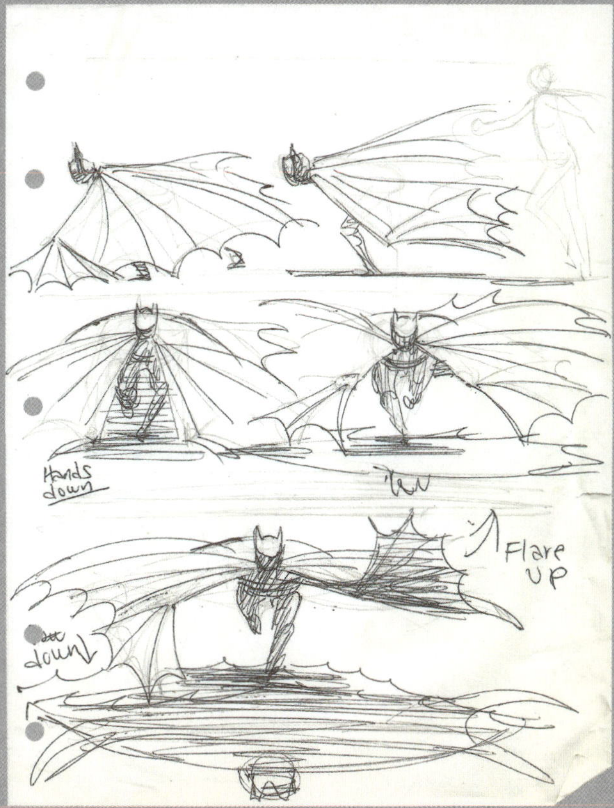

needed and a credit on all future appearances of the Man of Steel, just before the movie's release on December 10, 1978 convincing audiences worldwide in their belief that a man could fly.

"It was the Donner movie that gave us that leverage," Adams recalled to me in 2011, citing the element that aided the victorious result. For Siegel and Shuster, justice in part had been served, and they would fulfill their sides of the bargain until Shuster died in 1992 at the age of 78 with Siegel following in 1996. But that wasn't the end of the story by any means. As well as being a consummate artist, Neal Adams was an early and dependably vocal exponent of creator rights within the comic book industry who researched his subjects thoroughly and was instrumental establishing the procedure in the major comic book publishing house of returning original art to its creators. In 2011, Adams said to me, "When I was fighting for the return of original art, I didn't just go to the offices of Marvel and DC and say, 'Hey, please return the art.' I went to the companies and said, 'Do you believe that you bought this original art?' They would say 'Yeah, yeah of course we bought it.' Until I said, 'Well, did you pay sales tax on it?' If I buy some art, I have to pay sales tax on it. It's the law. If I didn't pay sales tax, I didn't buy it. Or the State of New York will come down on you and say, 'Guess what Marvel/DC Comics, you owe 50 years of back sales tax on every page of art you bought.' It was a good year for all comic artists that year. That was the big deal. Everybody doubled their income that year! (Laughs)"

Pointing out this technicality shook the companies as Gene Colan confirmed in a signed affidavit, supporting a Kirby estate legal case in the 1990s, "Marvel suddenly began returning original freelance artwork in the late 1970s because, as I understood it, they were very concerned they would otherwise owe a tremendous amount of New York sales tax on all the freelance artwork they had purchased over the years." It was not the only factor, as Paul Levitz wrote to me in 2018, "Original art began being returned at DC in 1974, partially in response to Atlas offering that to its contributors. As an assistant editor, I helped unbundle some of the stacks of older art that was removed from the warehouse and returned, but I played no part in the decision making."

Prior to this, management dictates at DC Comics involved the routine disposal of stacked original art boards by the cutting up and dumping of hundreds of previously published pages, many containing early stories of DC's flagship characters. Over at Marvel, Herb Trimpe recalled that "there was so much original artwork just lying around in the office — they didn't know what to do with it! Eventually, of course, they started to return it to the artists, and guys would trade pages with the inkers to put together a complete book." The return of the original art pages to the artists provided them with a much-needed additional income, allowing the sale to fans at conventions and seeding the burgeoning original comic art market of today.

But not all pages were returned to the penciller with the inker and writer each receiving a share (This situation incensed one artist so much that, rather than give the entire page, he meticulously peeled off every speech bubble and caption and mailed them instead to the writer.) Marvel staffer Irene Varantoff was appointed in charge of the warehouse now storing the stacks of original art in the mid-1970s and compiled "an exhaustive inventory" of all pages in the company's possession. A later inventory list from 1979 was published in *The Comics Journal* #105 in February 1986 and showed that the warehouse still held the original art for the majority of Ditko's *Spider-Man* work at that time, apart from six complete "missing" issues; a couple of pages absent from two other issues and all eleven pages of the origin story from *Amazing Fantasy* #15.

While artwork produced after 1975 would be returned to the artist, any artwork predating this would not be released until the mid-1980s with the proviso that the recipient signed a release form agreeing to accept the art pages as a "gift" from Marvel. Before the art, the bulk of which belonged to Kirby and Ditko, was returned in late 1982 many of the pages mysteriously disappeared from the warehouse, resulting in very few making their way back to the artists who created them. Ditko addressed the subject in an essay published in the January 1993 issue of *History of the Comics*, "I received story/art pages from three *Spider-Man* issues: Two complete issues (inside pages) and a third which had three pages missing. So, I was given, as a 'gift' a portion of 3 issues of the 41 *Spider-Man* books I did. There is nothing from the *Spider-Man* annuals (one of which included Doctor Strange as a guest star) and no covers of any kind. What happened to those 38 missing *Spider-Man* books and all the other missing pages and covers?"

P. Craig Russell recalled to me in 2018, "The return policy came into effect just about the time I started work on *Killraven,* and so all that artwork was returned to me. And when I say 'all' I mean that stand-up man Don McGregor refused 'his' portion of the artwork, deeming it, rightfully, the property of the artist. On the other hand, I came in just one year before the return of original art. So, my Ant-man series, single issues of *Iron Man* and *Doctor Strange* and a few short stories remained in the warehouse for about twenty years before they were returned to me. And while entire issues of Kirby and Ditko had gone 'missing' from the warehouse, all of my barely-professional early work was returned intact. NOBODY wanted to steal it!"

Circumstances were not dissimilar with Ditko's DC original art as Carl Potts, a Marvel editor during the 1980s, and who cites Ditko as his "first big comic art influence," wrote on his social media in 2013, "In the late 1970s, I found an original page from an early issue of Ditko's *The Creeper* for sale at a NYC convention for $25. Back then, $25 was a big chunk of my weekly food budget, but I really wanted a Ditko original! I bought it. During the late 1980s, while I was a line editor at Marvel, Ditko would occasionally stop by the offices and visit some of the editors. He liked to talk, especially about his objectivist philosophy and politics. It was usually a one-way "conversation" since he was a true believer, and his dogma seemed impervious to any doubt or questioning. Even though I'd heard he didn't give autographs, I told Steve about my cherished Creeper original, and I asked him if he'd sign it for me. He told me that none of his Creeper originals had been returned to him — the pages on the market were stolen from DC's offices. I felt horrible about this and decided I'd give the page to him. I brought the original page in to the offices and kept in my flat files. The next time Ditko stopped by my office, he began one of his long philosophical and political spiels. As he spoke, I rose from my desk, walked over to the flat files, removed the Creeper original and handed it to him. Without skipping a beat in his one-way conversation, he took the page, slipped it into his portfolio and carried on talking. He in no way acknowledged the exchange of the original art — not even a nod of his head."

Despite the grand art theft and with influential and resourceful individuals like Neal Adams promoting a better condition for creators' cause, industry improvements, like the return of original art and a royalty scheme payment for reprinted work came into being. Adams said to me in 2011, "It's true that today the companies pay artists royalties on trade paperback collections, but that wasn't always the way. I had to help argue the case for that as well. Their take was that they didn't have to pay royalties because it wasn't a book; it was a comic — a periodical. What defines a periodical? Two-thirds of the content is advertising. I just pointed out that a trade paperback collection has very little, if any, advertising — not dissimilar to a book. I also helped to raise page pay rates simply by communicating rates between artists. I would say, 'I'm getting this for this book, what are you getting?' Normally, the reply was 'Oh, I'm not getting that. But I will Monday.' I only step up if everything is wrong, and, quite honestly, at the time no-one else was stepping up. This was right from the beginning, back when comics were printed on toilet paper! With the very worst reproduction possible. The industry was a fucking mess. It really was. It needed straightening out. And from my point of view that sometimes involved taking people by the shirt fronts and yelling, 'No! You can't do that! This is a worthwhile and important industry, and if you don't do it right, I'll shake you until you do!'"

The royalty payments were small, as Dan Adkins stated in a letter published in *The Comic Reader* #168 (May 1979), "Marvel is now paying $3.00 per page for inks on reprinted work in comics and $1.00 per page for reprinting comics in paperbacks for inks. I got a big $1.00 check the other day for inks on a *Hulk* cover recently reprinted on a paperback," but a reward hitherto offered. Less of a benefit was the introduction of an "agreement" form at Marvel that wielded the phrase "work-for-hire" with immediate and retrospective impunity. Gene Colan stated, "Nobody at Marvel ever told me they considered my artwork to be 'work-for-hire.' My Marvel checks in the 1960s had writing on the back stating that I was granting or transferring all my rights in my artwork to Marvel but did not state my artwork was 'work-for-hire.' It wasn't until the late 1970s the words 'work-for-hire' were inserted in the statement on the back of the checks. In 1978, Marvel editor Jim Shooter insisted that everyone suddenly sign a form 'agreement' issued by Marvel which said that all artwork and materials created in the past or in the future are to be considered a 'work made for hire.' I was required to sign the form if I wanted to continue to work for Marvel."

Slightly more progressive over at DC was the implementation of the first written contracts for freelancers, as Paul Levitz, who cites their introduction as one of his proudest achievements in the industry, wrote to me in 2018, "The first written standard contracts replaced the old 'back of the check' endorsements. They weren't long or complex, and didn't change the fundamental deal between DC and freelancers, but put it all in writing and so made it enforceable (at least in theory). That was in 1977, and over the next few years the deals were expanded to included payment of reprint fees, royalties and other improved terms. This was put in place by Jenette Kahn, Joe Orlando and myself, with Dick Giordano joining the discussions when he came back on staff in late 1980." In 1985, Jenette Khan, Paul Levitz and Dick Giordano collectively issued a statement to clarify DC's stance on the ownership of original art. It read, "We, the publishing houses, are paying only for the right to reproduce the work. The ownership of the page, the actual object, belongs unequivocally to the artist, and the artist alone. The return of artwork is an artists' inalienable right."

Thirteen years after leaving Marvel Comics, Steve Ditko returned to the company in 1979, but the terms for his acceptance of assignments this time around were not unconditional, nor was his tenure one devoid of friction. "Marv Wolfman called me after Charlton shut down to work with him on Marvel material, and my return to Marvel had to have some others trying to take advantage of it," Ditko wrote to me in 2014, continuing, "I was sitting in Jack C. Harris's DC office, talking, when Marv Wolfman called him — a courtesy call — asking Jack if it was alright with him if he spoke to me. I was a freelancer; Jack had no objection. I said I'd work with Wolfman/Marvel, but I would not do any Spider-Man or Doctor Strange — that was my condition. Some writers (at Marvel) tried to sneak in panels dealing with J.J. Jameson's paper, etc, which I left blank for someone else to fill in."

Marv Wolfman recalled to the author in 2018, "He made it clear upfront that he would not draw Spidey or Doctor Strange characters. I did ask him at one time if I could put in a minor character, but he said no, so I didn't. I wanted to keep working with him and I didn't want to do anything that would offend him. I honestly don't remember any of the circumstances that led to me calling him. I would love it if I had anything to do with Steve's coming back to Marvel. I'm thrilled he did and was even more thrilled that I got to work with him and talk to him about Spider-Man and comics. We talked about his differences with Stan on Spidey and such. What ideas Steve had versus what ideas Stan had and that they didn't always gel. Based on what Steve said I saw lots of his ideas for Spidey were great, but so were a lot of Stan's. Having worked with many artists, Steve included, that give and take usually strengthens a joint project. There's no reason to ever get insane about differences. If you value your partner's contributions and you find yourself on different sides of this idea or that, it's best to drop the idea completely and come up with something new you both can accept. It's fiction and you can always come up with a better idea. When I was a fan, I remember writing to him and asking if he'd draw a picture that I could use in one of my fanzines. He sent me a gorgeous Mr. A page that he drew just for me. Although we did not share the same politics, I truly loved his art and really liked talking with him about comics."

Writer Tom DeFalco, who joined Marvel in 1978 and would eventually rise to Editor-in-Chief for a seven-year period during a turbulent time for the company between 1987-1994, was then a writer assigned to Ditko's first return work for Marvel in 1979, taking over from Kirby on his creation *Machine Man*. DeFalco recalled to the author in November 2018, "My first contact with Steve was over the phone, shortly after I submitted my first plot for *Machine Man*. When I was assigned the title, I was told Steve wanted to read my first plot before he decided if he was going to stay on the book. I used to put my phone number on all my plots or scripts so that the artist could call me if he/she had any questions. Steve called me, and we had a long conversation." A conversation that opened with a startingly direct question from Ditko, "Are you Tom? What gives you the right to write about heroes?" DeFalco continues, "We discussed heroes and the traits we associated with heroes. While I no longer remember the details, I'm sure we agreed on some things and disagreed on others, but I do believe we stayed on the phone for over an hour. I forget when I eventually actually met him in person."

As the 1980s dawned, the apparently motiveless murder of John Lennon, gunned down outside his Central Park-facing home The Dakota on December 8, 1980, was a pivotal event in the development of the new decade that seemed to usher in a period where an imagined world of peaceful co-existence was insidiously replaced with the harsh reality of power gained by the accumulation of material assets where capitalism is king and "greed is good." For Ditko, however, it's speculated but not confirmed that it was a time of financial struggle, and while the slender assignments from both Marvel and DC he received were welcome, they barely provided enough income for his needs.

Rich Buckler remembered Ditko searching for work around this time in 1982 and wrote to the author in 2010, "I didn't meet Steve Ditko until the 1980s when I worked for Archie/Red Circle Comics and, as Managing Editor, created their line of superhero books. After a long interview with Steve at Archie Comics' Manhattan offices I hired him to draw *The Fly*. That was a surreal time for me, to be sure! I was in the enviable position to hire the likes of Gray Morrow, Jim Steranko, Alex Toth, Jack Kirby, Steve Ditko! All of them industry giants! I remember finding it a bit peculiar that Steve stubbornly refused to talk at all about his *Spider-Man* work. He was adamant about that. That work was all behind him, he asserted. He hated for comparisons to be made between then and now. His emphasis was on new work and always moving forward."

Ditko reiterated this to me in a letter from February 2014 when he wrote, "As a freelancer, my focus had to be on what was next, what had to be done. The last job is history. The movie actor Robert Mitchum was once asked, 'What's your favourite movie role?' and he answered, 'The next one'."

The conviction of Ditko's notions of heroism and their immovable constraints, sparked one particular incident where a storyline in current issues of *Iron Man* saw a plot development that ran contrary to his beliefs. "I also refused to do a drunken Iron Man splash page — someone else had to draw, ink it. The anti-hero was becoming well entrenched at Marvel and DC," Ditko wrote to me in 2016 referencing the Marvel assignments he would accept or disregard during his return to the company. Writer David Michelinie, who, along with writer/artist Bob Layton, introduced the memorable storyline in the pages of the comic book, wrote to me in 2019, "When I was first assigned to *Iron Man*, I had never read an *Iron Man* story. So, to prepare for the assignment I read the previous six stories (sometimes in plot form) that led up to my first issue. And I saw a character whose world was crumbling: a rival corporation was mounting a hostile takeover of Stark International, the government was trying to regulate The Avengers, S.H.I.E.L.D. had apparently gone from friend to foe, and Tony Stark's love life was in the dumps. I thought that the natural thing for a real person to do under those circumstances would be to look for some sort of stress relief, a way to ease the pressure if only temporarily. And it had long been established that Tony was a social drinker, so it seemed to me that the temptation to seek escape in the bottle would become stronger and stronger. I pitched the idea to Bob, he liked it, so we developed it and brought it to Jim Shooter. To his credit, Jim's only proviso was, 'Do it well.' I've heard from people I've never met, and never will meet, about how reading the Tony Stark alcoholism saga helped them understand the behaviour of an alcoholic friend or relative, and how it even helped to bring estranged family members closer."

But for Ditko it was the antithesis of how a hero should act, and when assigned to draw the issue of *Iron Man* which called for an opening page showing an inebriated Tony Stark wearing his armour, he adamantly refused. Marie Severin stepped in to draw the first page of *Iron Man* #160 (July 1982). Michelinie continued, "I never actually met Steve, and we never worked together directly, only through an editor. As I recall, he illustrated a couple of my Indiana Jones stories, and back-up stories with a couple of characters I created, Chance and Solo. Of course, having the latter published in *Spider-Man* annuals, drawn by the original Spider-Man artist, was pretty cool."

While not prepared to draw any characters from Spider-Man, Ditko was not averse to his new work being published in the title itself, and his last co-creation for Marvel was introduced as a back-up feature in Amazing *Spider-Man Annual* #22 (January 1988). Writer and co-creator with Ditko of *Speedball*, Tom DeFalco recalled to me, "We did some work together on *Speedball*. I wrote the character's bible and asked Steve if he'd like to draw it. He read the bible and agreed to do it, designing the costume for the character. I think I wrote the first few plots and then Steve took over the plotting. I don't recall ever asking him to make any changes. Steve was a total professional and knew how to tell a visual story better than almost anyone. He didn't need much direction. Around this time, he would often come into the Marvel offices, I had a coffee pot in my office, and he would drop in for a coffee and a conversation. Steve and I talked about a lot of things, but we rarely discussed comics. We had too many other subjects to cover. When he came in the people in the office who knew him greeted him, but I don't recall anyone going out their way to especially bother him. Over all the years I saw him, Steve always looked like Steve to me. The man didn't seem to age."

At Marvel, Ditko was assigned the pencilling duties on *ROM, Spaceknight*. a comic book based on an action figure toy. P. Craig Russell wrote to me in 2018, "I loved doing finishes over Ditko's *ROM* layouts. He was a very structural layout artist, cubes and spheres and all. It was left to the finisher to provide the atmosphere and mood and that's just what I like to do. I endeavoured to adhere as close to Ditko's style as possible, and though you'd never confuse us, we did have a similar linear/clean-line approach to drawing. He did give me one large panel that was a close-up of a woman's face, but all he drew was an oval with minimal detail. I knew if I simply finished it myself from scratch it would be a Craig Russell face so I researched my Ditko collection, found a similar closeup of an anxious woman's face, traced it, projected it onto the page, copied that off, and inked it. Presto, Ditko face!" Comics historian Tom Field said, "I saw a *ROM* script (that Ditko was pencilling) and almost every Marvel character was guest starring in that issue! There was a description that reference a bunch of heroes bursting onto the scene, including Spider-Man. Spidey's name was circled in red pen on the page with a trail leading to a margin note that read 'Oh, really??' Needless to say, Ditko didn't draw Spider-Man. A few years later, when bookshelf edition comics were all the rage, one Marvel editor told me that Ditko had been offered life-changing money to draw one last, stand-alone Spidey story, but it wasn't even a consideration."

Over the next decade, Ditko would produce work for Marvel that saw print at the time, including *Captain Universe*; *Micronauts* and *Wargod* and work that was shelved during the period but printed later. One of these was a *Hulk/Human Torch* story that reunited Ditko with writer Jack C. Harris, although they were not to meet again. "It was all through the editors," Harris wrote to me in 2018. "I would give my written material to the editor and he would return Steve's pencil drawings for me to dialogue. We actually never met face-to-face during the Marvel work." On another assignment, a story was repurposed by the artist as Wolfman remembered, "What happened was Steve and I were going to take over the Marvel *Godzilla* book. I remembered his giant monster comics he did at Charlton and was looking forward to doing it with him. But soon after Steve pencilled the story Marvel lost the Godzilla rights, and rather than throw out all those great pages, I did some research into real Japanese mythology and found a giant monster idea that would fit. Although the pages were already pencilled, I asked Steve to change the look of the monster as he inked it so it wouldn't look anything like Godzilla. He did that beautifully. Meanwhile, I took the altered pages and wrote them so the story would be closer to the Japanese myth than the Godzilla story they had originally been intended to be. It's tricky to do and make it seamless, but in the end, it worked, and I got to write another Ditko story. Steve and I also did a *Tomb of Dracula* black-and-white story as well as working on multiple issues of Machine Man together."

When Ditko returned to the Marvel offices, the man in charge from 1978 to 1987 was Pittsburgh-born writer/editor Jim Shooter, a prodigy comic book writer at the age of 13 and a controversial figure during his reign as Editor-in-Chief. Bob Layton wrote to me in 2013, "It was a double-edged sword. Jim had a very abrasive management style that alienated a lot of the creative staff. At the same time, he was instrumental in a lot of positive changes to the company. But to be perfectly honest, Paul Levitz and Dick Giordano were way ahead of Marvel on the issues of creative rights. Although Jim takes credit for it, the truth is that Marvel merely countered what benefits DC initially offered in order to hold off mass defections by their top creative players. Marvel's creator royalty policy didn't come into existence until much later. Jim Shooter was a brilliant writer and a very persuasive individual. But, somewhere down the line, the work became about *him* and not the stories. Ultimately, it became a pattern of personal behaviour that eventually led to his downfall."

While Danny Fingeroth remembers that "Jim took a chaotic, sometimes brilliant, sometimes awful, line of comics that was perpetually missing printing deadlines (and paying penalty fees for it) and instilled a consistency and general level of quality into the books—that were now mostly on time. While there was a certain homogenizing quality to this, it also enabled unique talents like Frank Miller, Bill Sienkiewicz and John Byrne to thrive and do great work. In general, Shooter also enabled better pay for staffers and freelancers. He had flaws and rubbed some people the wrong way, but I think he's one of the people responsible for Marvel surviving and thriving during his reign as EIC."

David Michelinie pointed out that, "There were a lot more benefits for writers and artists introduced by the time I left, most courtesy of efforts made by Jim Shooter. Unfortunately, there was also a split between the two factions, pro-Jim and anti-Jim, which I think was one factor involved with Jim's ultimate departure," while Roy Thomas bluntly recalled, "In the early 1980s I left Marvel to work exclusively for DC for a time. This came about because I felt Jim Shooter had deliberately misled me (that's the polite word for it) about the contract I would be offered, had I stayed at Marvel."

Largely unaffected by Shooter, Ditko continued to balance his Marvel assignments alongside ones for DC and assorted small press publishers while forever nurturing his ultimate objective of self-publishing. Maintaining a low-profile policy of no interviews or appearances, the artist was perceived to be a strange, hermit-like creature in the imaginations of some fans as Brian Bolland, celebrated British comic artist whose work includes Judge Dredd and the 1988 graphic novel *Batman: The Killing Joke*, shared in a relevant memory on his social media in 2014, "Shortly before going to New York in the early 1980s, I was talking to a guy in a London comic shop about Steve Ditko. He jokingly told me he'd heard that Ditko was a deformed dwarf, and he slid his artwork through a panel at the bottom of his door. Later I was in New York at DC, and Ditko was standing alone in a corridor in front of a board displaying all of this month's comic book covers. One of them (to my immense pride) was by me. My friend, Joe Staton, said, 'Brian, let me introduce you to Steve Ditko.' I was so in awe of the man that I started to babble. The first thing I could think of was to tell him the story about how he was a deformed dwarf! He didn't seem amused. He said, 'Stories about people can be exaggerated.' He looked at all of the covers and said — 'They're all terrible'. Joe and I slowly moved away!"

While the major comic book publishers were all searching for the next big thing to boost their flagging sales, the slow but steady rise of specialist comic book stores necessitated a delivery system to distribute the product and with the acquisitions of pioneer distributors Bud Plant and Capital City, Steve Geppi formed Diamond Distribution in 1982, a company that would eventually distribute all comics books to outlets worldwide. This emerging combination of store, product and distributor led to a resurgence of interest in creators self-publishing their own work through a number of small publishers that had formed with the possibilities now available to them. At the vanguard of this, writer Mike Baron and artist Steve Rude's character Nexus was a costumed adventurer far removed from the standard archetype.

As the deliverer of justice from an alien being that's the self-appointed conscious of the human race, Horatio Hellpop is force-fed nightmares showing the deeds of mass murderers across the galaxy, and Nexus is compelled to seek those individuals out and execute them for their heinous crimes. Operating from a moon he names "Ylum" orbiting a dead planet, Nexus' solitary home eventually becomes a refuge for myriad races fleeing oppression across the universe, documenting the societal changes and conflicts the gathering brings. Birthed in the independent publishing scene of the early 1980s, and cradled in the infant days of the direct sales comic book market, Nexus moved to First Publishing where the rights to the character were tangled up and held from its creators but in a rare case of publisher/creator solidarity, the rights were graciously returned when Nexus found a home at Dark Horse comics in the early 1990s.

"When First dissolved and Nexus was bought by Dark Horse, it was shortly thereafter that head publisher Mike Richardson gave us the rights to Nexus back. It was a fairly unprecedented act, according to our industry's rights coveted history. With editorial despots like Martin Goodman, Bob Kaniger, or Mort Weisinger, such a move would've been considered unthinkable and probably awarded with a mandatory prison sentence!," Steve Rude wrote to me in 2015, adding, "I hope to always be associated with Nexus. It's the most personal and therefore the most rewarding work I'll probably ever do."

For the mainstream comic book industry, Rude has produced sporadic but memorable work including a *World's Finest* mini-series for DC along with a number of one-shot Marvel titles featuring the heroes rendered in Rude's nostalgically precise style. One of the books was a cross-over featuring Superman and Hulk, which initially was planned to be written by Stan Lee as Rude recalled, "When I found out I was to draw an entire 48-page book from Stan's single, bare-bones paragraph, I got a little worried, but a new writer was then brought on board to provide me with a full script. From there, other books for Marvel progressed to mini-series on the X-Men, Spider-Man, Thor and Captain America."

The spirit of creator-owned freedom also reared its head in England in the early part of the 1980s as Dez Skinn left his editorial and writing duties at Marvel UK to launch an ambitious new publishing project. It would not only introduce the writer Alan Moore, whose articulate and highly-original work would later dominate the industry in the latter part of the decade; create the impetus for DC to establish its mature audience Vertigo Comics imprint and also provide the springboard for one of the medium's modern-day classics and, through artist David Lloyd, offer a visual iconography that was adopted in the real-world as a symbol against oppression some 30 years later. Lloyd said to me in 2013, "Dez was passionate about comics and wanted to do his own thing. After he left Marvel, he set up his own company Quality Communications, and his first periodical was *Warrior*, an anthology magazine. He wanted to use the kind of character mix he'd used in *Hulk Weekly* with writers like Steve Dillon and Steve Moore but with completely new characters. Dez couldn't offer the page rates major publishers could because he was independent, so

Opposite page: Letter from Ditko to the author discussing comic book editors and economics from 2014.

2/ The anti-Ditko started when I did the first Question story/art for Charlton Press.

A comic fan magazine publisher attacked me, the Question violating their THE standard of fiction and fantasy.

The attacks just spread.

My first work for DC comics had editors split on my doing any work for them/DC's fiction/fantasy and I heard of editors who wanted me and pressured by others not to use me.

So a comic book industry that started out doing fictional, fantasy characters became restrictive, not open to someone's fiction/fantasy or hero.

The superhero comic industry editors confessing such fear of a different fiction/fantasy story ideas, art—what a humiliating confession.

Charlton Press editors wisely let the artist develop his own style, styles, even story ideas, etc.

DC editors were more like kings.

Marvel's Lee, personal picky, not intrusive but still, his Marvel had a pile of rejected art pages, a couple of my covers, rejected stories in their "vault", etc.

Why should any comic book fiction/fantasy story/art become so anti, not fit to be published?

It can be because comic book editors, fans, fan publications can't stand the comparison

the compensation offered to his contributors was that we had complete creative freedom to do what we wanted to do and we owned the characters we created. *V for Vendetta* would not have existed without this freedom to do whatever the hell we liked."

Lloyd continued, "The scripts from Alan on *V* were not as detailed as I hear he's produced for others and neither of us knew how it was all going to end. The element of *V* that was detailed was the outline of the world it was set in. Alan had worked out this fantastic universe of where this character would live and how it happened; after a nuclear interchange; what happens to society and the world that is left. It was very much based on Germany in the 1930s — after hyper-inflation and massive unemployment – that was the model for the world in *V for Vendetta*. Detailing a similar reason for the rise of fascism, with the people reaching out for a saviour, not really caring if he was a monster because they needed saving. We translated that to a future Britain. I went through a few designs which either didn't work or weren't satisfactory for the character. The Guy Fawkes thing was just one of those crazy brain waves you have and it worked — it fit perfectly with what we wanted to do. And, of course, that design kicked off a lot of creative developments."

Having been faithfully interpreted in the 2006 movie starring Hugo Weaving and Natalie Portman, the Guy Fawkes influenced mask design began to appear across news media worldwide when it was first worn by members of the Anonymous section of the Occupy Wall Street movement in October 2011. "I think it's fantastic that something I created has had such an impact — and the mask represents the spirit and the philosophy of the original work," Lloyd commented to me, adding, "So though people are using it for different reasons it still represents its original purpose — as an all-purpose symbol of resistance to oppression — something that it very important for us all. I consider *V for Vendetta* the most important work I've ever done."

Ditko's 1960s work on Charlton's *Action Heroes* line was paid homage or borrowed heavily by Alan Moore and Dave Gibbons when they created *Watchmen* in 1986, a seminal deconstructionist view of the superhero genre that became one of the industry's perennial sellers in collected editions. Some main characters in the series were reimagined versions of Ditko's originals (The Question became Rorschach; Captain Atom became Dr. Manhattan and Blue Beetle became Night Owl) with Alan Moore recalling of their origins for an interview published in *The Comics Journal* # 116 in July 1987, "Originally, *Watchmen* grew out of me sending in a proposal for the Charlton characters. Dick Giordano liked it but couldn't use it because it would have made the Charlton characters unusable thereafter. So, he said, 'Why not come up with some other characters?' which I did. These were loosely based upon the Charlton characters, although I don't think there's a recognizable similarity now. The Rorschach character

Above: Ditko, pencils and inks, original artwork for the "wrap" cover from ***The Collector*** fanzine, 1972, published by Bill Wilson, ©1972 Estate of Steve Ditko.

was created to fill the gap he made in the plot. What I was trying to do was come up with this quintessential Steve Ditko character, someone who's got a funny name, whose surname begins with a 'K,' who's got an oddly designed mask. That struck me as a Ditkoesque touch, having that blot crawling around on the face. And also, somebody who takes the philosophic aspects of Mr. A a great deal further and into a world perhaps a lot grimier and more realistic than the very clean world that Steve Ditko's characters inhabit."

Despite the graphic novel's phenomenal success and subsequent far reaching influence, it had little impact on Ditko who wrote to me in 2015 when asked about it, "Allen (sic) Moore's 'version' of the Question, Blue Beetle, etc. I might have, probably did, see, read something about it but have no memory about it." As for the character of Rorschach, Ditko has been quoted as summing him up as "just like Mr. A, except he's insane." The only known recording of Ditko's voice appeared in Ken Viola's 1987 documentary film *The Masters of Comic Book Art*. While refusing to be filmed for the production, which also included on-screen interviews with Will Eisner, Jack Kirby and Frank Miller, the now 60-year-old Ditko gave Viola a brief audio recording talking about his independent work. It appeared in the documentary as a voiceover, accompanying relevant on-screen art panel examples of his work and Ditko referring to modern versions of superheroes as "Today's flawed superheroes are superior in physical strength but common, average, ordinary in mental strength and rich in super-powers but bankrupt in reasoning powers."

With The Punisher picking up guns as his "super-power"; Frank Miller's *The Dark Knight Returns* series depicting an embittered, aging Batman, repugnant at the modern world and finally presiding over The Joker's death; Wolverine forever holding back a berserker rage and the flesh-slicing weapons within and Watchmen offering a bleak picture of dysfunctional superheroes in a dysfunctional world, the angst that typified 1970s costumed dramas was replaced with ultra-reality and a parade of grimacing, stubbled-chinned vigilantes.

"Comic book fans who later became editors, writers, wanted flawed heroes, anti-heroes to suit their own unwillingness to seek higher standards," Ditko wrote to me in September 2014, adding, "It seems comic book companies, publishers, editors, too many writers and artists, all want the comfort of the anti-hero, where we're ALL grey, so no-one can judge anyone or anything."

"It's tough to do multiple stories with a psychotic mass murderer as your 'hero,' and I know because I did it!" writer David Michelinie said to me in 2019 referencing the Sony movie franchise that launched the screen career of one of his co-creations for Marvel and a perfect example of an increasingly popularity of anti-heroes. Michelinie continued, recalling the character's introduction, "This is the word-for-word description I gave for Venom's first appearance in my plot for the last page of *Amazing Spider-Man* #299: '(Mary Jane) sees a white smile form beneath the eye-shapes. Not a pretty smile; a scary smile. Like that of a predator sure of a quick kill. The form then steps from the shadows, and we can see that it is dressed in a Spider-Man costume, but it is definitely not Peter Parker. Besides the feral smile, the man's body is huge, bulky, massively muscled — like Arnold Schwarzenegger on a good day. MJ backs up, terrified, as the stranger reaches a hand out towards her, his lopsided animal smile stretching to the point where it almost connects behind his head.' Creating Venom, I thoroughly enjoyed working with Todd McFarlane. He was a solid professional, told a story very clearly, stuck to the plot, and drew pictures that were fun to write dialogue for. Most people I talk to these days, associate the ever-lengthening tongue of Venom with Todd. Not so. Go back and look and you'll see that super-licker started when Erik Larsen took over the pencils. I was never contacted by anyone in regard to the Venom movie, but I did receive some small remuneration as specified in a contract I signed with Marvel. Also, Todd and I received a stand-alone credit at the end of the movie, which I thought it was entertaining. With Venom and also Carnage, creating characters that have become part of the Spider-Man world for over 30 years is very gratifying indeed. Other than that, and even though it's been retro-deleted by the endless reboots, I was proud that I was able to make the marriage between Peter and Mary Jane work during my time as writer of the series. I didn't want to marry Peter and Mary Jane in the first place. But that was a decision made by the higher-ups at Marvel. I was given the option of getting them married or quitting the title, which was my dream job. So, I decided to give it a shot and do the unthinkable: make the marriage a happy one, with none of the bickering and jealousy and separation that readers would likely expect. And I think I made that work. My memory is that *ASM* was selling about 325,000 copies a month when I started writing it and was selling around 375,000 copies when I left. Though I do remember that an anniversary issue sold over a million copies."

Ditko's productivity had changed little from 1972, when he created 256 comic art pages and 31 covers, with his output at the end of 1989 at 251 pages but just seven covers and though he would work within the comic book industry for a few more years, the artist would, for the next twenty-five years and right up until the end of his life, direct most of his efforts into creating self-published, small print-run, black-and-white publications that contained new art and strips along with essays, freely espousing his Objectivist views. "Comic companies not wanting to use me because of my Charlton Question and *witzend* Mr. A gave me more opportunities to get into self-publishing with Robin Snyder," Ditko wrote to me in November 2014, defiantly adding, "I should thank those editors for not wanting to use me."

© 91 S. DITKO
BURRIS
AL JAPER
EXPLODER
MESSA JUBI

Chapter Six

A "Self-destructing" Industry and its Hollywood Saviours 1990-2017

"Stan jumped up and embraced Steve as soon as he entered the room. They seemed very happy to see each other and their discussions lasted maybe a half-hour to an hour," recalled Tom DeFalco of a meeting that took place between the two previous collaborators of historic productivity in the early summer of 1992. That year, Marvel launched a line of comic book titles with reimagined versions of some established characters, Spider-Man included, set in the future, corporation-controlled world of 2099. The promotion for the event played up Stan Lee's return to writing comics, bringing with him a singular brand new character for the line named Ravage, and this led to the reunion meeting with Steve Ditko. DeFalco recalled to the author in 2018, "Stan wanted Steve to draw *Ravage 2099* and I think Stan just thought it would be fun to team up with Steve again. I arranged a meeting between them, but Steve wasn't interested in drawing the character. If I remember correctly, Steve wasn't all that intrigued with the idea of drawing a character who was essentially a garbage man. Ravage just didn't press his creative buttons."

In the first time the two men had been face to face since the difficulties over Spider-Man in 1965, when they inhabited the same orbit again the meeting was amicable, according to DeFalco, "It was a real thrill for me to see Stan and Steve together and I think that Steve left the door open for future collaborations, but nothing ever came of that. He and Stan left on cordial terms." It would be the last time the two great comic book creators would ever meet. While DeFalco initially suggested Ditko as a choice of artist on the series, it was Jim Salicrup who called him with the invitation to attend the meeting that took place in Marvel's then-President Terry Stewart's office, familiar surroundings for Lee as it was his own office back in the days when he was in charge, just before his departure to California.

One of the "future collaborations" that De Falco mentioned was a pitch from Lee for the pair to reunite to produce a one-off Spider-Man graphic novel ("Think of all the money we'll make!," Lee impressed on Ditko, according to Salicrup, who was also present at the meeting). But Ditko opined how he could never care about the character as much as he originally had and declined the invitation, much to Lee's obvious disappointment. "In the seven years I was Editor-in-Chief I saw Marvel transform from a small company that couldn't give its licenses away to start on the road of becoming the large corporation it is today with its major motion pictures and merchandising industry," DeFalco said, adding, "Stan and I used to talk on a regular basis, and we spent a lot of time together. He taught me so much about comics and dealing with creative people. I will always be in his debt. Steve was a creative genius and an incredible visual story-teller. He created and co-created a lot of characters that will never be forgotten. My own proudest achievements in my comic book career is co-creating *Spider-Girl* with artist Ron Frenz and initiating the Marvel Masterworks hardcover reprint collection series."

The final meeting between Ditko and Lee took place at Marvel's offices at 387 Park Avenue South, located between 27th and 28th Street, where the company had moved from Madison Avenue in the early 1980s, following a succession of different owners with its parent company Marvel Entertainment Group now in the hands of Revlon executive Ron Perelman, who took the company public in 1991. At these spacious offices, Ditko would deliver his final assignments for Marvel Comics, passing or entering on occasion, a conference room with glass doors etched over completely with a frosted webbing design in celebration of the publisher's flagship character and enduring evidence of Ditko's past contribution to its present standing.

Among his last deliveries was a story introducing a character named Squirrel Girl, first appearing in *Marvel Superheroes Winter Special* 1991 and widely quoted in media articles as Ditko's last co-creation for Marvel Comics. But the artist was quick to point out, in a letter to me from February 2016, that this wasn't the case, "Squirrel Girl, She wasn't my idea, creation. It's the writer — Will Murray's creation, I just did the visuals. (During that time) I did a lot of pencilling that other artists inked." Ditko continued with occasional assignments for Marvel with his very last work for the company, an Iron Man story, appearing in the one-shot *Shadows and Light* (February 1998). A previously unpublished 21-page story produced around this time with writer Jack C. Harris eventually saw print in *Incredible Hulk and The Human Torch: From the Marvel Vault* published in 2011.

Opposite page: Ditko, pencils and inks, original artwork for a page from ***Mr. A***, 1991, ©1991 Estate of Steve Ditko.

His final work for DC included a Spectre story published in *Legends of the DC Universe 80-Page Giant* #1 (September 1998) and a *Tales of the New Gods* story written by Mark Millar that only saw print in a collected trade paperback edition in 2008. A Ditko-drawn Batman story was promised in the solicitation for *Gotham Knights* #7 (September 2000) but never materialized. Former DC editorial assistant Valerie D'Orazio wrote on her social media in 2007 that she had delivered the script to Ditko's office but later "found out that he rejected the script on the grounds that it had a supernatural basis and that he didn't do stories with supernatural elements in it."

In tandem with these, the artist also produced work for Topps Comics and Valiant Comics, two emerging players in a burgeoning ensemble of new publishers entering the field via the direct sales market and its supply to the ever-growing number of comic book speciality stores. At the end of 1991, Marvel was rocked by the mass defection of some of its star artists, Todd McFarlane, Jim Lee, Rob Liefeld, Marc Silvestri, Erik Larsen and Jim Valentino who had conspired to leave and form their own, independent publishing company Image Comics, producing their characters in a creator-owned environment and extending the same deal to other writers and artists.

Its embryonic period saw a combination of the artists' popularity and the speculative buying of retailers and consumers producing sales figures on comic books like *Youngblood*, *Wildcats* and *Spawn* as high as the major publishers top-tier books with its success typified by its visually-forceful style, presenting many one or two-page spreads revelling in the spectacle of its varying art styles, similar to the early days of Marvel Comics with Liefeld taking Kirby's dynamic naïve art immediacy to less inspired places and McFarlane providing the quirky details prevalent in Ditko's work. Marvel's stock price fell for a time in reaction to the formation and initial success of Image Comics, but a series of late-shipping books hampered its reputation for a time, and its threat largely diminished. Image would, however, develop as a lasting presence in the industry and an effective platform for creators' self-copyrighted work, with a notable success in writer Robert Kirkman's *The Walking Dead* and its subsequent adaptation to television.

After a failed bid by Jim Shooter, lawyer businessman (who in a previous career in music artist management launched the career of Cyndi Lauper and handled other acts such as The Psychedelic Furs) Steven J. Massarsky and an investor group to purchase Marvel Comics in 1988, the consortium formed Voyager Communications a year later with Valiant Comics established as its comic book imprint. From 1991, the company released a number of successful titles licensed from Western Publishing, including *Magnus, Robot Fighter* and *Solar, Man of the Atom* along with new characters such as *Bloodshot* and *Shadowman*. With Valiant gaining over 5 percent of market share from industry leaders Marvel and DC by 1992, the newcomer had an air of the creative underdog also in a similar fashion to Marvel's first taste of success in the 1960s, but within an industry measuring its growth by a transitory speculator boom, its triumph was short-lived.

Bob Layton, Iron Man's definitive artist of the 1980s and co-creator of the War Machine character, remembered Valiant to the author in 2014, "We started up in 1989, in a fifth-floor loft in downtown Manhattan. The place was a total rat-trap-literally. From the very beginning, we were operating behind the 8-ball. Jim Shooter surrounded himself with people who were very loyal to him, but not big on hard work or making deadlines. We (the Production Department) were always breaking land speed records trying to get product out, solicitations, mock-ups. It was much worse working with Jim Shooter at Valiant than at Marvel. Most Valiant fans will not want to believe anything I say, and it's hard to get the truth past the revisionist history that's been generated over the years by certain disgruntled parties. However, I kept a daily journal of every event that transpired at Valiant, from the day I started, to the day I exited. I can recall every day in vivid detail, thanks to those journals. Granted, it's written from my perspective, but the chronology is historically accurate. Nine months into the start-up, Triumph (the venture capitalists that funded Valiant) dismissed CFO Winston Folkes and placed Fred Pierce in our offices to spy on Jim Shooter's business activities and report back to them. (They now had a crisis of confidence in Shooter's business acumen.) In a repeat of his history at Marvel, Shooter's relationship with upper management became antagonistic in nature. They were incredibly upset that their investment money had gone up in smoke, and we weren't even out of the gate yet. Every day, the staff lived under the threat of closure at a moment's notice. Not a fun time. Barry Windsor-Smith and I were best friends at that time in my career. He had also had a tumultuous relationship with Marvel management and was looking for other creative venues. Although he was dubious of Shooter and the rumours that constantly swirled around his career, I was able to convince him to join Valiant as our premiere penciller. Without Barry to give the company credence with the buying public, there would have been no Valiant. Valiant was a grand experiment that had incredible highs and unbelievable lows. In many ways, it was the Camelot of comic book companies — a wondrous time that this industry will probably never see again. Once Triumph ousted Shooter, we became a very tight-knit family, with everyone sharing in the work and benefits. We all knew it wouldn't last, but it was great while it did. Many of us keep in touch — twenty-some years later, because of the bond that we shared as cogs in a huge, creative dream machine. The entire industry failed at the time, not just Valiant. Marvel was forced into Chapter 11 bankruptcy around the same time. I'm going to tell you exactly what happened to Valiant and why we had no control over its eventual demise: Triumph, by the end of 1993, had made a small fortune off of Valiant. We were netting around 30 million dollars a year and they had more than satisfied their investors. If you understand how venture capital works, they are always short-term investors. Once Triumph had made sufficient profits, they ordered CEO Steve Massarsky to sell the company. They wanted out. They were in the venture capital business, not the publishing biz. They didn't give us a choice." David Michelinie also recalled, "When I first started writing for Valiant, both Jim Shooter and Bob Layton were old friends of mine. As might be expected, they both valued writing and story, and it was exciting to be a part of creating a whole new universe of characters. Slowly, however, artists began getting preferential treatment, and petty squabbles became the norm in the offices. Sad, but I suppose inevitable."

Layton had previously edited the publication *Charlton Bullseye* ("We had total access to Charlton's unpublished library of material, and this included all the unpublished Ditko material") and worked briefly at Valiant with Ditko, who provided pencils and layouts on various titles including *Magnus, Robot Fighter* and *Solar, Man of the Atom*. When Shooter left Valiant to set up Defiant Comics, Ditko followed and with the editor/writer created a brand-new title *Dark Dominion* that only appeared as a #0 issue reproduced across a trading card set. Layton wrote to me, "Ditko did eventually work with me at Valiant, and we had a very friendly and respectful relationship. Many a day, Steve would plop down at my desk and tell me stories about his early Marvel days. At times, it was surreal for this boy from Indiana to be swapping tales with one of the true legends of the comic industry."

Another "true legend" passed on February 6, 1994 when Jack Kirby died of heart failure at his home in Thousand Oaks, California, where the artist had been living with his family since moving out from New York back in 1969. He died a wealthy man, with a 10 million dollar estimated estate value, but that was a relatively low figure in comparison to the billions of dollars the library of comic book characters Kirby had created generates for its legal owners. With sporadic work in animation and the comic book industry leading up his official retirement in 1987, Kirby had experienced a particularly bitter fight in attempting to regain his historic, and lucrative, original 1960s artwork back from Marvel Comics.

Originally offered just 88 pages in exchange for signing a release declaring all his art was created as a work made for hire, assuring that Marvel retained all rights, Kirby responded with a public damnation of the situation declaring the company to be "thugs," and by 1985 Marvel had relented by releasing around 2,000 of the estimated 12,000 pages Kirby had drawn back to the artist, on receipt of a signed document that waived his right to any claim of copyright over the hundreds of characters he had created for Marvel Comics. The vast majority of the artwork that Kirby drew for the company, around 10,000 individual pages and covers, were stolen from the Marvel offices, and the warehouse used to store all original art and command high prices at auction today, with their exact provenance unclear. Later in 1996, the estate of Jerry Seigel contested that the Copyright Act of 1976 allowed them to terminate their grant of copyright on the character of Superman, 56 years after copyright had originally been established with a five-year window allowing them to serve notice of their intention to do so. It meant that for a time the Seigel family held 50 percent of the rights to Superman with Warner Brothers now in a position of renegotiation for the full rights. In 2001, a deal was settled with a one-off payment of 3 million dollars, an annual stipend of $500,000, royalties paid on future appearances and a credit for the writer thereafter.

It wasn't the end of the legal drama, however, with an opportunist attorney persuading both the Seigel and Shuster families to stage another copyright challenge with an emphasis on Superboy. By 2014, following several appeals, the ruling was that the 2001 agreement was a complete transference of rights, with full ownership of both characters reverting back to Warners. For a time at least, as all copyrights eventually expire, initially within a 75-year period, but the Copyright Term Extension Act, eligible on certain copyrights, extended that period to 95 years from when first established, ostensibly meaning that in 2033, the original superhero will enter into public domain and herald a new round of legal wrangling, with Kirby's characters and Ditko's Spider-Man following suit around 2057. The estate of Jack Kirby, comprising the four children the artist had with his life-long wife Roz, used a similar case of termination of copyright in 2009 to launch a series of legal proceedings against Marvel,

Opposite page: Stan Lee, 2011, ©2011 David Currie.

resulting in an undisclosed settlement with the family in September 2014 in what was simply the close of another chapter in a seemingly never-ending battle.

In the comic book industry's own continual battle for sales, the market had shifted from promotional events, such as the *Death of Superman* in 1992, to a proliferation of high-priced gimmick covers, enhanced through a variety of production methods, embossed, lenticular, holographic, die-cut and so on, along with a trend in "variant" covers, limited editions bearing a different image, all fuelling a growing emphasis on comic books as a collectable commodity and igniting a speculator boom that enabled the doors of many a comic book store to open. In late 1994, Marvel made a dramatic and ultimately ill-fated move to control the distribution of its own product by purchasing Heroes World Distribution, then the third largest player in the field with Capitol City and Diamond Distributors all having access to every publisher's range. With Heroes World now appointed as the sole distributor of Marvel comics, both Diamond and Capitol immediately responded by seeking to negotiate exclusive deals with all the other publishers with comic book retailers caught in the middle, besieged by added paperwork, disparate ordering systems, reduced discounts and general confusion. With the company, originally founded by Ivan Synder, previous head of licensing in Marvel's merchandising department back in the early 1970s, ill-equipped to deal with the complexities of shipping Marvel comics out weekly to thousands of worldwide accounts and multiple shipping and billing errors resulting in lost business lawsuits, the company went out of business by 1997, with Marvel returning to Diamond Distributors as the last player standing and a company now enjoying exclusive distribution rights to all major North American publishers of comic books.

By now, the speculators had fled the market, and this, combined with the after-effects of the distribution wars, caused many of those dispirited retailers to close the doors they had optimistically opened just some years previously, and the number of comic book stores fell to under half its previous amount. "The means of distribution and control are always held by big companies, and Marvel and DC have been running the show for many decades, and there's nothing really to keep them from running the shows for more decades to come," artist David Lloyd said to me, continuing, "I've got nothing against DC; it's all been good experiences with them, and if it weren't for DC, *V for Vendetta* wouldn't be where it is now But the point is this: It's not good for any medium to be dominated by just two major companies that decide how the public perceive the medium to be. Which is generally a bunch of superheroes running around — everything else is side-lined or second choice. Of course, the movies have heightened this perception — it's now all about source material for Hollywood."

Back in the early to mid-1990s, Marvel was aggressively expanding with multiple company acquisitions, including trading card companies Fleer and Skybox; toy manufacturer ToyBiz and Italian-based publisher of sticker-books Panini adding to its purchase of Heroes World. Now faced with a volatile and diminishing market, the company reported a loss in late 1995 followed by the departure of nearly 300 employees; merged with ToyBiz (creating a new division called Marvel Studios) and eventually, in December 1996, the entire group of companies filed for Chapter 11 bankruptcy with Marvel stock delisted on the New York Stock Exchange in the darkest days for the company since the Comics Code debacle of the 1950s.

"When I first got there in the late 1970s, it seemed like it was a business that would soon be gone, and that situation didn't seem to bother anyone," editor Danny Fingeroth wrote to me in 2019, continuing, "It felt like it was looser, less structured, than it became. We were working for a corporation, but it seemed more like we were working for a high school or college magazine. By 1995, it was clear just how important Marvel's intellectual property was, whether it was presented in comics or on TV or in the movies or in videogames. It wasn't playtime anymore. The company's characters were going to be involved in big business one way or another for the foreseeable future. Even if the comics went away, the characters were too valuable and popular to ever disappear. That's true today more than ever."

With investor Carl Icahn replacing Ron Perelman, who was later to pay out 80 million dollars in settlement of a lawsuit accusing him of diverting funds, the company rose from its calamity, changing its name by 2005 to Marvel Entertainment, in emphasis of its intention to finance its own character movie productions.

As the 1990s and the millennium itself came to a close, Stan Lee's public profile remained high, and by now he had long relinquished any duties at Marvel other than as a figure head who drew a 1 million dollar salary from the company as "Chairman Emeritus." This came to an end in 1998 when Marvel used its bankruptcy procedures to void the lifetime employment contract with Lee, and later that same year, with the advent of the internet, Lee formed "Stan Lee Media" designed to originate, produce and web-distribute new superhero creations, in association with former lawyers Peter Paul and Arthur Lieberman. It would end in disaster, with the company filing for Chapter 11 bankruptcy by 2000 while under investigation for illegal stock manipulation after going public through a reverse merger with a trading shell, with Paul eventually convicted and serving jail time and Lee cleared of any implication or involvement in the scheme.

Undaunted, Lee formed POW! Entertainment in 2001 in partnership with Lieberman and Gill Champion, as another web-active development company for media properties. In November 1998, Lee had taken a claim to Marvel for half

Opposite page: Ditko, pencils and inks, explaining the division of labor in the creation of Spider-Man from his self-published ***The 32-Page TSK! TSK! Package***, 2000, ©2000 Estate of Steve Ditko.

ownership of Spider-Man, the X-Men and other characters since Marvel had cancelled his previous rights assignment during its bankruptcy. It resulted in a reinstatement of his 1 million dollar annual payment along with a 10 percent share of movie and television profits. With the coming of the billion-dollar grossing 2002 *Spider-Man* film, Lee invoked the contract and sued Marvel for unpaid share payments. A 2005 settlement between the parties was never revealed but rumoured to involve a 10 million dollar pay out.

In interviews to promote his new endeavours, and validate his spokesperson salary, mention was often made of his contribution to Marvel characters with the editor often perpetuating, or failing to correct, the belief that he was the prime creator of the Marvel stable of characters. An article in *Time* magazine, published November 16, 1998, had referred to Lee as "Spider-Man's creator" motivating Ditko to write his own letter to the magazine, published December 7, 1998, to correct the error by noting that because of his visual contribution to the character, Spider-Man "was a collaboration of writer-editor Stan Lee and artist Steve Ditko as co-creators." In an open letter dated August 18, 1999, Lee responded with the following clarification, "I would like to go on record with the following statement…I have always also considered Steve Ditko to be Spider-Man's co-creator. When I first told Steve my idea for a shy, teenaged high-school science student who'd be bitten by a radioactive spider, thus gaining the ability to stick to walls and shoot webs, Steve took to it like a duck to water. Steve's illustrated version of Peter Parker/Spider-Man and his coterie of supporting characters was more compelling and dramatic than I had dared hope it would be. From his very first panel, Steve created and established the perfect mood and gestalt for Spider-Man. Also, it goes without saying that Steve's costume design was an actual masterpiece of imagination. Thanks to Steve Ditko, Spidey's costume has become one of the world's most recognisable visual icons. Nor can I forget to credit Steve with the many, many brilliant plots he furnished as the strip continued to increase in popularity with each passing month. So adept was he at story telling that Steve eventually did most of the plotting and illustration which I, of course, continued to provide the dialogue and captions. I write this to ensure that Steve Ditko receives the credit to which he is so just justly entitled."

In replying to Lee's letter, Ditko noted that the giving of credit is often diminished by the words chosen to relay the information, in this particular case, the use of the word "considered." Ditko wrote in *The 32-Page Tsk! Tsk! Package* in 2000, "What is needed to be considered, pondered and for how long? The issue is: Either Steve Ditko is the co-creator of Spider-Man or Steve Ditko is not the co-creator of Spider-Man. A is A or A is not A. Is it so difficult for Lee to admit, write, 'Steve Ditko co-created Spider-Man with me?'" The open letter by Lee did not signal an end to his apparent claims of sole authorship or negligence in naming collaborators. A year later, in an interview in the *Tampa Tribute* (December

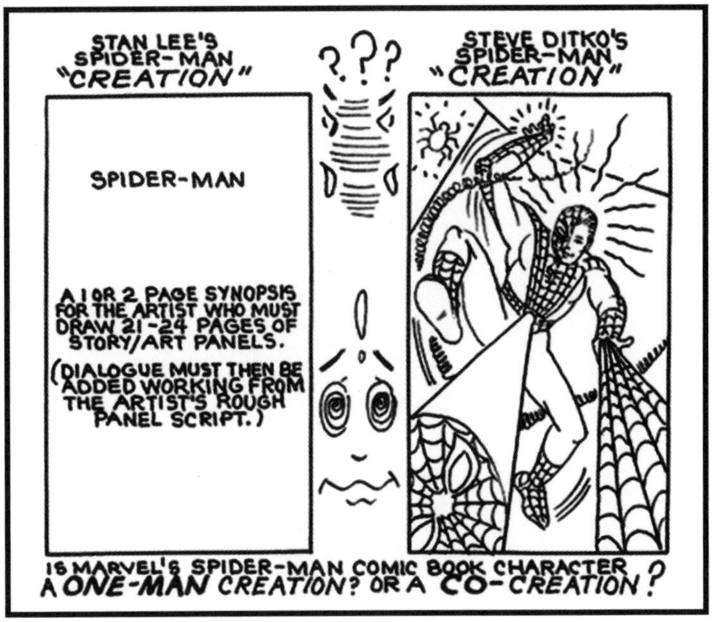

7, 1999) when asked to name his favourite creation, Lee answered, "I don't know, Doctor Strange. Well, Spider-Man is the most famous character I created," along with an earlier throwaway line written in jest, but perhaps revealing more truth than intended when Lee stated in his Soapbox column for Marvel comics dated May 1999, "You know me, I'll take any credit that isn't nailed down!" Lee had made inconsistent statements over the years and with past articles bearing headlines such as "How I Invented Spider-Man" (1977), in which Ditko was mentioned just once, and the more recent *Time* article, the artist had begun writing his opinions on the subject of creatorship in his self-published *The 32-Page Tsk! Tsk! Package* in 2000 and later in *The Avenging Mind* published in 2008 where Ditko stated in an essay titled "He Giveth and He Taketh Away" that "It's actually very, very rare that Lee ever used the term 'co-creator' and actually named who the co-creator was."

In 2007, English television personality Jonathan Ross produced an hour long BBC documentary titled *In Search of Steve Ditko* presenting a knowledgeable appraisal of the artist's career and a telling interview with Stan Lee where his reluctance to share creator credit on Spider-Man is revealed on camera, seemingly confirming Ditko's observations of such. When pushed by Ross on the subject, a visibly annoyed Lee first asserts that he is "willing to say so" until negating his own statement with the admission that he still believed that the person who came up with the initial idea was the creator, "and then you give it to anybody to draw it."

At the end of the documentary and its "search" for its subject matter, the TV presenter, along with influential and acclaimed author Neil Gaiman, is shown on camera outside Ditko's office building requesting an audience. After a swift camera cut, Ross reappears declaring that they had spoken with the artist, but he had declined to be filmed for

the production. Gaiman wrote to me in 2019, recalling the meeting, "Jonathan just said to me, 'I'm going down to see Steve now, do you want to come along?' We remained in the hallway. He went in to get us some comics and came out again, but I did not see inside. He looked… well he looked like the photo of Ditko from the 1950s, just 50 years on. Greyer hair and balding, and he looked like he had spent a lifetime at the drawing board." Ditko was not aware of precisely who his two English guests, with their own celebrity status, were, and while the artist answered their questions and sent them off with a handful of his recent comic books, the meeting was relatively brief and the books remained unsigned. "We didn't ask him to sign them," continued Gaiman, "It would have felt like we were pushing our luck. He talked to us, answered our questions, and entertained us for 25 minutes. He gave us comic books. It was enough. I read his comic books growing up and fell in love, not with his Marvel work, but with the work he did for the small horror titles that were reprinted in the UK, such as *The Mysterious Traveller* and the like. I found *Doctor Strange* reprints which I loved, and *Spider-Man* reprints as well. I think Ditko was vital to the creation of Marvel. For me, Peter Parker and Doctor Strange were black-and-white before they were colour. And then I fell in love with his DC work. The Creeper, Hawk and Dove, they were beautiful and strange and the stories were weird. Interestingly weird. I think his Doctor Strange is definitely in my DNA. I don't think his Spider-Man was. The Creeper might be in there somewhere." In reference to Ditko's career and the difficulties the artist often encountered, Gaiman wrote, "I don't think he was ever unemployable. I think that mainstream publishers did not want to publish his comics as mainstream comics, but they were published. And he found an audience. Meanwhile, he still did work for bigger publishers. I wish he had been properly recompensed for what he did with Spider-Man and Doctor Strange, because it would have made it easier for him to self-publish and create the stories and material that he wanted to get out into the world. But I do not believe, and I do not think he believed the publishers were under any obligation to publish anything he did."

Above: Ditko, pencils and inks, for the original cover art for ***A Ditko*** #15, 2011, ©2011 Estate of Steve Ditko and Robin Snyder.

With the bulk of Ditko's independent work from the 1960s and 1970s first collected in the two-volume *The Ditko Collection* published by Fantagraphics 1985/86, the majority of the artist's new work and vintage reprint packages from 1988 onwards were published with Robin Snyder, an editor who had first worked with Ditko at Charlton, DC and a variety of other companies. These include: *Static* (1988); *The Ditko Package* (1989); *The Mocker* (1990); *Laszlo's Hammer* (1992); *160 Page Package* (1999); and a total of 26 in a series of 32-page comic books since 2008 including new Mr. A stories and new character creations including Miss Eerie, The Outline, The Cape, The Grey Negotiator and The Hero, in addition to regular contributions to Synder's *The History of Comics!*.

Ditko wrote to me about his self-published work and its lack of coverage in the mainstream industry saying, "Comic books fans, fan publications, don't want to report on my and Robin Snyder's material, unless it's negative in some way. It has to be embarrassing for comic book fan publications since me and Robin have been putting out material for 25 years. (In 2013) It's a 25th Anniversary of Robin and me putting out material on personal histories of writers, artists and my stories, art. Everything adds up. When Robin started publishing his *The Comics,* there were issues in comics he wanted to cover, etc. I'm not a writer. But the issues — stolen art, etc — affected me, so I agreed to do some writing on them. It just grew. Comic book fandom continues to be childish, resentful, because they can't have their own way. I'm amazed at how shabbily so many comic book fans treat themselves by always wanting to have their own way with others. But it's not only in the area of comic books. It involves all areas of life and its global."

Robin Snyder said of Ditko on his social media in December 2018, "Ditko's ideas helped shape this publication in the beginning, and his constructive criticism, suggestions, articles and artwork have sustained it over all these years. Without Ditko, *The Comics!* would have been a different, smaller, poorer production."

Marvel's domination of the block buster cinema industry began outside of its own auspices beginning with New Line's production of *Blade* in 1998, with licences sold to 20th Century Fox and Sony yielding its first real superhero successes with Bryan Singer's *X-Men* in 2000 (providing the first outing for Hugh Jackman as Wolverine and Sir Patrick Stewart as Professor X, roles both actors would reprise frequently enough for them to share the awarded honour of *Longest Career as a Live-Action Marvel Superhero* in the Guinness Book of Records 2018), followed by the phenomenal-for-its-time box office receipts generated by Sam Raimi's *Spider-Man*, which opened in American cinemas on May 3, 2002. Teased the previous year with an advance trailer showing the web-slinger capturing thieves escaping by helicopter in webbing suspended between the twin towers of the World Trade Centre, the trailer and its accompanying poster showing the New York landmark reflected in Spider-Man's eyes were swiftly pulled following the horrific, society-changing, traumatically live streamed televised attacks of September 11, 2001. By the time of the film's release, the resilience and community spirit of New Yorkers seemed personified on the screen by an ordinary local hero from Queens, with one scene showing a crowd of onlookers uniting to help Spider-Man deter The Green Goblin from his nefarious activities. A worthy and predominantly faithful translation of Ditko's original character template to movies, actor Tobey Maguire played well against Willem DaFoe's maniacal performance as the Goblin, but its dark and bloody climatic battle sequence betrayed the director's horror genre background, creating a confusion of style in its closing narrative.

Sequels of both franchises would ensue, over various reboots and cast refreshments with the iterations of Marvel characters emerging as a worthy box office competitor to DC movie heroes Superman and Batman, the latter of which introduced the sombre *Darker Knight* to cinemas beginning with Tim Burton's *Batman* in 1989 and the subsequent revision of the franchise in 2005 with *Batman Begins.* With the acquisition in 2009 of parent company Marvel Entertainment, including the comic book division and all its intellectual properties, by The Walt Disney Company for an estimated sum of around 4.24 billion dollars, the resources were present to solidify the development of Marvel Studios and the production of its own character movies. Becoming the world's most successful film franchise with a global box office gross approaching 18 billion dollars, Marvel Studios has released 23 films at the time of writing this book, launching with *Iron Man* in 2008 up to *Spider-Man: Far from Home* in 2019, presenting its characters in the closely knit continuity of its skillfully realised Marvel Cinematic Universe. With the 2018 release of *Black Panther* becoming the first superhero film to win Oscars for Best Costume Design, Best Production Design and Best Score, the franchise is set to continue for some years to come, albeit without the cameos of Stan Lee that so elevated his worldwide celebrity status.

Jack Kirby would never live to witness the spectacular acceptance for his creations as movie stars and unsurprisingly, the event held little appeal for Ditko, who wrote to me in September 2015, "I have no interest in seeing these Marvel character movies. I didn't really follow those characters when I worked on Spider-Man, and no reason to follow after I quit Spider-Man. The Spider-Man movies seem to be a mixed bag. I just saw the first Spider-Man and Superman movies, and I don't go to any other of those comic book hero movies. They are made for world-wide appeal. Movie producers want to appeal to the widest range of potential ticket buyers globally and new technology has made it possible to create fantastic special effects but I'm not sure about Hollywood's designer brains — the *Fantastic Four* failed again at the box office, but *The Ant-man*, never a popular comic book, was a surprising movie success. Not all changes will make sense. There will be the usual plusses and minuses." *Doctor Strange* director Scott Derrickson compared Ditko to reclusive American writer J.D. Salinger when he said in 2016 to *The Hollywood Reporter*, "He is private and has intentionally stayed out of the spotlight like J.D. Salinger." Adding, "I hope he goes to see the movie, wherever he is, because I think we paid homage to his work." Ditko wrote to me in 2017, "I have mixed feelings with the additions and eliminations, Tilda Swinton as the Ancient One, Doctor Strange with a side-kick etc. But whoever has the rights can add and subtract from the original any way he chooses. The movie had a problem with trying to match a panel's frozen magic effect with its continual, ever-changing view of what is seen. Movies can't translate a frozen panel action effect into a comparable moving image. Every medium has its uniqueness that makes it stand out." The uniqueness of comic books, a visually instantaneous medium that attracted Ditko so intensely he devoted his life to producing his own, was not defined exclusively by the superhero genre in the artist's mind, nor the sentimentality attached to the nostalgic reverence given to characters beloved in youth. With Ditko's admission that he had no interest in seeing any of the superhero movies including numerous versions of Batman and his dismissive rejection of the opportunity to draw a character he once loved so much in childhood, it was clear that when the artist was done with something, he was most assuredly done.

The success of Spider-Man as a movie franchise in the early part of the 21st century focalized some attention on Ditko's contribution to the character, with failed attempts to interview the artist from media journalists reinforcing the mystique of his rigidly-guarded private life and igniting rumours and speculations regarding his continuing silent counsel. While Ditko was known to diligently collate together issues of original art, package them neatly in brown paper, and store them at his family home back in Johnstown

AMAZING 15-P.9
AS HIS FIRST TV SPECTACULAR ENDS, PETER PARKER BREATHES THE FIRST SWEET SCENT OF FAME AND SUCCESS!
I'M FROM LIFE! WE'LL PAY ANY PRICE FOR A PICTURE SPREAD!
SIGN WITH ME! I'LL PUT YOU IN THE MOVIES!
WAIT! WE WANT AN INTERVIEW!
SEE MY AGENT, BOYS! I'M BUSY!
WHEW! RID OF 'EM AT LAST!
HEY! WHAT'S GOIN' ON??
STOP! THIEF! STOP HIM! IF HE MAKES IT TO THE ELEVATOR, HE'LL GET AWAY!
MADE IT!
I'M SAFE NOW! THAT COP CAN NEVER GET DOWN TO THE LOBBY AS FAST AS I CAN IN THIS HIGH-SPEED EXPRESS ELEVATOR! LUCKY THAT GOON IN A COSTUME DIDN'T STOP ME!
WHAT'S WITH YOU, MISTER?? ALL YOU HADDA DO WAS TRIP HIM, OR HOLD HIM JUST FOR A MINUTE!
SORRY, PAL! THAT'S YOUR JOB! I'M THRU BEING PUSHED AROUND --BY ANYONE! FROM NOW ON I JUST LOOK OUT FOR NUMBER ONE --THAT MEANS--ME!
I OUGHTTA RUN YOU IN--
SAVE YOUR BREATH, BUDDY! I'VE GOT THINGS TO DO!
AND, A FEW HOURS LATER...
PETER, YOU KNOW THAT MICROSCOPE YOU'VE ALWAYS WANTED? YOUR UNCLE AND I BOUGHT IT FOR YOU THIS AFTERNOON!
GOSH, THAT'S TERRIFIC!
YOU'RE THE GREATEST FAMILY ANY FELLA EVER HAD!
THEY'RE THE ONLY ONES WHO'VE EVER BEEN KIND TO ME! I'LL SEE TO IT THAT THEY'RE ALWAYS HAPPY, BUT THE REST OF THE WORLD CAN GO HANG FOR ALL I CARE!
8
9.

when he began his career, rumours now circulated that he cared so little for his own original art he would use them as cutting boards in his office, with a nearly two-foot stack of pages pushed up against a wall behind a curtain available for the task. A veritable fortune in original art assets that the artist never chose to offer for sell, the most valuable artwork he ever created was, for the most part, not within his choice to determine its destiny. In 1992, a Sotheby's auction sold the complete interior artwork to *Amazing Spider-Man* #31 for $24,200 and Ditko noted that, "Issue 31 is one of the 38 issues available as 'gifts' to non-producers," indicating that it was among the missing artwork unreturned to him. While the artist received many of the 5-page fantasy strips he had done for Marvel and the majority of his Doctor Strange work ("I received most of the Doctor Strange art pages"), the lion's share of his Spider-Man artwork was long gone before the company agreed to return what was left to him. Its value has substantially increased over the decades since it was first produced, in 2002 Heritage Auctions sold the complete 22-page story of *Amazing Spider-Man* #10 for $161,000; by 2012 the splash page of *Amazing Spider-Man* #12 reached $137,425, and by 2017 a single interior panel page from issue 25 sold for $105,000. To date, no original covers from the Spider-Man series drawn by Steve Ditko, all of which went "missing" from Marvel's warehouse, have ever come to the market.

In late 2008, the complete 11-page Spider-Man origin story art pages were anonymously donated to the American Library of Congress in Washington, together with all the other Steve Ditko art published in *Amazing Fantasy* #15. A phone call to Ditko seeking a comment on the Library's acquisition from the *Chicago Tribune* in September 2008 elicited the response, "I couldn't care less." Sara W. Duke, curator of Popular and Applied Graphic Art at the Library of Congress commented on the donation to me in 2019, "I was first contacted in 2008. I received a cold call, and will admit that at the time I knew *Action Comics* #1 was Superman, but did not know that *Amazing Fantasy* #15 was Spider-Man. I accepted the offer because while we have a spectacular editorial cartoon and comic strip drawing collection, the Library is rather weak on comic book illustrations. And then I did research and my jaw dropped! I never communicated directly with Mr. Ditko, the donor did and was told that the art was a gift and theirs to do with as they wished. As an Ayn Rand objectivist, Ditko didn't care. The art was donated as a permanent gift and neither the Ditko nor the Kirby covers were included in the gift." Duke continued, "The art is stored in a box. Each page is individually housed in a lignin-free 40-ply archival folder in which a mylar-D insert has been taped. Inside the insert is permalife paper to absorb any off-gassing from the original art. The box is stored in a vault that

Opposite page: Ditko, pencils and inks, original artwork for an interior page from ***Amazing Fantasy*** #15, April, 1962 ©1962 Marvel Characters. Right: Steve Ditko, pencils and inks, cover from ***The Amazing Spider-Man*** #37, June, 1966, ©1966 Marvel Characters.

is monitored for temperature and humidity, around 68 F and 50 per cent relative humidity year-round. We've had the art since 2008, and it's popular, but I haven't kept count of the number of requests nor the number of guests that come along. Plus, individual pages have gone out on loan to Australia, New York, and Seattle, as well as one page that was included in an exhibition here, *Timely and Timeless*."

Liberated from what Ditko would term as the "looters" of the original art collectors' market, the artwork now enshrined in the nation's capital is available for viewing by any interested individual following the Library's two-week appointment procedures. "I do my best to honour the spirit of the gift," Duke said, continuing, "The donor selected the Library, and I want to make it as accessible as possible. I never turn away people, but they do have to be able to visit on a weekday — the Prints and Photographs Division is closed at the weekend. Researchers have to be over 16 and obtain a Library of Congress researcher card. People are more than welcome to come." While not at liberty to reveal the identity of the donor, Duke remarked, "I will tell people that it is not Marie Severin, it is not Steve Ditko and it is not Stan Lee," adding that it's worth the trip to view the pages. In reference to the art itself, Duke said to the author, "When you see the art, you see the dialogue. And in this case, there is real dialogue between Stan Lee and Steve Ditko that show they were both very creative forces in the creation of Spider-Man. There are marginalia notations in Stan Lee's hand writing, some of which Steve Ditko honoured and ones where he didn't. You don't get a sense of that from the published version of the comic book, but in the original art it really shines through."

The notes would have been added by Lee while the art was still in pencil stage as instructions to Ditko before the artist inked it, and they were less employed to alter plot narrative but mostly cosmetic in nature or designed to appease the edicts of the Comics Code. As in one example from a panel on the third page, where a car narrowly avoids Peter Parker, sending him crawling up a wall in avoidance and instantly aware of his new super powers, Lee writes underneath the panel, "Steve, make this a sedan, no arms hanging, don't imply wild, reckless driving." which Ditko observes and makes the required change. Or, more tellingly, in another from a panel from the eighth page, which shows the villain's face as he flees from the scene of his crime, "Steve, omit crook! Show door slamming!," Lee writes, but Ditko ignores the directive, aware of the story's final revelation and the necessity to reveal the identity now in order to set the later scene and enable Lee to script his famous "With great power there must also come, great responsibility" line. Keeping the identity of the soon-to-be murderer of Uncle Ben secret at this stage in the story seemed oddly contrary to its ultimate point. It was almost as if the scripter didn't know what the ending would be until he looked at the very last page.

With the major comic book publishers today adopting a similar stance of non-acceptance of unsolicited material as mainstream book publishers and still operating a work-for-hire arrangement for those they do employ ("Work-for-hire is still a thing and the Image model still hasn't changed things across the board." Tom DeFalco wrote to me in 2018), each respective universe of characters has seen very little in the way of new and original additions to their ranks, as the publishing houses produce an endless recycling of their existing inhabitants represented in first issue relaunches, derivative new characters based on established franchises and repetitive promotional event stories such as *Civil War* (2006); *Secret Invasion* (2008); *Avengers vs X-Men* (2012); *Avengers: Standoff!* (2016); and *War of the Realms* (2019).

The departure of DC Comics from Manhattan in 2015, relocating its headquarters to Warner Brothers' Burbank, California headquarters, signalled the end of the decades-held domination of New York as the centre of the comic book industry with an upswing in sales for online comics and collected editions supplanting the dwindling sales figures of their printed pamphlet origins, a regular edition of such retailing at just under four dollars, a day's average pay back in 1962. "The heyday of the monthly newsstand comic book has passed," artist P. Craig Russell wrote to me in 2018, continuing, "When Marvel cancelled *Killraven* I was told it was because of its sales figures, a mere 75,000 copies per issue. People would kill for those numbers today." (For comparison, estimated sales figures for comic books dated April 2018 saw the anniversary issue of *Action Comics* #1000 heading the top 500 at under 450,000 sales; *Amazing Spider-Man* reaching 233,000; *Batman* at 125,500 but titles outside of the top ten such as *Avengers* achieving just 60,000 and titles near the bottom of the chart like *Doctor Strange: Damnation* or *Astonishing X-Men* selling meagre amounts under 1000 copies.) Danny Fingeroth wrote to me, "Comics, be they superhero comics or Indy personal vision comics/graphic novels, will always be around. And there will always be some of them in print, since humans do seem to like paper as a delivery system for entertainment and information. But I imagine we're going to continue to head to most readers using some electronic method of experiencing comics, if only because you can click a button and download something within seconds. The old divisions between what's print and what's film and what's video and what's internet-native seem to be breaking down. People consume stuff on screens, whatever the original source of the material was. Having said that, I hear there's been a renaissance of print book sales lately, and that's more than fine with me."

No longer contributing to the mainstream industry, Ditko nonetheless retained an awareness of its activities through his correspondents and any press article mentions. In a letter from 2016 he wrote, "I didn't follow what was going on in comics when I wasn't relevant to comic book fan editors. I get some ideas, information from correspondents, about what is taking place in comics. Now, I only occasionally see what Marvel or DC is publishing. Certainly, the old heroes fighting crime — Marvel heroes all in New York City is impossible with all the changes in technology, etc. So comic book 'heroes' have to exist in some future fantasies. I have no idea what attracts todays comic book fans, what kind of changed heroes, like in the far-out movies. The new publishers, editors, writers, artists are more in tune with their now generation and have some ideas of what appeals, like with the new costumes, odd kind of villains, super villains etc. Reprints do reveal the history of the changes, but modern people want their own kind of lifestyle reflected in comics so the anti-hero will dominate everything. 'Captain America — sleeper agent for Hydra' — or Captain America infiltrating Hydra by posing as traitor revealed at his trial, etc. There have been stories, movies about double, triple agents. There's a proper logic in ongoing fiction/fantasy that allows a lot of creative explorations — but not contradictions, like an alien Spider-Man etc. Comic books are fictions and fantasies; someone is always trying to manipulate comic book followers for continuing interest and reactions. So many want to be 'creators' with others' created property, like one 'idea' — Spider-Man as an 'ALIEN'! So, editors, writers, want to also recreate a creation." Ditko continued, "Marvel and

DC for a long time dominated the 100 best monthly selling comics. Recently, seven different titles appeared on the charts. There's always been a problem with outlets that sell comic books. Who, where can ALL the published comic books be carried, who can afford the monthly risks, etc.? Re-evaluations continue. Today, DC, Marvel, the comic book industry is more of a manufacturing business, they are heavily into spinoffs: Reprints, toys, costumes, commercial gimmicks, movies for a GLOBAL MARKET. Marvel and DC keep flooding the market with titles. It makes it harder for other comic companies to get carried, have space in comic bookstores. Their standards are pragmatic, flexible for greater profit."

Devoid of any modern communication device, Ditko would reply on print as the source of his information including its coverage of popular culture and varied adaptations of characters the artist co-created decades earlier. "I read that the Broadway Spider-Man production ran into all kinds of problems, trouble. A big money loser. Like with a lot of projects, the original idea has to be changed by the 'truly creative.' Some changes are necessary, but there has to be some valid reason," the artist wrote to me. Ditko, a reader and contributor to comic books since the birth of the industry, also witnessed the astonishing evolution of comic book conventions from their obsessively niche origins into the huge, culturally important, media-led, mass gatherings of devotees and idea-hawkers from all areas of creativity they are today. "Comic conventions changed from being all comic book related to now movie- dominated and with comic book sales declining. There are always positive/negative changes, but it's not easy to know what actually causes the changes, positive or negative. (You see) A lot of Spider-man costumes at conventions, street fairs etc. – from the sensible to the ridiculous. There are also other comic characters that are favourites for someone to dress up as. The movies add or subtract something with the hero costumes that often don't make sense."

With major retrospective exhibitions of original comic book art now regularly held worldwide, including one recent show devoted exclusively to Ditko's work (*Ditko Unleashed: An American Hero* that ran from September 29 to January 8, 2016 in Palma, Majorca, Spain) and the rise of the worldwide appeal of superhero genre movies, the originators of such fantasies are posthumously being attributed their places in the pantheon of great American artists from all disciplines, recognising their significant cultural contributions to the arts. "Technology keeps changing faster today," wrote Ditko to me in September 2014, continuing, "When I started doing comics, the original art page size was 12" x 18". I don't know the exact technology but printers found out they could copy four pages instead of one, if there was a smaller original art page. So, all original art pages now had to be done on the new reduced size page. Everything keeps changing with every new generation."

From his first attempts to break into the comic book industry as a young man in the early 1950s to his elderly years spent in the city, Steve Ditko had been a resident of New York for over 66 years and reflected on the many changes he had seen over that time in a letter to me from February 2014 saying, "It's difficult for me to experience a familiarity with my early New York years. One can't walk a block in my area without some construction going on — tearing down, building anew — businesses failing, empty stores, new ones starting up. Variety and confusion, but normal for NYC. We had a colder, longer winter, but as a business, tourist city, snow is quickly removed so no real problem getting around, although I'm in an area of cold, wintry blasting winds. Every area has its problems like with flooding, earthquakes, etc. Weather predictions continue to be more a guessing game. But we continue to survive. N.Y.C people have become like robots fixated on some gadget they're holding, watching or photographing something. It's become more important to their life than awareness of what is actually going on around them — where they are going, like crossing a street. Mindless behaviour has to affect one's ability to focus, distraction on something else has to affect their judgement, and there are always penalties." Adding, "Recently, the New York newspapers had some material on the Banksy artist, material etc. I didn't get too involved in it. NYC went through that years ago with the graffiti 'artist's, with their spraying subway cars/trains, private property with their 'art.' It's the old violating the rights of another's property, be it public or private. History has all kinds of public exhibitionists doing 'their thing.' Yes, 'making a statement' was a popular defense, justification, contradictions of all kind continue. I don't get involved in trying to understand someone's nonsense."

Living in the city that was a common backdrop to his comic book stories, Ditko rarely left New York — apart from regular family visits to Johnstown, every year at Christmas, and often twice a year — but spent the majority of his time in solitude within the closed doors of his Manhattan apartment and the office he maintained off Times Square until the end of his life, invisible in a population approaching two million contained in an area of just 23 square miles. His office, on the seventh floor of a twelve-storey building at 1650 Broadway, faced the elevator and was a long and narrow area, roughly 30 x 9 feet, where, beyond its small reception area, were orderly stacks of boxes and shelves full of books on art and philosophy in varied forms, files and magazines with artwork and proofs attached to the wall. At the back of the office, where the window afforded a view over 51st Street, Ditko would sit at his drawing board with all the materials he required before him, creating comic strip art as he had done for most of his long life.

"I work with radio music, one reason to drown out traffic noise," he wrote to me in 2013. Now producing artwork exclusively intended for his own publications, unlike many other artists who regularly accepted private commissions to supplement their income, Ditko never joined their number throughout the whole of his career. In 2016, he wrote to me

32 PAGES ALL NEW ART
©2012 S. DITKO
#1 2 3 4 5 6 7 8 9 10 11 12 13 14 15
#16
SIXTEEN
YOU

saying, "I don't do any commissions. They are just interrupters of plans, schedules, dead-ends." Nor did the boxes stored in his office contain a collection, or even a selection, of any early career comic books that he contributed to, including his 1950s/1960s Marvel comic books, as he confirmed to me in a letter from 2015, "I don't have any copies of the early comics, I gave all of them to my nephew years ago." Mark Ditko confirmed this to me and added, "He sent me boxes and boxes of his older comics, which I still have." A voracious reader, Ditko would travel the world from his chair and read books, newspapers and magazines regularly, informing him and keeping his knowledge current.

Communication in the traditional letter-writing fashion was an important part of Ditko's daily routine, and he held a number of correspondents at any given time over his life with whom he exchanged letters, books and clippings. Mark S. Ditko clarified this to me saying, "I collected over 100 letters from his studio floor through his mail slot, since he hadn't been there for a few months. We could barely open the door from the amount of mail behind it." Within my own correspondence with the artist, we exchanged views and news on topics both global and local to our respective locales, one example being when I recounted the first visit to Bath on June 3, 2016 of the second man to walk on the moon, Buzz Aldrin and how his sold-out talk at The Forum and predetermined decision to sign all copies of the book he was promoting to attendees resulted in a wrist-straining four-hour session for the then-86-year-old ex-fighter pilot and astronaut. Ditko wrote, "That's quite a spectacle with Buzz Aldrin, his unbelievable achievement. Four hours of signing — WOW! He probably wished he was back on the moon!" Or in response to when the spectre of Brexit first loomed on the British political landscape, "Brexit — politics —yes — uncertainty in the change, affecting everyone, but that's to be expected in politics — power and more power."

A book that I gave him containing photographic views of my own home city of Bath, garnered the following insightful comment on a place in England the artist would never visit or actually see in person, "Bath has an enviable history and one that has retained its unique origins, its character. Additions seem more complimentary than adversarial. It's the details that give the unique identity that dominates Bath — all closer to plant and human life, of being a part of continuity and not some strange environment. Bath's architectural structures are a delightful treat for the eye in which there are many parts but all within a pleasant unity. At times it looks as if it was not built but just grew, the result of the then-inventive, imaginative, man's mind."

As time went by, the phone calls and knocks on Ditko's door became fewer with even reporters looking for a soundbite in coverage of another Marvel movie featuring his creations deciding it to be a fool's errand. Ditko wrote to me in July 2014, "No, I'm not bothered by newspapers etc. about any new Spider-Man movie or anything else. It's probably too well known I don't comment on the past or on anything I'm not really involved in." Even Ditko's most determined fans would have found difficulty in breaching the formidable building security as Mark S. Ditko related to me in 2019, "It took my Dad, Steve's own brother, and myself about 20 minutes to get the building manager to let us through." But within the narrow walls of his office, the artist continued to produce, despite the fact that it could be argued he was "making all his nowhere plans for nobody" as his audience had diminished to all but a handful of faithful followers in publications of small print-runs produced through the assistance of crowd funding.

An alternative view, perhaps, is that it was the culmination of a lifetime objective to achieve complete creative freedom, a vindication of the steadfast approach he employed to obtain it and a necessary vehicle which kept the individual engaged, active and creatively explorative, with his still sharp and agile mind reaching out in thought to transcend his earthly boundaries in a spirit that echoed the astral flights of Doctor Strange. "The ever-expanding universe keeps growing, changing with new discoveries being made about the past, now and the future," he wrote to me in 2015 continuing, "It's certainly an exciting time for those professions involved. Mars seems to be an intriguing example of having once been a living, breathing planet with some kinds of life forms. On Earth, they are always finding evidence of some earlier meteor impact somehow never believed possible, never imagined. Archaeologists continue to find, discover new startling facts about man's early life. And Earth still keeps many secrets, most well-kept because of its slow, long-changing history. Will they find actual life on some other planet or are we the only one with life? The universe is VERY OLD; planets with life could have existed."

While back down on terra firma, his views on the human condition, perhaps amplified and consolidated by his own personal life experiences were uncompromisingly objective in condemnation. He wrote to me in June 2016, "Aristotle, 4BC, defined man as a 'rational animal.'" Too many have chosen to be irrational, unreachable, so (exists) anti-man, anti-life, anti-existence. It's been said the issue is still between Plato (the mystic) and Aristotle (man, the rational animal). One can't reach minds that refuse to be reached even with national, social issues, problems etc." Concluding, as a man approaching 90 years of age, "The irrational dominates the world."

Opposite page: Ditko, pencils and inks, cover for ***A Ditko*** #16, 2012, ©2012 Estate of Steve Ditko and Robin Snyder.

Epilogue
The Death of an Artist 2018

On July 13, 2018, six days after the announcement of Steve Ditko's death, Stan Lee appeared on his official Twitter account to present a brief video saying, in a faltering voice that was testament to his own advanced years and rapidly deteriorating health, "One thing occurs to me, I really cannot let the week go without commenting on Steve Ditko. Steve was certainly one of the most important creators in the comic book business and his talent was indescribable. I worked with him for many years and was always impressed with how he saw everything in terms of photos and pictures and movement and scenes. He told the story like a fine movie director would. I think that he will be very greatly missed by the public, by his fans. I'm sure there will be lots written about him as time goes by and I will be one of the guys who buys the first book. You made a real impression here in the world. Excelsior."

The final years of Stan Lee were mired in rumour, lawsuits and restraining orders against former managers; Los Angeles Police Department investigations into reports of elder abuse against him and evidence he was far from happy. The death of Joan, Lee's wife of 69 years in July 2017, impacted hard on the nonagenarian, ultimately leaving him bereft and ready to join her. Suitably, one of the final people to visit Lee and also present in the last photograph ever taken of the comic book creator was Roy Thomas, his protégé of the 1960s, who spent some time with Lee just a few days before his death. As a consequence of the modern information age, which dictates that speed is of the essence when a death is announced, with everyone eager to be among the first to offer condolences, a deluge of postings on social media appeared to commemorate Lee's passing. Among them, SpaceX founder Elon Musk tweeted, "The many worlds of imagination and delight you created for humanity will last forever"; actor Seth Rogen said, "Thank you for making people who feel different realize they are special"; while *The New York Times* noted the "humanizing neuroses" in the heroes he'd helped to create and Alice Cooper humorously recalled, "My absolute favourite thing about Stan Lee is that when he had me drawn for the comics it was with great abs! Thanks for that Stan." As with Hugh Jackson's erroneous thanking of Lee for Wolverine, the late writer would have had little or nothing to do with the way the rock singer was drawn (by Tom Sutton, incidentally), but the world found much to legitimately thank him for.

While, either through personal or corporate intent or the result of a bad memory, he may have elevated his importance in the creation of Marvel's bankable heroes, much to the chagrin of Jack Kirby, Steve Ditko and others, his media-friendly personality became a familiar face in the promotion of comic books over generations, and he fulfilled a role that very few others could have. With Lee, Kirby and Ditko, all three creative individuals produced, if not their definitive best, but arguably the most enduring work of their respective careers in collaboration together, and whatever their personal conflicts may have been, the inspired results of their associations relied on input from all parties for its specific alchemy to work. "Without Lee, Kirby and Ditko, there is no Marvel Comics, maybe no comic book industry and certainly, no popular culture industry as we know it today," Danny Fingeroth wrote to me in 2018. "I liked Stan," recalled Marv Wolfman, "He was a really great comics writer who was doing things we'd never seen before. As good as he was as a writer, he was probably even better as an editor. He was also someone who clearly loved and understood the comics medium. Jack was a visual genius and his art was utterly amazing. He took us places we'd never seen before. He was also a great guy. I met Jack and his wonderful wife, Roz, back in my early teens, and he was one of those great people who, when you met him was even better than you had hoped."

While not as extensive or prolonged as the coverage that resulted from Lee's death, in the flurry of activity across social media about Ditko's passing, which had already peaked days before the editor's eulogy, DC Comics said, "Steve Ditko was one of the most amazing creators in the history of comics and showed us there is a hero in all of us." Marvel Comics said, "Today, the Marvel family mourns the loss of Steve Ditko. Steve transformed the industry and the Marvel Universe, and his legacy will never be forgotten." Writer Brian Michael Bendis who helped invigorate the *Spider-Man* franchise with his rebooted version *Ultimate Spider-Man* in 2000 and later co-creation of Miles Morales said, "I spoke to Steve Ditko on the phone once. I got to thank him for creating Spider-Man and

Opposite page, left to right: Steve Ditko, sister Anna, sister Betty and brother Pat, in this family photo taken the late 1990s, ©2020 DitkoVerse/ Mark S. Ditko.

putting food on my table. I hope he really heard me." Referring to Ditko's legacy, Paul Levitz wrote to me in 2018, "Steve gave us one of the true treasures of American comics in Spider-Man, and set the standard for surrealism in so much of his other work. He also was a key supporter of the evolution of the indies, particularly with his *Mr. A* work."

Under the headline "Mere Spider Cents," journalist Julia Marsh wrote an article for the *New York Post* on August 27, 2018 revealing some post-death details and a revelation that the "reclusive creator left an estate of an estimated 1.5 million dollars." Many were surprised to learn that Ditko had left an estate of such value, despite the article rightly declaring it a "relative pittance" in comparison to the billions of dollars his creations had earned for the owners of Marvel. But the figure was not substantiated at the time. "It's possible that he's not worth that much," said Ditko's lawyer Howard Borkan after the estimated figure was provided by Ditko's surviving brother Patrick, 83, who, along with his sister Elizabeth Russak, 87, emerged as his only immediate heirs and inheritors of his estate as Ditko did not leave behind a will. Borkan added that he only learned about his client's career as a comic book artist legend from reading his obituary, despite the fact that Ditko had first come to him years back seeking legal advice to help renegotiate the lease on his apartment. "Until he passed, I didn't know what he had done," Borkan said in the article, adding that he only knew Ditko as a "very nice man" whose hearing had gone in his final years. In the same article, Patrick declared, "I know nothing about his finances or anything about his personal life," adding that his brother "was never in it for the money."

Both siblings still lived in Johnstown, and Patrick revealed that his older brother last visited the family's hometown a few years before. In the months leading up to his death, Ditko had been hospitalized for "age issues" and was three months in arrears on the rent on his West 51st Street apartment when he suffered a fatal heart attack. This was because "he was in the hospital," his lawyer said. Ditko was eventually released from hospital care and died alone in his apartment not long after. "His body was not found until a few days later when the NYPD had to be called to gain access to the unit," Borkan said in court papers. It was then, and only then, when Ditko's lawyer and neighbours discovered exactly who the old man, with the ink-stained fingers, had been that they realized his importance to popular culture. The details of Steve Ditko's funeral and how and where he was laid to rest were not made public by the wishes of the family since presumably Ditko left no instructions. But while New York was the city he lived and worked in, Johnstown was the home he returned to often and with Ditko's father, Stephen Ditko, who died in 1966 aged 66, and his mother, Anna Ditko, who followed him in 1970 aged 68, both laid to rest at Johnston's Saint Mary's Byzantine Catholic Cemetery in a combined grave with a headstone that bore the simple epitaphs "Father" and "Mother," it would not take a detective of the stature of Batman to speculate further.

Ditko's comfortable financial position at the time of his death indicates that he may have accepted some payment or payments from Sony or Marvel Studios for movies that featured his characters, despite rumours that he once returned a cheque to Sony. He was, after all, duly credited as "co-creator" on all of them. Ditko may have received and considered due a payment for the *Doctor Strange* movie, a character that can unambiguously be solely credited to him and would have received semi-regular royalty payments from Marvel for sales of reprinted volumes of his past work, as with all writers and artists of the publishing house, along with any pensions he may have had. He lived frugally, dining in the fast-food outlets of Times Square and spending his money on art material supplies along with the generous donation cheques he would send to the Randian Society.

Right: Ditko, pencils and inks, original artwork for the splash page from ***Strange Tales*** #117, February, 1964, ©1964 Marvel Characters. Opposite page: Ditko, pencils and inks, specialty illustration featuring Spidey and Doctor Strange, with Ditko in the ink bottle. Page 139/142: Ditko, pencils and inks, cover from ***The Amazing Spider-Man*** #7 and interior page original artwork from the same issue, December, 1963, ©1963 Marvel Characters. Page 143: Ditko, pencils and inks, original cover art for ***Out of This World*** #6, November, 1957, ©1957 Charlton Comics.

For all his contributions to popular culture, Ditko did not die a particularly rich man, but with a million or so dollars in his account, he was not struggling either. For comparison, Stan Lee was worth an estimated 70 million dollars at the time of his death. With two hefty volumes of hardcover omnibus editions collecting all of Ditko's pre-superhero Marvel work with Lee in 2019, along with the ongoing work of Mark Ditko and the Ditko Estate to preserve and promote his legacy under the umbrella title of "DitkoVerse" and the continuation of publications by Robin Synder with reprinted and previously unpublished work by Ditko with *The Return of Mr. A* and its 2019 release leading the charge, the artist looks set to be represented in many ways together with the new compilations of his back catalogue for years to come, adding to the library of material already reprinted in various forms and editions. In early 2019, the complete eight pages of original art for one of the *Doctor Strange* stories that Ditko never received back from Marvel in 1985, *Strange Tales* #117 turned up for sale at Heritage Auctions with hundreds of pages of Ditko's Marvel and DC art yet to surface. What will become of the mountain of highly valuable original artwork that would have been part of his inherited estate? Perhaps the family, wishing a permanent presence of the artist in the city he loved, might one day request a section of MOMA or the Guggenheim to be devoted to the artist as a lasting tribute to his extraordinary talent. Framed original art pages of *Spider-Man* and *Doctor Strange* would be the prize exhibits together with other covers and panelled pages spanning his entire career. Collectively, and in such settings, the curators of the art would be proclaiming, "Here is great American art. Here is a master of a chosen field. Here is an example of an iconoclast whose visionary abilities touched many lives. Here is history of our culture." An accolade and a recognition that most artists would dream of.

But if the ghost of Steve Ditko joined the throngs of tourists observing his pen-and-ink art pages displayed on the walls, the artist would simply shrug and walk away, by his own estimation the true purpose of the work already met. When I asked about his creation of Spider-Man and its potent effect on generations past, present and future, Ditko wrote to the author in February 2013, "The authors of fables, etc, don't need to or can know the effect of the truth, moral of their fables, tales, etc. They are expressions of their own beliefs, insights, truth. (In history) fables, fantasies were a safe way to express ideas, truths, while living under cruel, powerful rulers, tyrants, in very harsh, dangerous times. No one can think or live for future generations. Life is now."

In his final essay, posthumously published in February 2019 within the title "Down Memory Lane," Ditko's last published words quoted an old toast when he wrote, "Here's to those who wish me well and those that don't can go to hell." But in summation of the inner drive that led Steve Ditko to create iconic, beloved and challenging comic book characters, I would prefer to close this book with the legendary artist's more sanguine conclusion from a 2015 letter to me, "No one was ever forced to work for any company or to 'create' beyond his job. The only important audience is oneself, in doing something worthwhile, new and novel."

DEDICATED TO: My wife Sue, my daughter Yasmine, my son-in-law Joel Lucy, and my grandchildren Mersim, Arabella, Oliver, Daisy, Charlie and baby Gianna, born during the pandemic year of 2020 — to a heroic future for them all.

IN MEMORY OF: My parents Alexander (1928-2002) and Gwendolyn Currie (1930-2013) for teaching me that love is the only super power that truly counts.

ACKNOWLEDGMENTS: Special thanks to my lovely wife Sue who supported this project from the beginning and helped me every step of the way. Thanks also to my life-long friend Keith Gale for reading the early drafts; for the support of Sam Wakeman, Phil Rugg, Paul Fflokes Davies, Wayne Powney, Dylan Almond, Ross Williams, Ailsa Wright, Daniel and Sabrina at Hermes and all my family and friends. Special thanks to Mark and Patrick Ditko for their invaluable insights and dedication to the legacy of Steve Ditko.

ABOUT THE AUTHOR

David worked as a journalist in London in the 1980s, when he also wrote two books on David Bowie *The Starzone Interviews* (1985) and *Glass Idol* (1987). The title *Starzone* began life as a comic strip fanzine David produced in the 1970s. He returned to his home city of Bath to open and run two comic book stores in the West of England for nearly twenty years and was a regular article contributor to *Comic Heroes* magazine. David also worked as an actor for a time, appearing in the films *Spider-Man* (2002); *Vanity Fair* (2004); *The Other Boleyn Girl* (2008) together with numerous television work. He writes and performs music with his band *Unlegal People* and solo as David Romain and is currently working on his first novel in the fantasy genre titled *Miracle Fields*. His next book for Hermes Press is *The Grand Illusion of David Bowie*, due in 2021, collecting together his photographs of Bowie together with his memories of the superstar. In the spirit of the song "That's Life," David has also worked as a tour guide, armchair salesman, a chocolatier, astronomy museum attendant and a social media manager.

APPROVED BY THE COMICS CODE AUTHORITY
the AMAZING SPIDER-MAN
IND.
MARVEL COMICS GROUP 12¢
7 DEC.
A MARVEL SUPER-SPECTACULAR:
"the VULTURE'S RETURN!"
THE VULTURE LOOKS TOO SURE OF HIMSELF! HE MUST HAVE A FOOL-PROOF PLAN TO DEFEAT ME! BUT--WHAT CAN IT BE?
HERE IS SPIDER-MAN AS YOU LIKE HIM... FIGHTING! JOKING! DARING! CHALLENGING THE MOST DANGEROUS FOE OF ALL, IN THIS-- THE MARVEL AGE OF COMICS!

Index

SPIDERMAN #7 P11
GOT TO SPIN AROUND IN AIR-- TO SLOW MY RATE OF DESCENT! MUST BREAK FALL! WILL TAKE ALL MY SPIDER STRENGTH! SPIN... KEEP SPINNING--KEEP-- -OOOF-!!
SPIDER-MAN IS FINISHED! MY REVENGE IS COMPLETE! NOW THE VULTURE IS SUPREME!
LOOK AT THE SHOCKED CROWDS BELOW! THEY SAW WHAT HAPPENED!
NO MAN WILL EVER DARE DEFY ME NOW!
THE VULTURE DEFEATED SPIDER-MAN!
POOR SPIDER-MAN! DESPITE WHAT JAMESON'S EDITORIALS SAID ABOUT HIM, WE COPS ALWAYS FELT HE WAS ON OUR SIDE! HE'LL SURE BE MISSED... WHOEVER HE WAS!
LOOK! HE'S FLYING OFF NOW! LIKE A CONQUERING HERO!
BUT, ALTHOUGH BADLY SHAKEN UP, THE COSTUMED TEEN-AGER IS STILL ALIVE... SAVED BY HIS AMAZING SPIDER STRENGTH!
GOT TO GET UP--CAN'T STAY HERE--CAN'T LET ANYONE DISCOVER ME--
LUCKY TO BE ALIVE! DIDN'T THINK I'D MAKE IT...
OHH! MY ARM! MUST HAVE LANDED ON IT!
FEELS LIKE IT'S BROKEN!
GUESS I CAN'T COMPLAIN! IT PROBABLY SAVED MY LIFE! IF I HADN'T BEEN ABLE TO SPIN AROUND... IF I HAD LANDED ON MY HEAD INSTEAD... ZOWEE!
9
500
498
11

VANDERCOOK
OUT OF THIS WORLD # 6
OUT OF THIS WORLD
CDC
TALES OF THE UNKNOWN
FANTASTIC
DIFFERENT
Nº 6
OUT OF THIS WORLD
A CHARLTON PUBLICATION
10¢
RED
BLUE
UNUSUAL
STRANGE
BLACK
YELLOW
DITKO

Regards
Steve Ditko
Steve Ditko

EY! WAIT A MINUTE! E CAN'T GO THIS WAY! THERE ARE TOO MANY EOPLE! WE MIGHT...
LOOK OUT! YOU'RE GONNA GET YOURSELF KILLED!
SHUT-UP, WILLYA? WE HAVE TO TAKE A SHORT CUT, IF WE WANNA GIT THERE IN TIME!
ELL THEN, WHY DON'T WE JUST ALL THE POLICE! THEY COU... WHOOP!
WHAT'S BUGGIN' YOU? YOU KNOW HOW TO SWIM, DON'T YOU?
YES, I DO! IN FACT, I CAN OUTSWIM YOU! AND NOW, WITH MY INCREASED POWER I'M DOING BETTER THAN EVER!
AW, SO WHAT? THERE AIN'T NOTHIN' ELSE YOU CAN DO BETTER THAN ME! AND WE WON'T BE IN THE WATER FOR MUCH LONGER!